WESLEY

The Author

WILLIAM RAGSDALE CANNON is dean of the Candler School of Theology at Emory University and professor of church history and historical theology. There, and wherever he goes, he is extremely popular as a preacher. His sermons, which are marked by an eloquent sincerity, have power to command the hearts and minds of men. He is increasingly in demand for campus lectures and for leadership in youth and church assemblies.

Dr. Cannon is a native of Georgia and a graduate of the University of Georgia. From Yale he received his B.D. degree *summa cum laude* in 1940 and his Ph.D. in 1942.

Dr. Cannon is a frequent contributor to religious journals and the author of *The Redeemer* and *History of Christianity in the Middle Ages*.

THE THEOLOGY OF
JOHN WESLEY

With Special Reference to the Doctrine of Justification

By
WILLIAM RAGSDALE CANNON

ABINGDON PRESS
New York ● *Nashville*

THE THEOLOGY OF JOHN WESLEY

Copyright MCMXLVI by Stone & Pierce

Library of Congress Catalog Card Number: 46-5637

SET UP, PRINTED, AND BOUND BY THE
PARTHENON PRESS, AT NASHVILLE,
TENNESSEE, UNITED STATES OF AMERICA

PREFACE

IT IS A MISTAKE TO THINK THAT JOHN WESLEY IS ADEQUATELY DESCRIBED as an organizer, like Ignatius of Loyola, or as a sweet-spirited saint who attracted disciples through the magnetic spell of his personality, like Francis of Assisi. Both Ignatius and Francis did their work within the doctrinal bounds of the Roman Catholic Communion. But John Wesley pushed beyond the circumscribed territory of Anglicanism and of the other confessional denominations of the Reformation. Willingly or unwillingly, he bequeathed to posterity a Church. Methodism, based on his teachings, has its own theology, its peculiar doctrinal place in the economy of grace.

Yet Wesley himself did not take the time to write a textbook in systematic theology. Like Augustine and Luther before him, he was content merely to express his thoughts as occasions demanded, and his doctrines must be gleaned from writings produced at various and sundry times in response to various and sundry needs. Like all creative geniuses in religion, he did not start out to construct an entirely new system of theology. Rather, he was possessed of one central truth, that man is justified by faith and perfected in love; in the light of this truth old doctrines took on new meaning for him, and he saw the remainder of theology as aspects of his own theory of justification and final salvation.

This book deals, therefore, with the problem of salvation as Wesley faced it, and with the theology which emerged from the solution which he gave to that problem. Its purpose is to present in systematic form the theological opinions of John Wesley and to examine the major phase of the English Evangelical Revival of the eighteenth century in the light of its religious teachings: the convictions which produced it, and those doctrines which sustained and added strength and purpose to its life.

That Wesley was not systematic in the arrangement of his doctrines does not warrant the assumption that he was inconsistent or contradictory in his theological opinions. Once we have discovered the central purpose of his teaching, it is not difficult to group the individual beliefs around it and to see how they fall naturally into place as orderly parts of a harmonious system of divinity.

It is impossible here to cite by name those people to whom I am indebted for help in the successful completion of this task. Acknowledgment of sources of ideas and quoted matter is made in the footnotes. Credit to publishers is given in the full bibliography in the Appendix. The quotations from Calvin's *Institutes of the Christian Religion* are reprinted, by permission, from the John Allen translation, published by the Westminster Press. I am especially indebted to my former professors at Yale University and to my colleagues and students at Emory University: to the former, for the guidance they gave me in the research underlying this study; to the latter, for the encouragement they gave me in publishing the work and the patience they exercised in listening to my accounts of its progress.

WILLIAM R. CANNON

Candler School of Theology
Emory University, Georgia

CONTENTS

9

CONTENTS

The sacred road to God is sore beset
With weary pilgrims seeking truth in bands.
They yearn and search and strive, all asking rest;
They would escape with life from this hard land.
The fitful past, with its grim forms and shades,
Still chills the soul, still freezes with despair.
The future, though untried and e'en unmade,
Yet takes the heart with question and with care.
These pilgrims, you and I and all our kind,
So bent on quest, so restless to push on,
As if by searching we His face could find
And through our strength His truth and light put on.
O God, forgive our pride and vain conceit;
Thy love alone doth lead men to Thy feet.

INTRODUCTION

WITH THE PROBABLE EXCEPTION OF A FEW STATESMEN AND SCIENTISTS, perhaps a general or two, John Wesley has received more attention from the pens of biographers and has had more written about him than any other Englishman of the eighteenth century.[1] Time seems scarcely to have affected men's interest in him. When Wesley died on March 2, 1791, the first account of his life was ready for the press;[2] and since that date almost every year has seen some new sketch of his career or some new treatment of a phase of his work added to the sum total of Wesleyan material.[3] Most writers have been content merely to deal with the events of Wesley's life, with the day-by-day accomplishments in his long ministry, and with the organization of his religious movement, which later became a church. Thus Luke Tyerman, by all odds the most thorough and dependable of Wesley's biographers,[4] states the purpose which underlies not only his own work but also the majority of all the works that have been written on John Wesley when he writes: "I have tried to make Wesley his own biographer. I have not attempted what may be called the *philosophy* of Wesley's life. I leave that to others. As a rule, intelligent readers wish only to be possessed of facts. They can form their own conclusions; and care but little about the opinion of those by whom the facts are collected and narrated."[5]

To a certain extent that statement is true; but it is also true that

[1] F. J. McConnell, *John Wesley*, p. 9.

[2] John Hampson's *Memoirs of the Late Rev. John Wesley, M.A., with a Review of his Life and Writings, and a History of Methodism, from its Commencement in 1729 to the Present Time.* Hampson, a onetime follower of Wesley, left the movement in 1785 and became an Anglican clergyman. His work is bitter and vindictive.

[3] Maximin Piette, *John Wesley in the Evolution of Protestantism*, p. 203.

[4] The only modern work which is at all comparable to Tyerman's is J. A. Simon's four volumes and a fifth volume in the same series by A. W. Harrison, 1921-34. This work is valuable in that it examines Wesley in the light of modern scholarship and makes use of materials that heretofore have not been available.

[5] *Life and Times of John Wesley*, Vol. I, p. v.

readers are interested in ideas, in the thoughts which lie behind facts, and in the convictions which propel men's lives, guide their actions, and give meaning and purpose to all that they do. This book, therefore, attempts to reach a better understanding of Wesley's thought. It lies within the restricted area of what Tyerman has called his *philosophy of life,* or of what we might more properly call his teachings about man and God and about their relationship to one another.

Justification in Wesleyan Thought

In the body of these teachings Wesley's doctrine of justification was the measure and determinant of all else. A doctrine of justification is significant in any system of theology, because it has to do with the very heart of man's religious life—with the forgiveness of sins, and with the eradication of those barriers which separate man from God and which deny him the privilege of communion and fellowship with his heavenly Father. Especially is this true in the consideration of a system of theology which is the intellectual expression of a popular revival of religion. Wesleyan thought grew out of Wesleyan religion. If Wesley's avowed aim in life was the salvation of his own soul [6] and the souls of all men within the bounds of his ministry,[7] is it not reasonable for us to look for the clue to his theology in his teachings concerning man's justification before God, his present moral and spiritual restoration, and his final blessedness?

Relation of Wesleyan Thought to the Wesleyan Revival

Before turning specifically to Wesley's thought, however, it is necessary for us to consider the nature of the religious movement of which that thought was a part and to view the entire Wesleyan emphasis in the light of the factors which produced it. The Wesleyan Revival emerged in the eighteenth century; and it belongs as much to the time and place of its origin as the political enterprises of Walpole, the military campaigns of Marlborough, and the literary accomplishments of Johnson and Pope. It is not enough simply to admit the fact of the Wesleyan Revival as a phenomenon of history and then to pass over it

[6] *Works,* V, 3.
[7] *Ibid.,* VIII, 495.

14

by saying that it was merely a reflection of sixteenth-century Protestantism,[8] the shade of an old ghost cast across the ongoing stream of modern life. Any movement, by reason of the very fact that it is a movement and exerts influence, bears the marks of its own age and reflects the temper of the times in which it is launched. In the crises of religious history, as well as in the crises of political and social history, the problems at hand call forth their own solutions. A movement is never preconceived; it arises in answer to a real problem and offers itself as an attempt toward a real solution. To be sure, it may borrow from the past in the sense that its leaders utilize the experiences of those who have gone before. But at the same time it does not repeat the past; its duty lies in the present, and its accomplishments are forged out of the same stuff of which the other events of its own age are made.

The Revival and Eighteenth-Century Rationalism

The Wesleyan Revival arose, therefore, as a positive affirmation of scriptural Christianity in the face of the rationalistic and deistic philosophy which characterized the intellectual temper of the eighteenth century. Descartes had insisted that, if good sense is of all things in the world the most equally distributed, so that everybody thinks himself abundantly provided with it and so that no one desires more of it than he already possesses, then it follows that merely to be possessed of good mental powers is not sufficient; the important thing is to apply them well.[9] The eighteenth century took Descartes's advice seriously, and men began to think and to apply the powers of the mind to almost every department of human life. One cannot look back on the achievements of that age without a sense of wonder and admiration. Not only is there grandeur about the tasks which men undertook; there is also glory about those which they actually performed. The eighteenth century was an age of remarkable scientific advancement—an age which profited by the labors of Newton, Lavoisier, Boyle, Flamsteed, Halley, Buffon, and many others. It was an age of catastrophic political changes. Not only did it mark the collapse of the political policies of Louis XIV in the horrors and successes of the French

[8] Isaac Taylor gives this interpretation and claims there was nothing new or original in Wesleyanism.—*Wesley and Methodism*, p. 137.
[9] "Discourse on Method," *Works*, I, 81-82.

Revolution, but it saw also the conception of German nationalism in the might of Frederick the Great, the birth of American freedom in the courage of the Revolutionary War, and the growth of the British Empire in the vision of William Pitt. It was an age of literary and philosophical attainment. Though it did not give birth to many giants or produce any writer who even approached the measure of the stature of Shakespeare or Milton, it was not shorn of talent; and the general interest manifested in the pursuit of literature and philosophy was wider than it had ever been before.

But, most important of all for our purposes, the powers of the mind were now applied in all seriousness to religion. Theology ceased to be the subject which instigated the methods of thought and defined the limits of their operations and became rather the object of thought to which the methods of an emancipated philosophy were applied and concerning which a critical examination was undertaken. In other words, men no longer started with the premises of revealed religion, but they began at the point of their own discoveries and on the basis of those discoveries called into question the primary assumptions of the faith. Theology was removed from its exalted place as final arbiter in all matters of intellectual dispute and was summoned itself to appear as a defendant in the court and to justify its claims at the bar of un-aided natural reason. It cannot lie within the scope of this present undertaking to trace the development of the rationalistic movement in English religious thought from the overthrow of Aristotelian philosophy by Francis Bacon [10] through the repudiation of the use of implicit faith as an infallible guide to truth by Herbert of Cherbury,[11] the advocacy of materialism by Hobbes,[12] the establishment of reason as the only faculty by which man can achieve a direct vision of spiritual reality by the Cambridge Platonists,[13] and the reasonable, compromis-

[10] J. A. Dorner, *History of Protestant Theology,* II, 66.

[11] Herbert of Cherbury, *De veritate,* p. 289.

[12] Hobbes, though he insists on keeping philosophy and religion separate, none the less gives us a mechanical and materialistic view of the universe. Though he claims there is nothing in the *Leviathan* contrary "either to the Word of God or to good manners," it is still true that the implication of the work is not such as to bolster the Christian revelation, and did not serve as a defense of traditonal Christianity. Hobbes, *Leviathan,* "Review and Conclusion," chaps. xliii, xii, xiii.

[13] A. C. McGiffert, *Protestant Thought Before Kant,* p. 192.

16

ing supernaturalism of Tillotson [14] and Locke [15] down to the deism of
Tindal [16] and the skepticism of Hume.[17] Suffice it to say that the
extreme rationalistic interpretation of the deists flourished in the first
half of the eighteenth century and succeeded in cutting its mark deep
into the trunk of English religious life.

Perhaps Matthew Tindal is the best representative of the deistic
movement. John Orr tells us that Tindal brought together in his book,
*Christianity as Old as Creation: or the Gospel a Republication of the
Religion of Nature,* the various elements of deism of which the earlier
representatives of the movement had provided only fragments.[18] Tindal borrowed Herbert of Cherbury's and Wollaston's development of
the positive content of natural religion. Herbert named five principles
which he claimed to be common to all men: "I—That there is one Supreme God. II—That he ought to be worshipped. III—That Virtue
and Piety are the chief parts of Divine Worship. IV—That we ought
to be sorry for our sins and repent of them. V—That Divine goodness
doth dispense rewards and punishments both in this life and after it." [19]
These principles formed the basis of the whole deistic movement.
Tindal accepted Toland's repudiation of the mysterious and his rejection of the distinction between that which is contrary to reason and
that which is beyond reason. He agreed with Blount that what is neces-

[14] *Ibid.,* pp. 195-98.

[15] Locke, *Works,* VI, 148-49. See also John Orr, *English Deism: Its Roots and Fruits,*
pp. 84-113 (1934). Locke and Tillotson claim that rational propositions given from
without can be tested as any other propositions. Indeed, Tillotson felt that religion must
be accepted or rejected on the basis of its appeal to man's reason. Revealed religion is not
to destroy or to correct natural religion but merely to make it clearer and more effective.
Locke held we can gain religious knowledge and knowledge of God, not by intuition or
vision, but by the ordinary processes of rational demonstration.—*Essay on Human Understanding,* I, iv; IV, x. There are things which are above reason, however, such as the
resurrection of the dead.—*Ibid.,* IV, xvii, 23.

[16] Matthew Tindal's book entitled *Christianity as Old as Creation* was acclaimed as
the deist's Bible. It appeared in 1730, and its aim is to show that natural religion is a
pure and unalterable phenomenon and is not dependent on dogma or the deceits of
priestcraft. See chaps. vi, xiii of this work.

[17] David Hume published his *Essay on Providence and the Future State* in 1748, his
Natural History of Religion in 1757; and he wrote his *Dialogues Concerning Natural
Religion* in 1751, though this work was not published until after his death. These works
are directed against natural religion itself and end in complete skepticism.

[18] *Op. cit.,* p. 140.

[19] Herbert of Cherbury, *The Antient Religion of the Gentiles, and Causes of their
Errors Considered,* pp. 3-4.

sary to salvation must be known to all men and that revelation cannot be the special gift of God to the few. He accepted Shaftesbury's emphasis on ethics, Collins' insistence that prophecy must be considered as allegorical, and Woolston's rejection of miracles.[20] He set his teachings in an orderly system and offered them to the world.

At the very outset Tindal tells us that, since God is perfect, any religion that he gives to men must likewise be perfect and hence incapable of any improvement.[21] It is folly to contemplate the notion of a developing religion; the form of religion expressed in the Bible does not improve on religion as it was first bestowed upon man in creation.[22] "God has at all times given mankind sufficient means of knowing what he requires of them." [23] Revelation, therefore, is unnecessary and irrelevant to religion. If it is true that there is such a thing as revealed religion, then it came to free man from the load of superstition that he had heaped on himself.[24] However, Tindal does not accept the Bible as a whole or even the Gospels as constituting a revelation capable of freeing man from the load of superstition. He says that the Bible is filled with many unworthy things [25] and religion cannot shine through it in all its purity and truth.[26] But, if the Bible is clouded with errors, what, we ask, is the genuine content of that Christianity which is as old as the creation? Tindal, in his constructive statement, agrees with Lord Herbert of Cherbury in answering that true religion is belief in God and worship of God. But then he adds that it is, also, the seeking of one's own personal happiness and the co-operation with others in securing and promoting the common welfare of society.[27] Reason is man's ultimate guide, philosopher, and friend. No Gospel, writes Tindal, could be plainer than reason.[28] The law that is binding is the law that is given by reason. It is "a law which does not depend on the uncertain meaning of words and phrases in dead languages, much less

---

[20] Orr, *op. cit.*, pp. 140-41.
[21] *Christianity as Old as the Creation*, pp. 3, 49, 58-59, 118.
[22] *Ibid.*, pp. 2, 59, 115.
[23] *Ibid.*, p. 1.
[24] *Ibid.*, p. 7.
[25] *Ibid.*, pp. 22-23, 225.
[26] *Ibid.*, pp. 23, 54, 225.
[27] *Ibid.*, pp. 11-18.
[28] *Ibid.*, p. 22.

on types, metaphors, allegories, parables, or on the skill or honesty of weak or designing transcribers (not to mention translators) for many ages together." [29] Tindal reminds us that other religions have their sacred writings as well as Christianity,[30] that pagan cults cite miracles as well as the writers of the New Testament.[31] Then, too, there are actual disagreements in the Bible; for instance, one passage contradicts another. If the light of the body is the eye, then the light of the soul is the mind; and faith is made of the same *stuff* as reason, because in the last analysis faith is reason.

Such, in bare outline, was the philosophy of deism as it expressed itself in the English thought of the eighteenth century. Though traditional Christianity had many apologists, those apologists always attempted to meet deism on its own grounds; and, as one reads their works today, he finds them as cold and lifeless as the works of those whom they attempt to refute. Thus Leslie Stephen reminds us that the God the learned Warburton sought to defend sank in the course of argument "into a mere heap of verbal formulas."[32]

It would be erroneous to picture deism itself as the intellectual conqueror of the day. Such was not the case. The deist writings were, in comparison with the solid octavos and quartos arrayed against them—"very Goliaths among books"—but "shabby and shrivelled little octavos, generally anonymous, such as lurch in the corners of dusty shelves, and seem to be the predestined prey of moths."[33] Among the champions of orthodoxy stood such figures as Locke, Berkeley, Bentley, Clarke, Butler, Waterland, and Warburton. But the point is that rationalism had penetrated the ranks of orthodoxy; Christianity was viewed as nothing more than a correct set of opinions, a group of propositions which offer themselves to man's reason for acceptance or rejection just as any other "philosophical system, political principle, or financial investment."[34] Natural reason was the foundation of revela-

---

[29] *Ibid.*, p. 54.

[30] *Ibid.*, p. 163.

[31] *Ibid.*, p. 170.

[32] Stephen, *History of English Thought in the Eighteenth Century*, I, 367.

[33] *Ibid.*, p. 86. This literary comparison is used merely in regard to the number of the works and the ability of the defenders of the two groups taken as a whole. It is not used to prove that the deists' writings were not read or that they possessed no champions of ability.

[34] McGiffert, *op. cit.*, p. 195.

tion and the criterion of faith. Preaching, under the tutelage of rationalism, became dry, theoretic, and exclusively expository. Ministers, like philosophers, felt that they had to scrutinize severely every word they uttered and prove their points to the satisfaction of the most critical of the nonbelievers. Even the great Tillotson and Clarke read their sermons.[35] Warburton's sermons, in the words of his own biographer, were "masterly in their way, but fitter for the closet than for the Church. . . . They were written for the use of men of parts and learning." [36] The French literary critic Taine summarizes the situation adequately in these words: "A sort of theological smoke covers and hides this glowing hearth which burns in silence. A stranger who, at this time, had visited the country would see in this religion only a choking vapour of arguments, controversies, and sermons." [37]

The Wesleyan Revival, on the other hand, made no attempt to meet the intellectual attack of deism; it did not defend Christianity on a rationalistic basis. It was content merely to assert its own faith and to give testimony to the truth of God as it found that truth expressed in the Bible. In the writings of John Wesley deism is conspicuous more in the absence of attention paid to it than in any careful consideration of its tenets or any methodical refutation of its arguments.[38] The surest way to bring deists to Christianity, thought Wesley, was not by argument but by living example, by the positive affirmation of the principles of the Bible in character and in life.[39] The aim of the Wesleyan Revival, therefore, was to establish biblical Christianity over the land. Reason was not the mistress of revelation; [40] revelation itself was the starting point, for God had made his will known to man and had called on man for loyalty and allegiance.[41] Thus in his *Short History of Methodism* John Wesley writes that in 1738 he and his associates were of one heart and of one judgment and "resolved to be Bible-Christians at all events; and, wherever they went, to preach with

[35] Piette, *op. cit.,* p. 137.
[36] J. S. Watson, *Life of William Warburton,* p. 414.
[37] H. A. Taine, *History of English Literature,* II, 99.
[38] See his few references to deism: *Works,* I, 290, 532; II, 13-14, 164; VII, 196, 200, 298; VIII, 8, 6, 192-200; X, 77-78.
[39] *Ibid.,* X, 77.
[40] Piette, *op. cit.,* p. 123.
[41] Sermon LXXXV, secs. 2-3; Sermon LXIV, sec. 2; Sermon LV, sec. 15.

all their might plain, old Bible Christianity." [42] And in the preface to the very first edition of Wesley's sermons he announces the basis of his message:

I have thought I am a creature of a day, passing through life as an arrow through the air. I am a spirit come from God, and returning to God: Just hovering over the great gulf; till, a few moments hence I am no more seen; I drop into an unchangeable eternity! I want to know one thing,—the way to heaven; how to land safe on that happy shore. God himself has condescended to teach the way: For this very end he came from heaven. He hath written it down in a book. O give me that book! At any price give me the book of God! I have it: Here is knowledge enough for me. Let me be *homo unius libri.* Here then I am, far from the busy ways of men. I sit down alone: Only God is here. In his presence I open, I read his book; for this end, to find the way to heaven. Is there a doubt concerning the meaning of the thing I read? Does anything appear dark or intricate? I lift up my heart to the Father of Lights:—"Lord, is it not thy word, If any man lack wisdom, let him ask of God? Thou givest liberally, and upbraidest not. Thou hast said, If any be willing to do thy will, he shall know. I am willing to do, let me know thy will." I then search after and consider parallel passages of Scripture, comparing spiritual things with spiritual. I meditate thereon with all the attention and earnestness of which my mind is capable. If any doubt still remains, I consult those who are experienced in the things of God; and then the writings whereby, being dead, they yet speak. And what I thus learn, that I teach. [43]

The Wesleyan Revival ignored the rationalistic controversy about religion; its leaders felt little could be accomplished through argument; [44] they preferred the plain preaching of the Bible. And A. C. McGiffert, in his comment on the rationalistic movement in England, writes:

It is often asserted that in the controversy of the eighteenth century in England the victory was won by the orthodox apologists over both the deists and sceptics. Nothing could be further from the truth. . . . That religious faith and devotion still survived and flourished was due, not to the apologists, but to altogether different influences, of which the great evangelical revival was the most important. [45]

[42] *Works,* VIII, 349.
[43] *Ibid.,* V, 3-4.
[44] *Ibid.,* VIII, 350.
[45] *Op. cit.,* p. 243.

21

The Revival and Eighteenth-Century Morality

There was a second factor which characterized the birth of the Wesleyan movement. The Wesleyan Revival emerged as the moral counterpart of the immoral and corrupt tendencies which characterized the eighteenth century. Now it is not to be supposed by this statement that, apart from Methodism, or the Wesleyan Movement, there were no traces of spiritual or evangelical religion in England or that an absolute band had been placed on all moral practices and on all actions which savored of common decency. Too often this impression has been left by historians of the period; but "as long as the Bible and Prayer-book were read, as long as the great devotional literature of the past remained," [46] this was not altogether possible. In fact, the eighteenth century, like all other centuries, had some claims to honor and respect. Had not the Society for the Promotion of Christian Knowledge been founded just four years before the close of the seventeenth century, and did it not expand as time went on? Can anyone deny that ninety-six grammar schools were established before the year 1727, or that the Society for the Propagation of the Gospel in Foreign Parts was organized in 1701? [47] Addison himself wrote, "I have always looked on the institution of charity schools, which of late years has so universally prevailed through the whole nation, as the glory of the age in which we live." [48] And in a period of fifteen years, ending in 1712, London alone witnessed 117 such schools and an enrollment of nearly 5,000 children in them. The Society for the Reformation of Manners set itself enthusiastically to the task of combating bad morals and fighting crime.[49] It undertook the discovery and suppression of houses of ill fame, attempted to prosecute drunkards, Sabbath breakers, and swearers; and we learn from the fortieth annual report of the Society in 1735 that the number of prosecutions in London alone since the

[46] W. E. H. Lecky, *History of England in the Eighteenth Century*, II, 593.
[47] *Ibid.*, p. 594.
[48] *Guardian*, No. 105.
[49] Lecky, *op. cit.*, II, 594. It is interesting to note that on the Sunday of Jan. 30, 1763, Mr. John Wesley preached before the Society for the Reformation of Manners at the Chapel in West-Street, Seven Dials. This sermon, entitled the "Reformation of Manners," is preserved. It is Sermon LII in the series.

22

foundation of the Society had been 98,380.[50] There were still some traces of piety in the land.

Merely to cite the marks of goodness in a century, however, is not to erase its evils. The new movements in politics and the novel chances for increasing wealth had gone a long way in producing "a general indifference to all questions of religious speculation or of religious life." [51] The statesmen and scholars of the time paid little attention to religion; and drunkenness and foul talk were not held a discredit to Walpole, who as prime minister did not hesitate to act like a vulgar sailor. Marriage vows were no longer kept sacred, and Lord Chesterfield instructed his son in the art of seduction as a mark of a gentleman and a sign of a good education. The upper classes, so wrote Montesquieu, laugh at religion; it is simply not the thing to be brought up for discussion in polite English society.[52] Skepticism was spread abroad, especially through the upper classes; and, since it was of an indolent sort, it implied "a perfect willingness that the churches should survive though the Faith should perish." [53] Conditions among the poor were terrible. In fact, the masses of the people were "ignorant and brutal to a degree which it is hard to conceive, for the increase in population which followed on the growth of towns and the development of commerce" [54] had not been matched by religious and moral improvements. "The criminal classes gathered boldness and numbers in the face of ruthless laws which only testified to the terror of society, laws which made it a capital crime to cut down a cherry tree, and which strung up twenty young thieves of a morning in front of Newgate." [55] Police control was of the most inadequate sort, and frequently huge mobs broke out in London and Birmingham and burned houses, opened jails, and robbed and pillaged at will.

The slave trade was encouraged by the leaders of the nation; and as late as 1775 Lord Dartmouth, the secretary of state for the colonies and one of the most conspicuous leaders in English religious life, ex-

[50] Lecky, *op. cit.*, II, 595.
[51] J. R. Green, *History of the English People*, IV, 120.
[52] *Ibid.*, p. 121.
[53] Stephen, *op. cit.*, I, 375.
[54] Green, *op. cit.*, IV, 121.
[55] *Ibid.*

claimed in regard to slavery: "We cannot allow the colonies to check or discourage in any degree a traffic so beneficial to the nation." [56] Up to the year 1740 the number of Negroes introduced into the colonies of North America was around 130,000; but by 1776 that number had risen to more than 300,000.

The saddest fact of all was that, in the face of so great moral and spiritual needs, the Church itself was not equal to the task, for it had imbibed the spirit of the times. Green's description of the clergy furnishes us with a pitiable picture indeed. Many of the prelates were political appointees with no ecclesiastical and spiritual qualifications. One Welsh bishop frankly admitted that he had not seen his diocese more than once since his appointment. The system of pluralities made it possible for one clergyman to hold several churches at one time. Of course, each church had to be supplied with a preacher, but that necessity was easily relieved by the hiring of poor, indolent men without any consideration of their qualifications for the post.[57] Such was the moral situation in England; and, though one must admit the presence of some religious zeal, that zeal does not appear to have been widespread or to have been the sort which was at all *catching*. Genuine religion was on the decline, for in very truth a creed cannot "really flourish in which the faith of the few is not stimulated by the adhesion of the many." [58]

The Wesleyan Revival set itself to the task of restoring morality and decency to England. The keynote of its preaching was righteousness. Wickedness, thought its leaders and preachers, must be exposed; and ungodliness must be attacked even in high places. Thus on August 24, 1744, John Wesley preached his famous sermon before Oxford University on "Scriptural Christianity." In that sermon, after having described Christianity as leading to all inward and outward holiness and to the practice of good works, he turned boldly to his congregation and asked: "Where does this Christianity now exist? Where, I pray, do the Christians live?" [59] "Is this city a Christian city? Is Christianity, scriptural Christianity, found here? Are we, considered as a community

[56] Lecky, *op. cit.*, II, 16-17.
[57] Green, *op. cit.*, IV, 123-24.
[58] Stephen, *op. cit.*, I, 10.
[59] Sermon IV, part iv, sec. 3.

24

of men, so 'filled with the Holy Ghost,' as to enjoy in our hearts and show forth in our lives, the genuine fruits of that Spirit?" [60] Wesley told his congregation that it was not important to discuss theology but rather to live clean, decent, wholesome lives, to become in actuality "lively portraits of Him whom ye are appointed to represent among men." [61] Years later John Wesley wrote in regard to his movement that God raised up a few men to testify to that grand truth, which at the time was little attended to, that without holiness no man shall see the Lord.[62] And always in defending the validity of his preaching and the work of his movement John Wesley pointed to the moral successes, to the fact that men's lives were changed and that they produced in deeds and character the fruit of their faith.[63] In a letter to the Rev. Mr. Church, who had attacked his doctrines, Wesley penned these words:

I beseech you then to consider, in the secret of your heart, how many sinners have you converted to God? By their fruits ye shall know them. This is a plain rule. By this test let them be tried. How many outwardly and habitually wicked men have you brought to uniform habits of outward holiness? It is an awful thought! Can you instance in a hundred? in fifty? in twenty? in ten? If not, take heed unto yourself and your doctrine. It cannot be that both are right before God.[64]

Then he cited the accomplishments of his own ministry, which accomplishments are representative of the aims and achievements of the Wesleyan Revival:

The habitual drunkard, that was, is now temperate in all things. The whoremonger now flees fornication. He that stole, steals no more, but works with his hands. He that cursed, or swore, perhaps at every sentence, has now learned to serve the Lord with fear, and rejoice unto him with reverence. Those formerly enslaved to various habits of sin, are now brought to uniform habits of holiness. These are demonstrable facts. I can name the men, with their several places of abode.[65]

[60] *Ibid.*
[61] *Ibid.,* sec. 5.
[62] Sermon LXIII, sec. 13.
[63] *Works,* VIII, 475-77.
[64] *Ibid.,* p. 402.
[65] *Ibid.*

Such, in general, was the nature of the religious movement of the eighteenth century known as the Wesleyan Revival, or Methodism. Now we are in a position to consider the theology of that movement, more especially the teachings of John Wesley on the subject of justification.

Purpose and Method

The purpose of this book, therefore, is to set forth the Wesleyan view of the nature of the forgiveness of sins and the means whereby man is reconciled with God and is restored to communion and fellowship with his heavenly Father. The treatment of the subject falls into two main divisions: first, the development and formulation of the doctrine of justification; and, secondly, the relationship of the doctrine to other major theological concepts and the consequences of justification for man's moral and spiritual life. In the first division we shall treat the background out of which the doctrine arose and the positive and negative factors which influenced its formulation. We shall then define justification and attempt to ascertain its relationship to divine grace and human response and to set forth the conditions necessary to man's attaining its benefits. Finally, we shall note the marks, or signs, of justification in human life. In the second division we shall examine the relationship of justification to the concept of God, his power and his goodness, and attempt to ascertain the place of the justifying act in the moral government of the universe. We shall then consider justification in relation to the human need for it, the concept of man and sin; in relation to the divine cause or possibility of it, the concept of Christ and redemption; in relation to the instrument of its actualization, the concept of the Holy Spirit. Finally, we shall note the consequences or effects of justification in the moral and spiritual life.

Part One

THE DEVELOPMENT AND FORMULATION OF
THE DOCTRINE OF JUSTIFICATION

Chapter I

JUSTIFICATION BY FAITH AND WORKS

The Background of Wesley's Thought

THERE CAN BE NO DOUBT THAT THE INFLUENCES OF CHILDHOOD AND OF ADO-
lescence, the heritage of the family and of the school, are often "discernible, like the rings in the trunk of a tree," in the thought of mature
thinkers, and that "in spite of the natural decay and the violent eradication of certain component ideas, the final whole still indicates so
clearly the gradual growth of the intellectual possessions that it is possible to attempt a genetic analysis of the whole system by a study of
the various strata which compose it." [1] We dare not minimize the importance of this fact in our consideration of the subject before us. To
be sure, John Wesley was a synthetic thinker. He read widely; his in-
terests were various; and the scope of his intellectual curiosity was as
broad as the field of learning of the century in which he lived.[2] And yet
one idea was the focal point of all his thought and emerged as the uni-
fying principle around which diverse elements were gathered and by
means of which intellectual harmony was ensured. If he was interested
in electricity and studied the experiments of Benjamin Franklin, it was
only for the purpose of finding in that "electrical fire" a cure for paraly-
sis and other human infirmities and of thus restoring the body to
health and happiness, the natural condition for the receptivity of the
grace of God.[3] If he applied himself to philosophy and to the studies
of natural science, it was only for the purpose of showing man, in a
manner consistent with the secular learning of his day, the astounding
shortsightedness of human knowledge in the face of the mysteries of

[1] H. Boehmer, *Luther and the Reformation in the Light of Modern Research*, p. 248.
[2] The books which were read by Wesley cover the fields of geography, history, state-
craft, science, medicine, classical literature, oratory, biography, poetry, fiction, philosophy,
ethics, and religion. For a list of the books read and noticed by John Wesley in his
Journal, see the Everyman's Library edition of the *Journal*, Index, IV, 550-55.
[3] *Journal*, Fri., Oct. 16, 1747; Sat., Jan. 20, 1753; Sat., Feb. 17, 1753; Tues., Nov. 9,
1756; Mon., Jan. 4, 1768; Tues., Apr. 1, 1774. See also "A Plain Account of the People
Called Methodists," *Works*, VIII, 263-65 and passages from Wesley's correspondence,
Ibid., XIII, 88-89, 166.

the universe and of convincing him of the amazing power, wisdom, and goodness of the great Creator.[4] Salvation was the quest of Wesley's life, and all his thinking centered around this single goal.[5] But note carefully that salvation with Wesley was always a quest; and just as his life pictures movement and struggle, even so his thought exemplifies progress and development.

In this chapter, therefore, it is necessary for us to make a start in our examination of that development; and naturally we turn, first of all, to the ecclesiastical environment out of which Wesley came and to the home in which he was reared. In truth, a man is a part of all that he has met; and, if at the close of the year 1789 John Wesley was constrained to write, "From a child I was taught to love and reverence the Scripture, . . . to esteem the primitive Fathers, . . . and next after the primitive church to esteem our own, the Church of England, as the most scriptural national Church in the world," [6] is it not reasonable for us to expect to find some influences emerging from Wesley's home and from his Church and leaving their traces on his own doctrine of justification? We must, therefore, seek to understand the religious thinking of the age out of which Wesley came, to place the instruction of his childhood in its natural setting, and to see the man himself, not as some solitary religious figure totally removed from the currents of thought of his time, but rather as a man with a heritage and a whole stream of religious history flowing through his veins. In this chapter, therefore, we shall attempt to answer two questions: first, what on the eve of Wesley's birth was the prevailing thought among the theologians of the Church of England on justification; secondly, what was the thought of the parents of Wesley on this subject, and did their thought vary in any respect from the teachings which were predominant in the Church?

The Nature of Anglican Theology

In attempting to answer the first question, we are forced at once to recognize the peculiar nature of Anglican theological thought in gen-

[4] *Survey of the Wisdom of God in Creation, or a Compendium of Natural Philosophy,* Vol. I, pp. vii-viii.

[5] *Works,* V, 3; IX, 466.

[6] "Farther Thoughts on Separation from the Church," *Ibid.,* XIII, 272.

eral and to take into account the temper and spirit of that thought in
the consideration of any one of its doctrinal formulations. The theology
of the English Church on the eve of the eighteenth century was in a
peculiar sense the product of history. It had had its birth as the intellectual expression of and justification for a new church, a church both
English and Catholic, both national and universal. It had achieved its
manhood in a bitter struggle against the political intrigue and the
military might of Roman Catholicism. It had grown old and weak
in controversy and had died as a result of the quarrels and strife of
internal dissension; and yet, after the seeming triumph of Puritanism
and what appeared to be the complete eradication of the Anglican system from English national life, it had arisen again from the dead and
re-established itself, vigorous and supreme. Such a body of religious
thought, so closely allied to the temper and spirit of national life, itself
the effect, not the cause, of historical changes,[7] bore of necessity all the
marks of the influence of social and political movements. With Edward
VI and Archbishop Cranmer it had set its sails toward Geneva and
voyaged into the ports of Calvinism.[8] With Charles I and Archbishop
Laud it had put to sea again and had turned back in the direction of
the medieval Catholic faith.[9]

And yet, despite the circumstances of its origin and the vicissitudes
of its history, there was something more to Anglican theology than
the mere religious expression of social and political philosophy. At
heart it was spiritual. Its aim was to erect an intellectual system built
around the religious ideals of the English people. The seventeenth century saw the construction of such a system. In the Church of England,
Richard Hooker has become a name; for he it was, more than any

[7] Luther, Zwingli, and Calvin in a peculiar sense were the founders of their religious
movements, and these movements had social and political consequences. Anglicanism
did not have a religious founder in that sense and did not arise as a direct result of
religious fervor. Though many influences made the birth of Anglicanism possible, the
English Church was established as a political act under Henry VIII, when Parliament
adopted the Act of Supremacy in 1534. See J. R. Green, *History of the English People,*
II, 155, 158-160.

[8] "In the reign of Edward the doctrines of the Reformers were triumphant in the
Church of England."—J. Hunt, *Religious Thought in England,* I, 11. See Green, *op. cit.,*
p. 233.

[9] Green, *op. cit.,* III, 157-59; Hunt, *op. cit.,* pp. 168-72; Laud, *A Relation of a
Conference Between Laud and Jesuite Fisher,* pp. 125-56.

31

other man, who made the Anglican communion aware of itself "as an independent branch of the Church Universal . . . with a positive doctrine and discipline of its own and a definite mission in the wide economy of Grace." [10] On the foundation which he laid the divines of the seventeenth century built the structure of their theology; and, as we look back on that structure today, we see it, not as a compromise which evoked the support of the indifferent and merited the scorn of the sincere, but rather as an honest attempt to steer a middle course between the extremes of Roman Catholicism and radical Protestantism. The Bible, not the Church, contained for it, in the words of one of its bishops, "in all sufficiency and abundance the pure Water of Life, and whatsoever is necessary to make God's people wise unto salvation;" and yet the Church, too, was recognized by it as a "ministerial and subordinate rule and guide to preserve us and to direct us in the right understanding of the Scriptures." [11] The Bible, though affirmed as the only standard of the Anglican faith, was never quite freed from the Church in the true Protestant sense; and Dorner is entirely correct when he states that the English always showed an extreme mistrust for the private judgment of the laity and tended to let the clergy interpret the Bible for them.[12] *Sola fides* was incomprehensible apart from *salus extra ecclesiam non est.*

The Development of the Anglican Doctrine of Justification

The doctrine of justification, in common with the theology of which it was a part, underwent many changes and received many and diverse formulations at the hands of the various divines who dealt with it. Anglicanism was a roof which covered many opinions; and side by side in the house of the same tradition sat Calvinist and Arminian, sat the followers of Abbot and those of Laud.[13] Even more, the temper

---

[10] P. E. More, "Spirit of Anglicanism," in *Anglicanism,* ed. P. E. More and F. L. Cross, p. xix.

[11] F. White, *A Treatise of the Sabbath Day,* pp. 11-12.

[12] J. A. Dorner, *History of Protestant Theology,* I, 51.

[13] Every parish priest had his own personal opinion, and theological controversy was so pronounced that in 1623 James I issued directions that no preacher under the rank of bishop or dean should speak on such issues as predestination, election, reprobation, or the universality, efficacy, resistibility, or irresistibility of God's grace. Charles I likewise insisted on this of his clergy.—A. W. Harrison, *Arminianism,* p. 133.

of a particular period picked its favorites and conferred its popularity, so that *justification by faith* was the slogan of the age of Elizabeth, while that of *justification through the Church* was characteristic of the time of Charles I. Dr. Thomas Secker, then Bishop of Oxford, was unquestionably correct when in the year 1745 he reminded Wesley, on the occasion of Wesley's having made the fervent claim that his own doctrine of justification did not differ from that of the Church of England, that the doctrine of the Church of England itself differed from period to period; and that, in having professed deference and veneration for the teachings of the Church, he ought at the same time to have said whether he meant the Church and its pastors of the year 1545 or of the year 1745.[14] The doctrines of the two periods were not the same. This is true; but at the same time we must realize that, during the century which elapsed between the death of Elizabeth and the ascension of George I, there did develop a doctrine of justification which succeeded in gaining the allegiance of the Church and of establishing itself as the Anglican position. Despite the shades of variation in the interpretation of detail, there was a general way of interpreting the doctrine of justification which was accepted by the leaders of the Church and which was set forth by them as its official teaching. Once again, this doctrine was peculiarly English. It did not lean toward extremes. In the minds of its champions it avoided both the Scylla of Romanism and the Charybdis of Calvinism. It received its classic formulation in the *Harmonia Apostolica* of Bishop Bull. This doctrine of justification, together with the theology which dominated the Church after the Restoration and which interpreted the Prayer Book and the Thirty-nine Articles after the Savoy Conference of April, 1661, breathed the spirit of Archbishop Laud and bore the label of "Anglican Arminianism," a term designed not so much to link it with the Arminianism of the Continent as to separate it from Calvinistic Puritanism and to tie it to the faith and the tradition of the Church of the Apostles and of the Middle Ages.[15]

The foundation for such a doctrine of justification was laid as far

[14] Quoted from collection of Secker's letters to Wesley found in Henry Moore, *Life of John Wesley*, II, 280. This quotation is found in Wesley's correspondence with Secker, *Works*, XIII, 63.

[15] See H. O. Wakeman, *The Church and the Puritans*, p. 8.

back as 1586, when Richard Hooker delivered his sermon entitled "A Learned Discourse of Justification, Works, and How the Foundation of Faith Is Overthrown." [16] In this sermon Hooker defines for us the marks of agreement in the doctrine on this subject between the Church of England and the Church of Rome and, also, enumerates the points of disagreement between the followers of the See of Canterbury and those of the See of Peter. Both churches agree that all have sinned and, as a result of original sin, even infants have their natures defiled, destitute of justice, and averted from God; that God alone doth justify; that no man attains unto justification except by the merits of Christ; and that "although Christ as God be the efficient cause and Christ as man be the meritorious cause of our justification, yet in us also there is something required. . . . Christ hath merited to make us just: but as a medicine made for health doth not heal by being made but by being applied, so by the merits of Christ there can be no justification without the application of his merits." [17] Here Hooker sets Anglicanism within the stream of historic Christianity; there is no break. Man is not sufficient unto himself in the Pelagian sense. Justification is God's act made possible through the merits of Jesus Christ.

And yet the Church of England cannot agree with the Church of Rome in its conception of the nature of grace, namely, that the justifying righteousness of Christ is a quality infused in the human soul,[18] that it can be increased by works and diminished by sins.[19] In Hooker's opinion, to agree in this doctrine would be to admit that divine grace is a part of human nature, something inherent in us, a quality that is ours "just as our souls are ours." [20] Rather, the righteousness wherein we are justified is not our own but Christ's. It is objective. It remains outside of us. For Christ's sake God forgives us and accepts us as perfectly righteous, as if we had fulfilled all that is commanded in the law when in reality we have not obeyed one single precept.[21] The application of justifying grace to our sinful souls comes as a single act of God on us; and all the Ave Marias, crossings, papal salutations, and

[16] See note 30 in Keeble's edition of Hooker's *Works*, III, 483.
[17] *Ibid.*, p. 486.
[18] *Canons and Decrees of the Council of Trent*, Session VI, chaps. vii, x.
[19] *Ibid.*, chap. xvi.
[20] Hooker, *op. cit.*, p. 490.
[21] *Ibid.*

34

such like are of no effect either in preparation for or augmentation of this grace.[22]

Hooker is not prepared, however, to go in his theology all the way into the Camp of Geneva. The validity of man's election to justification does depend on his own consent; [23] his will is consulted, and nothing is given him except by his own deliberate advice and choice.[24] Not only so, but as soon as man is justified, God actually works righteousness in him [25]—that is, he sets in operation certain human processes which enable man to do good works, actually to co-operate with God and to become in a real sense his co-laborer. Though Hooker discards the Roman conception of the nature of grace by refusing to equate the good man does with the righteousness of Christ whereby he is justified, he none the less stops short of the teachings of Luther and Calvin that man is impotent, that he can initiate nothing worth while, and that his good works are no more than the signs and seals of God's act.[26]

True, Hooker laid the foundation, but those who followed were not too careful how they built thereon. Hooker stood at the beginning of the period; and, though he was no lover of Calvinistic discipline, he still had a profound respect for its theology. He left man helpless in his sinfulness and consistently refused to set any conditions on the divine bestowal of grace, as if "man could call God to a reckoning or hold Him in his debt books." [27] It is with William Laud and Lancelot Andrewes that we note a complete break with Calvinism and a fresh emphasis on man and the part he plays in his own justification. In his *Relation of a Conference Between Jesuit Fisher and Himself,* Laud boldly confesses that man has no way of knowing the truth of Scripture and of finding his road to heaven except by faith; but then he adds that faith itself is a human assent, "a mixed act of the will and of the understanding" in which act "the will inclines the understanding to yield full approbation to that whereof it does not see full proof." [28]

[22] *Ibid.,* pp. 488-89.

[23] Calvin holds that the validity of election does not depend on man's consent, as if we suppose "man to be a co-operator with God" or "that the will of man is superior to the counsel of God."—*Institutes of the Christian Religion,* III, xxiv, 3.

[24] Hooker, *op. cit.,* II, 540.

[25] *Ibid.,* pp. 539, 545.

[26] *Ibid.,* III, 507.

[27] *Ibid.,* III, 494.

[28] Laud, *op. cit.,* pp. 105-6.

Thus with Laud faith itself becomes man's own act made in co-operation with the Spirit of God; and even grace, God's gift, "is never placed but in a reasonable creature and proves by the very seat it hath taken up that the end it hath is to be but spiritual eye-water, to make reason see what 'by nature only it cannot' but never to blemish reason in that which it can comprehend." [29] Man by his nature as a rational creature is constrained to judge and to attempt to appraise the merits of faith and to weigh everything at the bar of reason, even the Word of God.[30] Lancelot Andrewes states that man himself must take the initiative and act in order to have faith.[31]

The Anglican Doctrine of Justification on the Eve of the Eighteenth Century

Now it will be impossible for us to trace in chronological sequence the development of this Arminian modification of Hooker's doctrine of justification through the writings of the many divines of the seventeenth century, for their name is legion.[32] But it will be possible and absolutely necessary for us to reconstruct, somewhat in detail, the salient features of the doctrine in its finished form and to present in a systematic fashion what at the close of the century had come to be the accepted teaching of the Church. This new emphasis on man's co-operation with God in the act of his own justification must be understood, not as an isolated phenomenon, affirmed for practical purposes and yet nowhere theoretically explained, but rather as an integral part of a well-thought-out view of justification.

Consider, to begin with, therefore, that the term "to justify" bears in the theology of this period a legal meaning. It is a term taken from the law court and is understood in the sense of "to acquit" or "to pronounce guiltless." In no case does it mean actually to purify from vice

[29] *Ibid.*, pp. 74-75.
[30] *Ibid.*, pp. 75-76.
[31] Andrewes, *Works*, VI, 21. See also II, 156-57, 322, 371; and III, 186-202.

[32] A. W. Harrison gives a brief but interesting sketch of the rise of Arminianism in general in England in his book entitled *Arminianism*, pp. 157-84. This is helpful in furnishing the names of some of the divines who were prominent Arminians. It is not footnoted, however, and there is no way of checking the sources. The subject is treated historically, and the doctrinal niceties in general are not dealt with. Justification is of course not treated specifically at all. The only way to get at the seventeenth-century doctrine of justification is to study first hand the writings of the divines themselves.

or to liberate from the habit of sinning. Rather, as Bishop Bull points out, the word "justify" is directly opposed to the word "accuse" or the phrase "lay to the charge of" "and therefore necessarily signifies to acquit an accused person and decree him free from accusation."[33] In every trial there must be a judge who pronounces sentence; there must be an accused person who is tried; and there must be a rigid law by which judgment is fairly given.[34] Always in this trial the judge is God, the accused person is man, and the law is either the law of Moses or else the law of Christ. Christians will be tried, of course, by the law of Christ.[35] But if "to justify" be but to give a legal pronouncement, then it follows that the author of justification is none other than the judge who pronounces the sentence. Man is, then, in a very real sense justified by God. He is pardoned. He is freed from guilt.

Why, we ask, is man pardoned? What prompts God to free him from guilt? If to justify does not mean to purify—if to pronounce guiltless does not mean to cleanse from actual sin—then it follows that one of two things must be the case: either God's justifying grace does not concern itself in the least with man's moral state but rather operates arbitrarily, freeing him from the punishment and yet leaving him in the practice of his sins; or else God's justifying grace does concern itself exclusively with man's moral state and operates according to moral law, coming as a consequence of, not as a means to, righteousness, freeing a man from punishment only when that man himself is actually free from sin. To affirm the former of these alternatives is to call into question the moral nature of God and to throw into jeopardy all ethical standards and all moral requirements. It is to separate religion from morality. It is to sever the bond that unites belief with practice. Such a course leads to uncontrolled antinomianism, to the wild frenzy of those children of God who behave like the children of the devil. It signifies the repudiation of all law and the establishment of a so-called "spiritual freedom" that knows no bounds and accepts no limits. To affirm the latter of these alternatives is to subordinate the religious significance of justification to a mere adjunct of moral practice. Morality becomes the standard by which all things are measured. Religion is subjected to

[33] Bull, *Harmonia Apostolica*, pp. 6-7.
[34] *Ibid.*, p. 19.
[35] *Ibid.*, p. 20.

37

its rule, and God's act in justification is nothing more than a judge's sentence. By his own laws he appraises man's life, and in the exact scale of justice he weighs offences against merits, and rewards or condemns according to human deserts. To be sure, the pronouncement of justification, the decision as to man's fate, is God's own act; but the means of its achievement are within man's power, and the deciding factor is the moral quality of man's own deeds. Why is man pardoned and freed from guilt? Because he deserves to be pardoned. He has merited the sentence of innocence.

Anglican theology, committed as it was to this legalistic conception of justification, accepted the second of these two alternatives and frankly confessed that man must work out his own salvation with fear and trembling. Man has endeavored to escape from the eye of divine justice; but, says Jeremy Taylor, nothing in the end "can escape but innocence." [36] And even James Ussher, who was far from going all the way with William Laud in his theology, none the less states in one of his sermons in the section devoted to conversion unto God, redemption, and justification: "Think not all will be surely well, because thou hasteth to shake hands with God at thy journey's end, when thou hast not walked with Him all the way." [37] Lancelot Andrewes writes: "With God verily it is a righteous thing to let every man receive for any kind of good he hath done. Yea, even the heathen for their moral virtues." [38] And George Bull clinches the point by saying: "Justification signifies that love of God, by which he embraces those who are already leading a holy life, and determines them to be worthy of the reward of life eternal through Christ." [39] What does this mean? Have we in pushing human freedom and responsibility to its final issue discovered that the Anglican theology of the seventeenth century was nothing more than an English brand of Pelagianism, or even worse, that it did not rise above the principles of the deists; for, though it affirmed God's existence and his justice, at the same time it ascribed to him no active role in man's salvation? What in its teachings became of the atonement, we ask? Was it nothing more than a moral example set before men? We

[36] *Works*, VIII, 335.
[37] *Whole Works*, XIV, 24.
[38] *Op. cit.*, II, 90.
[39] *Op. cit.*, p. 7.

miss the truth altogether if we carry the issue this far. Anglican theology still affirmed the atonement as an objective act, satisfying God's righteous justice as well as making its appeal to man's sense of guilt and shame. True, in its teachings man himself meets the conditions which make possible his justification before God, but God provided him with the means by which to meet those conditions.

If man had had within himself the power to fulfill the conditions and to meet the moral requirements and actually had done so, God would have justified him and given him the reward of eternal happiness. But the Anglican divines of this period recognized that man does not possess that power and cannot meet those conditions in his own strength. "Furthermore, we were all first enslaved by sin, and brought into captivity by Satan, neither was there any possibility of escape but by way of redemption. Now it was the law of Moses that, if any were able, he might redeem himself: but this to us was impossible, because absolute obedience in all our actions is due unto God, and therefore no act of ours can make any satisfaction for the least offence." [40] The means for man's justification, therefore, must come in the first instance from Christ. Thus John Pearson, speaking as the mouthpiece of his century, tells us why Christ in literal truth is our Saviour. The first reason why he deserves this appellation is that he has declared unto us the only way for the obtaining of eternal salvation. In other words, he has set forth the requirements which God demands that we meet in order to obtain justification. But a second and stronger reason why Christ deserves to be called our Saviour is that he has procured salvation for us and wrought it out in our behalf. Finally, Christ must be accepted as our Saviour because he confers salvation on us. Thus in the actual giving of salvation to us, which itself is the reward for what he suffered, we find the ultimate ground and the conclusive proof of his right to the title of Saviour. [41]

Final salvation, together with justification, which itself must precede salvation for the reason that it is God's declarative act that man is liberated from guilt and delivered from punishment and hence entitled to salvation, comes to man, not through his own deserts, but

[40] J. Pearson, *An Exposition of the Creed*, p. 113.
[41] *Ibid.*, p. 114.

alone through the merits of Jesus Christ. The Anglican theology of
the seventeenth century did not forget that fact. At the heart of its
theory of justification was a cross. Christ, merely out of

charitable pity toward us purposely came down from Heaven, and took our
flesh upon Him, that He might therein undergo those extreme acerbities
of pain, and those most ugly indignities of shame for us. . . . That He
should lay down His life, pour out His blood, should be aspersed with the
worse crimes, and clothed with the foulest shame, should be executed on
the cross as a malefactor and a slave, for His enemies and rebellious traitors,
what imagination can devise any expression of charity or friendship comparable to this? [42]

Christ . . . taketh upon Him our nature, bindeth Himself unto all, to
satisfy whatsoever might be exacted of us by His cleanness and pureness,
blotting out whatsoever stains or spots we are infected with in our nature.[43]

By reason of our insufficiency, Christ giveth us a bill under His hand
unto the Father, that all our debts are satisfied, all are reckoned up upon
His score, and therefore now being in Him we need not fear.[44]

Now the Anglican divines taught that Christ had made satisfaction
unto God for all mankind. They proclaimed universal redemption.
The doctrine of Christ's dying for none but the elect was ruled out of
their theology.[45] But immediately we ask, If Christ died for all, why,
then, are all not saved? On the basis of Christ's merits why does God
not pronounce all men as just and pardon them of their former offences? The Anglican theologians reply to this by saying that redemption, though universal, is none the less conditional.[46] But is not this a
contradiction? How can a thing be universal, unlimited, all-reaching,
entire, and at the same time be conditional, limited, partial, particular?
The answer is obvious. Redemption is universal considered in the light
of God's intention. Christ's atonement was intended for all mankind.
But redemption is conditional considered in the light of man's freedom.
"Christ died for all if all will take care to perform the condition re-

[42] I. Barrow, *Works*, II, 130.
[43] Ussher, *op. cit.*, XIII, 512.
[44] *Ibid*.
[45] H. Hammond, *Miscellaneous Theological Works*, II, 133-34.
[46] *Ibid.*, p. 138.

40

quired by Him." [47] Man must accept the satisfaction he made to God for him and actively claim it as his very own. Thus we may safely say that through the merits of Christ we are justified, acquitted, pronounced guiltless, only on the condition that we meet actively and completely the requirements set by him.

Bishop Bull's *Harmonia Apostolica* establishes the thesis that man cannot rest solely in the assurance that Christ died for him but that he must actively seek a reformation in his life in order to be capable of the benefits of the atonement. The Pauline conception of justification by faith does not exclude the teaching of St. James that man is justified by works. The two ideas are not separate and distinct philosophies standing in direct opposition to one another. Rather, they are two aspects of a single philosophy, complementary phases of one unified plan of salvation. Faith itself is not to be understood as belief, trust, confidence, or any other single virtue but rather as that which denotes the whole condition of the Gospel covenant and which includes in a single concept all the works of Christian piety. [48] In the last analysis faith is really a work, for it involves man's own act of assent to the validity of the Gospel teaching, his willingness to engage in works of repentance, and his humble desire both to be good and to do good. [49]

Critics trained in the tradition of the Reformation and familiar with the Confession of Augsburg, from which the eleventh article in the Thirty-nine Articles is taken, are led to question the validity of Bull's position. "We are accounted righteous before God only for the merit of our Lord and Savior Jesus Christ, by faith, and not for our own works or deservings: wherefore we are justified by faith only is a most wholesome doctrine, and very full of comfort." But the point is that the Caroline divines gave to the Thirty-nine Articles their own interpretation, and they were quite willing to agree with Bull that the phrase "justify by faith only," as used in the eleventh article, has only a figurative meaning and that the word "faith" must be understood in the sense of grace. [50] Naturally faith, in the sense of belief, in the merits of Jesus Christ is principally necessary in the achievement of justifica-

[47] *Ibid.*, pp. 138-40.
[48] Bull, *op. cit.*, p. 58.
[49] *Ibid.*, pp. 16-17, 18.
[50] *Ibid.*, pp. 198-99.

tion, but this faith must be established by works, or it is of no effect.

The Anglican Church laid great stress upon the sacraments and insisted on a regular observance of them on the part of the members of the Church.[51] They were considered among the good works necessary to the fulfillment of the conditions for justification, but more than this they were regarded as the means for the release of supernatural power into natural channels and the instruments for the achievement of moral goodness and the deeds of charity which flow therefrom. "Sacraments are the powerful instruments of God to eternal life. For as our natural life consisteth in the union of the body with the soul, so our life supernatural in the union of the soul with God. . . . Sacraments do serve to make us partakers of Christ." [52] Christ through the sacraments "driveth" his grace into those who use them in order to enable them to perform his will. Sacraments are moral instruments, "the use whereof is in our hands, the effect" in God's.[53] Of the two sacraments,[54] baptism signifies that God washes man thoroughly and purifies him from all sin, original and actual,[55] and enables him to begin the course of his Christian life; while the sacrament of the Lord's Supper, in which the body and blood of Christ are taken and eaten "after an heavenly and spiritual manner" signifies that God confirms and strengthens and keeps man in the Christian life and causes him to perform good works.[56] The sacraments, then, must be understood, not in the sense of supernatural operations which in themselves confer on man the right

[51] Laud, *Visitation Articles,* "Concerning the Parishioners," secs. 1, 9.

[52] Hooker, *op. cit.,* II, 220.

[53] *Ibid.,* p. 258.

[54] *Thirty-nine Articles,* art. xxv.

[55] *Ibid.,* art. xxvii. Anglicanism accepts baptismal regeneration. See Hooker, *op. cit.,* II, 263; I, 348-50; J. Taylor, *op. cit.,* I, 154-56. "A child is brought into the world, but it is carried out again to the Church, there to be born and brought forth anew, by the Sacrament of Regeneration."—Andrewes, *op. cit.,* II, 372. But an unbaptized infant is not necessarily damned or sent to *Limbus Infantum,* where he suffers *poenam damni* but not *poenam sensus;* rather, he may be saved without baptism by the grace of God. —See J. Hall, *Works,* VI, 248-49; F. White, *The Orthodox Faith and Way to the Church Explained and Justified in Answer to a Papish Treatise, etc.,* p. 177; J. Bramhall, *Works,* V, 176-78. This means that baptism is not by its nature or essence absolutely essential to salvation, but it is the usual means that God takes to regenerate and to purify and is thus by God's appointment the instrument of regeneration.—Hooker, *op. cit.,* II, 264-69, 304, 311. Hooker's position in regard to baptism remained normative for the Church.

[56] *Ibid.,* art. xxviii. See Andrewes, *op. cit.,* III, 128, 349; Barrow, *op. cit.,* III, 524-27.

to be justified by God regardless of his moral achievements, but rather as supernatural operations which enable man to perform moral acts and to achieve a quality of moral goodness which cause God to appropriate unto him the merits of his Son and to pronounce him justified.

Thus the conception of justification which was predominant in the Church of England at the opening of the eighteenth century was in the final analysis an attempt to hold together in a single system God's grace and man's responsibility. In doing this it laid its chief emphasis on man and on the requirements he must meet in order to be justified. Though it categorically affirmed that no man in himself can fulfill the requirements of perfect obedience and attain the right of justification, that all must be accounted righteous through the merits of our Lord Jesus Christ, it none the less set conditions on the appropriation by man of the gift of Christ's merits, and it established faith, in the sense of belief, and works, in the sense of moral and sacramental acts of obedience, as absolutely essential instruments for the bestowal of justifying grace. Man must take the initiative. Man must ask in order to receive, seek in order to find, knock in order to have the door of salvation freely opened.

The Doctrine of Justification Held by Wesley's Parents

Now we must inquire what precisely were the thoughts, the teachings, of Samuel and Susannah Wesley in regard to the doctrine of justification and whether or not they varied in any fundamental way from that interpretation of the doctrine which was predominant in the Church. Such an inquiry, on the surface, may appear ridiculous. Justification is a theological term, and it is hardly reasonable for us to expect to find it in general use within the family circle of an ordinary country home. But let us remember that the parsonage at Epworth was no ordinary home. Samuel and Susannah Wesley had discussed theology since their wedding day. Each possessed an independent and original mind. Though Susannah Wesley had been reared in the home of a dissenter, before she had reached "full thirteen" years of age she had begun to examine the literature on the "controversy between the Established Church and the Dissenters" and had reasoned her way back into the Church of England.[57] As a young lady, through a desire for absolute rationality in religion, she had embraced Socinianism, and only after her marriage had she been "drawn off from the Socinian heresy" by her "religious orthodox" husband and confirmed and strengthened in her new faith by the writings of Bishop Bull.[58] In her maturity, when she was forty or forty-one years of age, she had written an exposition of the Apostles' Creed, a document which proves beyond doubt her competence in the field of theology and indicates clearly the metaphysical temper of her mind.[59]

Samuel Wesley, the husband of this remarkable woman, though he possessed neither her practical ability nor her persuasive personality, was in his own right a careful student of divinity and a scholar of no mean repute. Like his wife, he had been brought up a dissenter and yet before his matriculation at Oxford had been so convinced of the error of the opinions of his youth that he had professed his willingness to "undergo the sharpest resentment from a sort of people who are none the best natured in the world . . . if thereby any small service may be done to the Church of England." [60] At the age of twenty-nine he had been one of the editors and chief contributors to the *Athenian Gazette,* a publication designed to improve knowledge in divinity and philosophy in all their parts and to commend this knowledge to the public in the best method possible for instruction.[61] Besides his poetic endeavors, which were constant and continuous, he had written *The Pious Communicant Rightly Prepar'd; or a Discourse Concerning the Blessed Sacrament.* Theology was no stranger to the Wesley fireside, and from early childhood John seemed to feel himself answerable to his reason and his conscience for everything he did.[62] Had not his mother insisted on "conquering the will" of her children because in her mind that was the "only strong and rational foundation of a religious education" and then on informing their understanding because

---

[57] J. Kirk, *The Mother of the Wesleys,* p. 32.

[58] *Ibid.,* p. 31.

[59] This document is preserved in its entirety and is printed in A. Clarke, *Memoirs of the Wesley Family,* II, 38-72.

[60] Samuel Wesley, *Letter of Country Divine Concerning the Education of Dissenters,* p. 3.

[61] L. Tyerman, *Life and Times of Samuel Wesley,* p. 139.

[62] L. Tyerman, *Life and Times of John Wesley,* I, 18.

she desired them to be "governed by reason and piety" and to have "the principles of religion" rooted in their minds?[63] Though Samuel and Susannah Wesley disagreed about many things and at one time almost separated because of a dispute over politics,[64] they nevertheless shared the same religious and theological opinions; and in this area Samuel Wesley was absolute master of his house.[65]

Let us turn now to a careful consideration of the theological views of the parents of John Wesley. Both Samuel and Susannah Wesley belong to that school of thought which we have styled "English Arminianism." In a letter to her son John of August 18, 1725, Mrs. Wesley writes:

> The doctrine of predestination, as maintained by the rigid Calvinists, is very shocking and ought to be abhorred, because it directly charges the most high God with being the author of sin. I think you reason well against it; because it is certainly inconsistent with the justice and goodness of God to lay any man under either a physical or moral necessity of committing sin, and then to punish him for it.[66]

Likewise Samuel Wesley repudiates the doctrine of unconditional election. He writes: "We cannot be satisfied by any of those scriptures which are brought for that purpose, that there is any such *election* of a *determinate number* as either puts a force on their *nature* and *irresistibly* saves them, or absolutely excludes all the rest of mankind from salvation."[67] Now both the father and mother of John agree that God does foresee all that will happen and foreknows all those who will make use of his grace. But in no case do they interpret this foreknowledge so as to overrule man's freedom. "God necessitates no evil action, yet He foresees all. If God tempts no man to evil, much less does He necessitate. Indeed, were He to do this, the nature of man would be destroyed, the proposals of rewards and punishments would be ironical, preaching would be vain, and faith also vain."[68] And Susannah

---

[63] See the letter of Susannah Wesley to her son John, dated July 4, 1742, on the education of her children.—*Journal*, Sun., Aug. 1, 1742.

[64] *Works*, XIII, 504.

[65] Tyerman, *Life and Times of Samuel Wesley*, pp. 125-27; Kirk, *op. cit.*, pp. 192-94; Piette, *John Wesley in the Evolution of Protestantism*, pp. 216, 218.

[66] Letter is printed in Tyerman, *Life and Times of John Wesley*, I, 40.

[67] *Athenian Oracle*, I, 178. Italics are Wesley's.

[68] *Ibid.*, II, 101.

puts the matter into a cryptic sentence: "Nor can it with more reason be supposed that the prescience of God is the cause that so many finally perish, than that one knowing the sun will rise to-morrow is the cause of its rising." [69] Man's freedom is indisputably affirmed. The rector of Epworth writes: "God made man upright, and a free agent. God's prescience presides over man's free agency, but doth not overrule it by saving man whether he will or no, or by damning him undeservedly." [70]

But what is the general conception of justification that we find set forth in the writings of Samuel and Susannah Wesley? Here again we find no deflection from the teaching which was predominant in the Church. If Bishop Bull defines justification in the sense of "acquitting" or "pronouncing guiltless," so Samuel Wesley declares it to be an act of God whereby he pardons and frees from punishment. "By God's justifying a sinner is meant His looking upon us and treating us as just and innocent persons, although before we stood guilty of heinous sins, and thereupon liable to grievous punishments." [71] Justification, therefore, is God's own declarative act that man is accounted innocent and is "esteemed righteous by God." [72] Note again that this is said to come, not through any merits on man's part, but solely through the merits of Jesus Christ.[73] Justification comes alone, writes Mrs. Wesley, "through Jesus Christ, the Mediator of the New Covenant, who gave his life a sacrifice by way of compensation and satisfaction to divine justice, by which God became reconciled to man, and cancelled the obligation which every sinner lay under to suffer eternal punishment." [74] The Wesleys, also, affirmed the doctrine of universal redemption as viewed in the light of God's intention and purpose. "Christ atoned so far for the sins of all mankind as to make them in a salvable condition." [75] "God really wills the salvation of all men, as far as is consistent with the liberty of man and His own purity and justice." [76]

[69] Tyerman, *Life and Times of John Wesley*, I, 40.
[70] *Athenian Oracle*, I, 58.
[71] *Ibid.*, p. 455.
[72] *Ibid.*, IV, 140.
[73] *Ibid.*, I, 455.
[74] Clarke, *Memoirs of the Wesley Family*, II, 66-67.
[75] *Athenian Oracle*, III, 531.
[76] *Ibid.*, p. 260.

The work of Christ must be appropriated by man. Man must fulfill actively certain conditions in order to be pardoned by God. True, God planned that man should be made salvable by Christ, but on condition of faith and a sincere, though imperfect, obedience to the law of God.[77] Here, then, we have reached the crucial point. What are the means of man's appropriation of the gift of Christ's atonement? Note carefully they are the same means as those set forth by Bishop Bull. Man attains the right to be justified by both faith and works. "Faith in Christ," writes Mrs. Wesley, "is assent to whatever is recorded of him in the Holy Scripture, or is said to be delivered by him, either immediately or mediately through the prophets and apostles."[78] Faith is belief. Like Laud, the Wesleys conceive of it as a human act, an act of assent and trust. This assent, however, is to more than just the "truths of the Gospel concerning Jesus;" it is likewise assent to the Gospel "influences and practices." Belief cannot stand alone. It must always be supported by the works of obedience.[79] Thus in a letter to one of her children, dated Jan. 13, 1710, Mrs. Wesley writes: "But, Sukey, it is not learning these things by heart (i.e., prayers, catechisms, creeds, Scripture passages) nor your saying a few prayers morning and night that will bring you to heaven; you must understand what you say, and you must practice what you know."[80]

The sacraments are to be understood in harmony with the Anglican conception of the period as divine instruments appointed by God as the means of aiding man to work out his salvation. The sacraments, writes Mr. Wesley, are "appointed for our perfection in Grace, as well as our conquest over our sins."[81] Baptism washes away the damning guilt of original sin by the application of the virtue of Christ's death, and through it we are admitted into the door of the Christian Church.[82] The sacrament of the Lord's Supper provides power and strength to conquer sin and fulfill the active duties of the Christian life. "If we impartially consider those among us, who do most frequently commu-

[77] Clarke, *op. cit.*, II, 47.
[78] *Ibid.*, pp. 47-48.
[79] *Ibid.*, p. 27.
[80] *Ibid.*, p. 39.
[81] Samuel Wesley, *The Pious Communicant Rightly Prepar'd*, p. 183.
[82] *Ibid.*, p. 200.

nicate, I am persuaded we should find them the most devout and rational Christians, and generally the best of men." [83]

Here, then, within the teachings of Samuel and Susannah Wesley, we find reproduced the doctrine of justification which was predominant in the Church of England on the eve of the eighteenth century. Faith is no longer represented as the free gift of God implanted in the human soul. Rather, it is itself a human act and takes its place among the works of moral endeavor. If man is said to be justified by faith and works, it must be understood that the two terms are essentially the same. Both have their roots firmly embedded in the soil of man's nature and grow through the watering of human achievement. Faith, virtue, reward—these three. The concern of the parents of John Wesley was for the salvation of their children and for the spiritual happiness of their immortal souls. The best way they knew to express this concern was, in the words of Susannah, by endeavoring to instill into their minds those principles of knowledge and virtue that are absolutely necessary in order to lead a good life here, which is the only thing that can infallibly secure happiness hereafter. [84]

> Virtue alone can deathless Laurels boast
> She gains the day when Life itself is lost. [85]

[83] *Ibid.,* p. 67.
[84] Clarke, *op. cit.,* II, 38-39.
[85] Samuel Wesley, *History of the Holy Bible in Verse,* CIII, 1-2. (Vol. I, p. 187.)

Chapter II

THE ALMOST CHRISTIAN

How a sinner may be justified before God is more than a problem in theology. It is a "question of no common importance to every child of man." [1] The correct answer to the question contains the foundation of all hope, for it points the way to a deliverance from sin and the consequences of sin, both in this world and in the next. [2] Any doctrine of justification must be viewed in the light of the religious needs which produced it. We learn, as Wesley wisely saw, not only from the oracles of God but also from the sure testimony of our experience. [3] In this chapter, therefore, we must face the religious problems of John Wesley's early life, see him in the very beginning of his struggle for salvation, and watch him in the school of practical experience as he discovers those truths which later become the teachings of Methodism.

Wesley's Religious Training in the Home

The very first fact that confronts us—and this fact emerges as a consequence of the theological view of justification held by the parents of John Wesley—is that John, together with his brothers and sisters, was trained for godliness in the home. He was taught, first of all, to believe, to give his assent to the truths of God's revelation in the gospel, to accept without question a proposition of faith on the authority of the revealer. "Divine faith," writes his mother, "is an assent to whatever God has revealed to us, because he has revealed it." [4] Yes, this unconditional belief is an absolute requisite to salvation. [5] Belief is the foundation of solid piety and sound virtue. [6] On the basis of these convictions Mrs. Wesley attempted to fashion the minds of her children

[1] Sermon V, intro., sec. 1.
[2] Sermon I, part ii, sec. 7.
[3] Sermon II, part i, sec. 11.
[4] Tyerman, *Life and Times of John Wesley*, I, 39.
[5] *Ibid.*, p. 40.
[6] Clarke, *Memoirs of the Wesley Family*, II, 23.

after a definite pattern of godliness. Under no circumstance did she neglect their timely correction for all faults. "When a child is corrected it must be conquered, and this will be no hard matter to do, if it be not grown headstrong by too much indulgence."[7] But why must it be conquered? Simply because self-will is "the root of all sin and misery, so whatever cherishes this in children ensures their afterwretchedness and irreligion: whatever checks and mortifies it promotes their future happiness and piety."[8] In fact, religion itself is nothing else than doing the will of God and not our own will. A child's will must be completely broken. "Heaven or hell depends on this alone. So that the parent who studies to subdue it in the child works together with God in the renewing and saving a soul; the parent who indulges it does the Devil's work, makes religion impracticable, salvation unattainable, and does all that in him lies to damn his child, soul and body, for ever."[9]

John Wesley was reared according to rules, and the highest authority he knew was mediated to him through the parental discipline of his home. This is an important factor in his moral and spiritual development, and one that we dare not minimize. For in it is involved the distinction between works that arise from slavish obedience and those that spring forth spontaneously as the creative expressions of a free soul. To be sure, Wesley was taught to say the Lord's Prayer as soon as he could speak; but then he was made to repeat it at rising and bedtime as long as he remained within his father's home. He was given a taste of the Prayer Book and the Scriptures, but after he had tasted them he was forced to take and to retain just as large portions of them as his memory could bear. Taking God's name in vain, cursing, swearing, profaneness, obscenity, rude, ill-bred names were never so much as heard by John Wesley as a child, and irregularities of conduct and behavior were alien to his nature as long as he lived.[10] The Wesley children were put into a regular method of living at the very day of their birth; and, if justification be the result of moral consistency and earnestness alone, then John Wesley was set on the road to its attainment from the very day he learned his name. He and his brothers and

[7] *Journal*, Sun., Aug. 1, 1742.
[8] *Ibid.*
[9] *Ibid.*
[10] *Ibid.*

sisters were admonished to fulfill all ecclesiastical and sacramental offices and to expect salvation only through faithful allegiance to the Church.[11] They were likewise told to join in all pious and charitable actions. Mrs. Wesley used to say time and time again, "May you still in such good works go on and prosper."[12] The moral and spiritual principles embodied in the doctrine of justification, accepted and taught by the parents of John Wesley, were given concrete expression in the regulation of the home and in the moral instruction of the children and in the daily activities of all the members of the family. In literal truth, theory was the guide to practice in the parsonage at Epworth.

Relation of Home Training to the Convictions of Wesley's Youth

But immediately we ask what the relationship is between the instruction Wesley received in his home and the moral and spiritual aspirations of his youth. This is a very difficult question, and one that causes us to pause before venturing an answer. First we must ask, Did Wesley undergo any moral changes; did he fall into any habits of conduct the repetition of which modified his entire character and changed the whole tenor of his life? To use Tyerman's oft-quoted phrase, did he enter the Charterhouse a saint and leave it a sinner?[13] Now it is important to note that Tyerman bases his affirmative answer to this question entirely on Wesley's own testimony; and this testimony, to say the least, is mild and causes us to wonder what Wesley thought a sinner really was. All Wesley says is that, since he was no longer restrained by rules, he became negligent of his outward duties and did commit outward sins. But he goes on at once to add that these sins were not considered scandalous in the eyes of the world, though he himself knew them to be wrong. In view of the strict standards under which Wesley was brought up and in light of the contrast he here draws between what society considers wrong and what he himself judges wrong, it does not seem likely that Wesley fell into any flagrant evils or committed any grievous sins.[14] But say perchance he did. We still cannot infer that such sins changed his character and modified

[11] Clarke, op. cit., II, 65.
[12] Ibid., p. 102.
[13] Tyerman, Life and Times of John Wesley, I, 22.
[14] See Piette, John Wesley in the Evolution of Protestantism, pp. 240-44.

the whole temper of his moral life. He himself invalidates such an inference at once by going on to say that he still read his Bible, said his prayers morning and evening, and actually hoped to be saved. This hope for salvation, he tells us, was based on the fact that he was not so bad as other people, that he still had a kindness for religion, and that he faithfully fulfilled the forms of religion.[15] This is substantially repeated in regard to his life at Oxford, where for five years he read the Scripture, several other books on the New Testament, and even felt short struggles, especially before and after Holy Communion, which he received thrice a year.[16] Wesley's character had not changed. The ideals of his life were high; the standards which he aimed for were far above those of most of his fellows. In other words, he had not adopted any new standard of values or geared his conduct with entire satisfaction to a form of action which he knew to be less than the best. If at home he had been taught that he "could only be saved by universal obedience, by keeping all the commandments of God,"[17] so in school and college he maintained this conviction even though he knew he was not fulfilling the moral conditions which it imposed.

Next we must ask whether Wesley underwent any radical intellectual changes, whether he modified fundamentally any of the religious convictions he had taken from his home. A boy coming from a conservative religious background and accepting without question the teachings of his parents on matters of faith is likely to meet in the new and strange life of a university many intellectual difficulties, to face problems which before he did not know even existed, and to give way to doubt, hesitancy, and perhaps even unbelief. To be sure, the new empiricism in philosophy was already beginning to be felt among the intellectually alert students at Oxford; the old scholastic treatment of problems in theology which had been revived in the universities during the reign of the Stuarts was rapidly falling into disrepute, and the scholarly defense of traditional Christianity against the onslaught of the deists was tending itself to water down through arid rationalism the vital elements of the faith. How did Wesley react in such a situation?

[15] *Journal*, Wed., May 24, 1738, sec. 2.
[16] *Ibid.*, sec. 3.
[17] *Ibid.*, sec. 1.

We know that he possessed an unusually keen and curious mind; he had a flair for scientific problems; he was a sharp logician; and nothing delighted him more than to overturn and humiliate all those who dared to debate with him on academic issues.[18] But, strange as it may seem, we find in the thought of the young Wesley absolutely no break with the conservative theological principles which dominated the thinking of his father and mother. Wesley's mind, though curious, was yet cautious; though always on the alert for new information, it was none the less hesitant to surrender any concept it had already acquired. Though he writes in July of the year 1725 that he cannot understand anything, even faith itself, except on rational grounds, and affirms that those things which contradict reason cannot stand on rational grounds,[19] at the same time he goes on to assure us that rationality itself is built on evidence and that he considers divine testimony to be the most reasonable of all evidence whatever.[20] Strange, unusual, mysterious events, therefore, found their place in his system of things; and he was as willing to accept them as to accept any ordinary occurrence provided they were consistent with facts and did not violate established truths.[21] Thus the religious skepticism engendered by deism seems to have passed him by; and even the rational appeals of Socinianism and English Arianism, which at one time had threatened his mother, seems never to have erected any barrier for her son. The forces which produced John Wesley's theology are not, therefore, to be found in the intellectual subtleties of various and conflicting modes of philosophical thought. Rather, they are to be found in the moral and spiritual endeavors of his life, in his earnest attempt to be something and to do something in and for the Kingdom of God.[22]

We may say, therefore, in answer to our previous question that the religious and spiritual aspirations of Wesley's youth (the period from June 24, 1720, when he passed his matriculation examination for Ox-

[18] See Piette, op. cit., pp. 238-39, 241, 546.
[19] Letters, I, 21-22.
[20] Ibid., p. 23.
[21] Ibid., pp. 13-14.
[22] I find no instance in Wesley's entire life when he was led to doubt any of the evidences of historic Christianity on the basis of philosophical or even intellectual considerations.

ford, down to May 24, 1738, when he was converted at Aldersgate) were directly related to the instruction he had received in his home and were built solidly on the teachings of his childhood. But at the same time we must examine the peculiar nature of those religious aspirations, consider carefully the factors that helped to form them, and note the channel of expression they took.

Factors in the Development of Wesley's Early Thought

The year 1725 stands out as a red-letter date in John Wesley's life. In that year, when he was twenty-three, he discovered, perhaps merely by accident, perhaps by the kindly suggestion of his father or a friend, Jeremy Taylor's *Rules and Exercises of Holy Living and Holy Dying*. We have seen already that prior to this date, though he had not surrendered any of the moral and spiritual aspirations that he had received from the training of his home, he had nevertheless been guilty of many acts of conduct which he felt were inconsistent with those aspirations. Now we find from his own record that after having read several parts of Taylor's book he was exceedingly affected and decided to dedicate all his life to God.[23] The section which most affected him was that which deals with purity of intention. In that section Taylor sets forth certain rules for our intentions. Of course in every action we must reflect upon the end, and in our attempting to perform the action we must consider why we do it. But Taylor insists that we let every action be begun with prayer, prosecuted under the continuance of its direction, and completed in its spirit. "Have a care, that, while the altar thus sends up a holy flame, thou dost not suffer the birds to come and carry away the sacrifice: that is, let not that which began well, and was intended for God's glory, decline and end in thy own praise, or temporal satisfaction, or a sin." [24] All the means and instruments of religion and of life receive their value from man's intention in the use of them. Many things ordinarily considered parts of our religion are yet of themselves so relative and imperfect that, without the purity of intention, they degenerate and become as other common and secular things. "Thus *alms* are for charity, *fasting* for temperance, *prayer*

---

[23] *Works*, XI, 366.
[24] Taylor, *Works*, IV, 25.

is for religion, *humiliation* is for humility, *austerity* or sufferance is in
order to the virtue of patience: and when these actions fail of their
several ends, or are not directed to their own purposes, alms are mis-
spent, fasting is an impertinent trouble, prayer is but lip-labour, humiliation is but hypocrisy, sufferance is but vexation." [25] And then Taylor
closes this section with a passage that must have made a tremendous
impression on Wesley, for later he remembered it in the presence of
wicked sailors on a perilous sea: [26] "Regard not how full hands you
bring to God, but how pure. Many cease from sin out of fear alone,
not out of innocence or love of virtue; and they, as yet, are not to be
called innocent but timorous." [27] The aim of Taylor's book is to convince man that, as God has given him an excellent nature and an immortal spirit, he has also appointed for him a work and a service great
enough to employ those abilities, and has ordained him to a state of
life beyond the grave, to which he can arrive only by that service and
that obedience.[28] On the basis of this aim Taylor carries his reader
through the duties of life and interprets each duty from the point of
view of religion and from what is expected of man by God. God is
present in all places, sees every action, and hears all discourses, and
understands every thought; [29] and man must practice the presence of
God, act as befitting the company of this ever-present guest.[30] Then
Taylor leads his reader before the awful consideration of death itself
and urges him to attend the call of the Lord that he be not caught by
surprise or found with sins uncanceled.[31] John Wesley, unlike the lady
who advised no one to read *Holy Living and Holy Dying* because it
had almost driven her out of her senses with fear,[32] resolved to dedicate
all his thoughts, words, and actions to God; for the book had succeeded
in convincing him that there was no middle way but that every part
of his life must be a sacrifice either to God or to the devil.[33] Wesley felt

[25] *Ibid.*, pp. 29-30.
[26] *Journal,* Sun., Dec. 18, 1735.
[27] Taylor, *op. cit.,* IV, 30.
[28] *Ibid.*, p. 11.
[29] *Ibid.*, p. 30.
[30] *Ibid.*, pp. 34-39.
[31] *Ibid.*, pp. 572-573.
[32] *Letters,* I, 19.
[33] *Works,* XI, 366.

he was strong enough to make the proper sacrifice and to conform to the standards Taylor had set.

In the same year [34] Wesley was advised to read seriously a book which he had frequently seen before but had never taken the time carefully to consider.[35] That book was *The Christian Pattern, or a Treatise of the Imitation of Jesus Christ* by Thomas à Kempis.[36] Wesley attributed the discovery of *The Christian Pattern* to the providence of God,[37] for through its pages the nature and extent of inward religion now appeared to him in a stronger light than ever before.[38] He saw for the first time that true religion must be seated in the heart and that God's laws must extend to a man's thoughts as well as to his words and actions.[39] He knew now what Thomas à Kempis, that "person of great piety and devotion," [40] meant in regard to both sincerity and purity; and from his work he learned "that 'simplicity of intention and purity of affection,' one design in all we do, and one desire ruling all our tempers, are indeed 'the wings of the soul,' without which she can never ascend to the mount of God." [41] But more than this, Thomas à Kempis reaffirmed what Wesley had already been taught in his home. The true Christian must seek to imitate his Lord. The very opening words of *The Christian Pattern* are:

"He that followeth me shall not walk in Darkness, but shall have the Light of Life," says Christ, who declares himself "The Light of the World," John viii, 12. The true Importance and Design of which Words is doubtless to instruct us, that the Way to be truly Enlightened, and to deliver our Lives from all blindness of Heart, is to make his Holy Life the Object of

[34] In *A Plain Account of Christian Perfection* Wesley gives as the date of having read *The Christian Pattern* the year 1726. This is obviously a mistake, for we possess Wesley's letter to his mother in which he tells of having read this book. The letter is dated May 28, 1725. His mother's reply to this letter, in which she states that she has à Kempis by her, bears the date June 8, 1725. Likewise, another letter of Wesley to his mother states that her reply has well satisfied him as to the tenets of Thomas à Kempis. This bears the date June 18, 1725. The date 1725 is confirmed also by the passage in the *Journal*, Wed., May 24, 1738, sec. 4.

[35] *Letters*, I, 15-16.
[36] *Works*, XI, 366.
[37] *Journal*, Wed., May 24, 1738, sec. 4.
[38] *Works*, XI, 366.
[39] *Journal*, Wed., May 24, 1738, sec. 4
[40] *Letters*, I, 16.
[41] *Works*, XI, 367.

our Imitation, and to form our Dispositions and Actions upon the perfect Model of that bright Example.[42]

A man's internal life must be spotlessly clean, and he must begin at home to reform and be sure "to do that effectually."[43] Yes, and it is the glory and the privilege of a good man actually to know that he is good, to possess a witness to his goodness in his own conscience.[44] After having read *The Christian Pattern* Wesley set out in earnest upon a new course of life. He put aside an hour or two a day for religious retirement, took Communion every week, watched against all sin, either inward or outward, and did so much good and lived so pure a life that he could find no reason to doubt that he was a good Christian.[45]

On March 17 of the following year, 1726, John Wesley was elected a fellow of Lincoln College,[46] and at the beginning of 1727 we find that he had taken up his abode in his new quarters. Sometime thereafter he met with William Law's *Christian Perfection* and *Serious Call to a Devout and Holy Life*. Law's *Christian Perfection* was first published in the year 1726, but his *Serious Call* was not offered to the public until 1729. The two books stand together in any consideration of the influence of Law on John Wesley. Wesley himself says of them: "These convinced me more than ever, of the absolute impossibility of being half a Christian; and I determined, through his grace, (the absolute necessity of which I was deeply sensible of,) to be all-devoted to God, to give him all my soul, my body, and my substance."[47]

The treatise on *Christian Perfection* takes a very practical view of religion, and Law defines his subject in such a way that it is difficult to find reasons for disagreement on any doctrinal basis. The mystical element, which later colored, even dominated, Law's thought, is not apparent either in the *Christian Perfection* or in the *Serious Call*.[48]

---

[42] Thomas à Kempis, *Christian Pattern, or Imitation of Jesus Christ,* p. 1. Wesley had just read the translation by George Stanhope, and that is the one used in this chapter. Later he made a translation of his own, 1735.

[43] *Ibid.,* p. 63.

[44] *Ibid.,* p. 75.

[45] *Journal,* Wed., May 24, 1738, sec. 4.

[46] Tyerman, *Life and Times of John Wesley,* I, 45.

[47] *Works,* XI, 367.

[48] See, for example, Law's *Spirit of Prayer, Divine Knowledge* (in Vol. VII of his *Works*), *Spirit of Love* (Vol. VIII).

Christian perfection consists in nothing but the right performance of our necessary duties, in our holy and religious conduct in every
state of life.[49] Every day we must live as members of the Kingdom of
God, for in very truth we cannot so much as belong to that Kingdom
unless it be within us. When the Kingdom of God is within us, then
the spirit of religion is the spirit of our lives. This spirit is seated in our
hearts and diffuses itself into all our motions. It makes us wise by its
wisdom, sober by its sobriety, humble by its humility. It is the principle
of all our thoughts and desires, the spring of all our hopes and fears,
the very temper, taste, and relish of our lives.[50] There seems, therefore,
to be the greatest necessity that we observe constantly all our daily
actions lest by negligence we fail to live up to the high calling of the
Christian life and load ourselves down with unrepented sins.[51] This
duty of a man to God is so great that it engulfs the whole of his life.

If a man had eyes that could see beyond the *Stars,* or pierce into the
heart of the earth, but could not see the things that were before him, or
discern anything that was serviceable to him, we should reckon that he had
but a *very bad sight.* If another had *ears* that received sounds from the
world in the *Moon,* but could hear nothing that was said or done upon
earth, we should look upon him as *bad* as *deaf.* In like manner, if a man
has a *memory* that can retain a great many things; if he has a *wit* that is
sharp and *acute* in arts and sciences, or an imagination that can wander
agreeably in *fictions,* but has a *dull, poor* apprehension of his *duty* and *relation* to God, of the *value* of piety, or the *worth* of moral virtue, he may
very justly be reckoned to have a *bad understanding.* He is but like the
man, that can only *see* and *hear* such things as are of no benefit to him.[52]

In this Law but strengthened and confirmed what Wesley already
believed. As far back as February 23, 1725, when his mother had written to him on the occasion of his decision to become a minister, she had
said that she expected him to prepare and dispose his mind for a more
serious and close application to things of a sublime and spiritual nature
and to resolve to make religion the business of his life. In this same
letter she had advised him, also, to apply himself to the study of prac-

[49] Law, *Works,* III, 5.
[50] *Ibid.,* p. 142.
[51] *Ibid.,* IV, 252.
[52] *Ibid.,* pp. 267-68. Italics are Law's.

tical divinity and to avert the great evil of engaging in trifling studies to the neglect of studies necessary in the preparation of the Christian life.[53] Two years later, on January 25, 1727, Wesley had written his mother that he had completely come over to her opinion "that there are many truths that it is not worth while to know and that it is great ill-husbandry to spend a considerable part of the small pittance now allowed to us on what makes us neither a quick nor sure return." [54] Duty, for Wesley as for Law, was at this period in his life the sublimest word; and his one aim was to love and obey God with all his strength.[55]

But there is another aspect of the thinking of Law in *Christian Perfection* and *Serious Call* which exerted tremendous influence on Wesley and strove like a giant to master and control his life. Law's temper in these two works is stern, austere, melancholy. The brighter side of Christianity is not emphasized, and the joy and glad tidings of the gospel are silenced by the uncompromising command of duty and of law. The world in which we live is a disordered, irregular state, a vale of misery, where vice and madness, dreams and shadows, variously please, agitate, and torment the short and troubled lives of men.[56] Absolute self-denial is required of us, and we must forsake by our own act and deed this life of time and seek to become citizens of eternity.[57] The world will pass as a dream, but goodness will abide forever and bring its rewards.[58] Nothing in all existence concerns the true Christian but the knowledge that he himself is an everlasting spirit that is going to God. "There are no Enjoyments here that are worth a Thought, but such as may make thee more perfect in those holy Tempers which will carry thee to Heaven." [59] Wesley, therefore, under the influence of Law, was convinced more than ever of the exceeding height and breadth and depth of the law of God. He pledged himself to keep the whole law of God, inward and outward, and he persuaded himself that, if he should keep this law, he would be accepted of God.[60] He now felt that the pursuit

[53] Tyerman, *Life and Times of John Wesley*, I, 32.
[54] *Letters*, I, 39-40.
[55] *Ibid.*, p. 138.
[56] Law, *Works*, III, 12.
[57] *Ibid.*, p. 48.
[58] *Ibid.*, IV, 29.
[59] *Ibid.*, III, 23.
[60] *Journal*, Wed., May 24, 1738, sec. 5.

of salvation meant, not only emancipation from the urges and desires of ordinary life, but an actual defiance of the world, a challenge flung in the face of all mankind. Every day he lived in the expectation that, whether his hand was raised against every man or no, every man's hand would be raised against him.[61] Mirth, gladness, joyous gratitude over the pleasures of this world, found no place in his stern philosophy,[62] and more and more he convinced himself that persecution must be the portion of every follower of Christ, wherever his lot is cast.[63]

The Humanistic Center of Faith

This phase of Wesley's life issued in the feverish attempt to justify himself through his own works and to win salvation of God through the moral and spiritual fruits of his own endeavor. First of all, he attempted to regulate in every detail the thoughts and actions of his life and to fashion himself into the sort of person that he thought God would like him to be. Nehemiah Curnock has provided us with a facsimile reproduction of the general rules that governed Wesley's conduct, drawn up by him on January 29, 1726, and entered into a private diary or notebook. This has been deciphered by Curnock and other experts and is now available for the use of scholars. Wesley's general rule in all actions of life was: "Whenever you are to do an action, consider how God did or would do the like, and do you imitate His example." [64] At this time in his life he resolved to employ all his spare time in religion, to keep all holydays, to avoid all drunkards and busybodies, all vain and light company, all idleness, all freedom with women, and all lusts and impure thoughts, to give up laughter and useless conversation; and he resolved likewise to begin every important work with prayer, never to leave off any duty, and always to consider the Scriptures and death.[65] Wesley fulfilled all the obligations of the Church and accepted without question all its doctrines and observed all the rubric in the Liturgy with exactness, even, as in Georgia, at the peril of his

[61] *Letters*, I, 113.
[62] *Ibid.*, p. 115.
[63] *Works*, XII, 46.
[64] N. Curnock's edition of *Journal*, I, 48.
[65] *Ibid.*, pp. 48, 52.

life.[66] In this also he sought for inward holiness, which he thought came from doing God's will alone.

It is interesting to speculate whether or not Wesley in this period between June 24, 1720, and May 24, 1738, became a mystic. Some have charged him with having embraced mystical divinity,[67] while others have denied the charges most vehemently.[68] There is absolutely no reason whatever for us to suspect that Wesley ever accepted any of the theological and philosophical tenets of mysticism. Though in his letter to his brother Samuel of November 23, 1736, he states that the rock on which he had nearest made shipwreck of the faith was the writings of the mystics, he hastens at once to add that he includes under this head all those who slight any of the means of grace. The entire letter is a consideration of the moral and spiritual practices of the mystics in relationship to the use of Holy Communion, the Scriptures, church attendance, service to other people, and so forth.[69] Wesley conceives of mysticism in this instance as a retreat from the world and as an attempt to purify the soul by isolating it from contact with the corrupt elements of human society. In this sense he did try mysticism as a means of saving his own soul and went through mental prayer and like exercises as the most effectual means of cleansing himself, but he found no comfort therein.[70] He tells us quite clearly, however, that he was never in the "way of Mysticism at all" and never concerned himself with anything in the works of the mystics except their views on the nature of inward religion,[71] or holiness.

But then, after having striven diligently against all sin in his own life, Wesley turned to outward acts of service in behalf of other people. These good deeds were of course part of the same effort to justify himself before God and to save his own soul. We know that in November, 1729, he joined himself [72] to a small group which had been organized by his brother Charles for the purpose of considering the

[66] *Works*, XIII, 272.
[67] E.g., G. C. Cell, *Rediscovery of John Wesley*, pp. 94, 97-98.
[68] E.g., Tyerman, *op. cit.*, I, 54.
[69] *Works*, XII, 27-29.
[70] *Journal*, Wed., May 24, 1738, secs. 7-8; *Letters*, I, 41-43.
[71] *Works*, X, 391.
[72] *Letters*, I, 124-25.

Gospels and engaging in good works.[73] This was the beginning of the Oxford Club, a little group of not more than twenty-seven members at its peak. Wesley, together with his companions in this group, began visiting the prisons, assisting the poor and sick in town, and doing what other good he could, either by his presence or by his small fortune, to the bodies and the souls of men.[74] He organized in behalf of this group a means of taking a collection among friends to help the unfortunate, and Nehemiah Curnock has published the first subscription list of September 29, 1730.[75] For the sake of the poor he denied himself all superfluities and many of the so-called necessities of life.[76] Finally, in the year 1735, Wesley broke away from the fourteen or fifteen friends who still composed the Oxford Club[77] and set sail with General Oglethorpe on October 14 for Georgia.[78] This missionary journey to the new world with its intended labor among the redskins marks the climax of this first phase in Wesley's religious development. His motives were still the same, and the only reason he left his work at Oxford for Georgia was the hope that he cherished of doing more good in America.[79] By doing good he thought perhaps he would prove to himself that actually he was good; for the chief motive of his life, to which all other motives were subordinate, was the hope of saving his own soul.[80]

Is it possible for us to say what view of justification Wesley held during this period of his life? Can we state what he actually thought about salvation? Or is this early phase of his thought confused, aimless, and devoid of any real center of unity? Does it express nothing more than a combination of youthful enthusiasm, which is eager to embrace any new opinion, with desperate fanaticism, which is anxious to attain a single end? In other words, are we led to believe that Wesley

[73] There were only three in the original group organized by Charles Wesley.—*Works*, VIII, 348.

[74] *Journal*, Wed., May 24, 1738, sec. 6. See the direct reference in Sermon LXXXIX, part vi, sec. 4, and the story of the young maid who was half starved and Wesley's reaction in Sermon LXXXVIII, sec. 16.

[75] Nehemiah Curnock, *op. cit.*, I, 91.

[76] *Journal*, Wed., May 24, 1738, sec. 6.

[77] *Works*, XIII, 304.

[78] *Ibid.*; *Journal*, Tues., Oct. 14, 1735.

[79] *Letters*, I, 191.

[80] *Ibid.*, p. 188; *Journal*, Tues., Oct. 14, 1735.

jumped from one camp of thought to another in his restless search for the meaning of salvation and eternal life, that at one time he accepted wholeheartedly Thomas à Kempis and then after a season turned away from him to the teachings of William Law? Not at all. There was a basic principle in Wesley's thought at this period in his life—the principle that man must be saved through moral goodness, through universal obedience, and through the rigid fulfillment of all the commandments of God. This principle defined his conception of justification and, like a magnet, drew unto itself all elements which helped to confirm, to clarify, and more especially to achieve its aim. The source of this principle lay in the religious instruction of Wesley's childhood, and through these early years of his development he measured and appraised all thought by this basic standard of goodness and obedience which he had derived from his home.[81] From Jeremy Taylor he learned that he could achieve goodness only by dedicating his whole life to God. Thomas à Kempis taught him that obedience must be centered in the heart. And William Law instructed him in the way of self-denial as the absolute fulfillment of God's law. Thus these men influenced Wesley at this period in his life, not in that they changed or even modified his basic conception of salvation or justification before God, but rather in that they taught him how to achieve morally and spiritually the conditions which that conception imposed.

In conclusion, therefore, we must say that the religious motives of John Wesley in the period from June 24, 1720, to May 24, 1738, stemmed entirely from an interest in himself.[82] Self-love was at the very center of his life. His neighbor and his neighbor's needs, though they engaged by far the greater portion of his activity, had no significance in and of themselves but were important only in so far as they contributed to his own salvation. Though he accepted as a dogma the

[81] Wesley sought the advice of his mother before he formulated any idea of his own or made any major decision. Her influence was absolute in its sway throughout this entire period. Consult his correspondence with her. Taylor, Thomas à Kempis, etc., were evaluated in the light of her opinions of them.—*Letters*, I, pp. 15-20, 21-26, 41-42, 46-49, 137-39, 196-97.

[82] See his letter to his father in which he refuses to apply for Epworth Church despite the benefits to his family because Oxford is more conducive to his own spiritual welfare. —*Letters*, I, 166-78.

redemption of sinful man through the death of Christ,[83] he had no conception whatever of the free gift of God's grace through faith, no consciousness whatever of the love of the Father shed abroad in the hearts of his children. He believed that the gift of Christ's atonement and, through it, of man's justification and salvation had to be achieved through man's own efforts, through moral goodness, through the performance of the commandments of God. Faith itself was man's own act, his assent to what God had revealed because God had revealed it.[84] With Wesley, therefore, faith and works stood together. They could not be separated. Yes, in reality faith itself was a work; for, if a man believes a thing because he is commanded, that is work.

[83] Sermon CXLI, part ii. There are eight sermons published from Wesley's manuscripts after his death but never designed by him for publication. Seven of these sermons were written in this period prior to May 24, 1738. These are Sermons CXXXV-CXLI in a complete edition of the *Sermons* or the *Works*. These are of importance in throwing light on his early religious doctrines.

[84] *Letters*, I, 25.

Chapter III

NEW WORLD OF FAITH

Wesley's Thought Before and After Aldersgate

JOHN WESLEY, ON THE EVE OF THE YEAR 1738, WAS THE SPIRITUAL PRISONER of his age. He was bound by the fetters of a theology the precepts of which he sought slavishly to obey. He possessed a knowledge of religion, "a form of godliness" prescribed in the gospel of Christ. He took care to avoid even the appearance of disobedience and went so far as to refrain from all conversation which was not spiritual, or at least good to the use of edifying. He engaged in good works, nor did he confine himself to cheap and easy offices of kindness but did actually labor and suffer for the profit of many. In all these endeavors he was sincere. His actions sprang from a real desire to please God and to do his will. And yet, according to his own words, he was "an almost Christian." [1] He possessed the religion of a servant, but not that of a son.[2] He desired to escape from sin and strove with all his might to break the chains of bondage and to be spiritually free,[3] but he was still a slave to the law and knew nothing of the genuine spirit of adoption, that abiding consciousness of the grace of God which enables a man to cry continually, "Abba, Father!" [4]

John Wesley, at the close of the year 1738, was spiritually free. He had been delivered from the fetters of his old theology, totally emancipated from a slavish obedience to precepts which he had found impossible absolutely to fulfill.[5] Now he knew what it was to be "an altogether Christian"; [6] he had crossed that narrow line which separates the religion of a son from that of a servant; he had felt the power of a new love, not that of aspiration and striving which has its center in

[1] Sermon II, part i, secs. 9, 13.
[2] Second corrective note in Wesley's own 1771 edition of his *Journal*, Wed., Feb. 1, 1738.
[3] Sermon IX, part ii, secs. 7, 10.
[4] *Ibid.*, part ii, sec. 9; part iii, secs. 1, 3; part iv, sec. 3.
[5] *Journal*, Wed., May 24, 1738, sec. 10.
[6] Sermon II, part ii, intro.

the self and which measures all things in the light of personal achievement, but the love of God which comes to the self, which engrosses the whole heart, takes up all the affections, and fills the entire capacity of the soul, and which uses the individual to the utmost extent of his faculties according to divine purposes and in the fulfillment of divine ends.[7] If righteousness remained dear to his heart, it was a new sort of righteousness, no longer built around a covenant of works, as if man by perfect and uninterrupted obedience could lay hold on and claim the gift of Christ's atonement,[8] but rather springing from the joyous submission to God's will and coming as the gift of free love, undeserved mercy, and fatherly affection.[9] Now Wesley was enabled to say that the believer had put off the filthy rags of his own righteousness and put on the spotless righteousness of Christ.[10] The Lord only was the foundation of his hope.[11] The center of his life was changed. He had gone through an intellectual and spiritual revolution. John Wesley had been genuinely converted.

The Significance of Aldersgate in the Development of Wesley's Theology

Now it is not our intention here to go into a psychological analysis of Wesley's conversion at Aldersgate, or to attempt to explain that experience in the sense that William James attempts to analyze and explain like experiences in his *The Varieties of Religious Experience.*[12] But in a work such as this, which attempts to deal with Wesley's theological development and to set forth his doctrine of justification, one cannot avoid the fact of Aldersgate and the actual results, intellectual and spiritual, of that experience in his life. From an examination of Wesley's writings, both his *Journal* and his *Sermons,* one is convinced of the marked change which took place in his thought, of the new emphasis which emerged, and in very truth of the birth of his own

[7] *Ibid.,* sec. 1.
[8] Sermon VI, part i, sec. 12.
[9] *Ibid.,* part ii, sec. 8.
[10] Sermon XX, part ii. sec. 11.
[11] *Ibid.,* sec. 13.
[12] This has been done by J. E. Rattenbury, *The Conversion of the Wesleys,* 1938, and S. G. Dimond, *The Psychology of the Methodist Revival,* 1926.

system of theology. Modern treatments of Wesley's life which minimize, or even erase, the significance of Aldersgate, must first and last set up their own criteria of what a conversion is, and on this basis judge and find valueless the phenomenon of May 24, 1738.

Father Piette, accordingly, contends that Wesley's genuine conversion was in the year 1725, when he discovered Taylor and à Kempis and resolved to devote his whole life to God.[13] But immediately we ask, From what standard was Wesley converted and to what new ideal was he drawn? We have seen already in chapter three that his fundamental conception of salvation was the same after he had read Taylor, à Kempis, and Law as it was before their discovery. But a fact far more significant than this arises, one which invalidates completely any thesis which attempts to set Wesley's conversion at a date in the year 1725, and that fact is that the very same problems which harassed his existence and tormented his life prior to the year 1725 continued in full force up to the date of his conversion on May 24, 1738. Prior to Aldersgate, Wesley was a sick soul; and, though he said that he had a fair summer religion, one that enabled him to talk well, yes, and even to believe what he talked while no danger was near, yet let death stare him in the face and his spirit was troubled and his good works crumbled into dust.[14] But, more than this, Wesley failed time and time again in the religious endeavors which he set about to perform; and, though the reading of Taylor, à Kempis, and Law set him on a new resolve to live the good life, he saw that resolve very imperfectly carried out and confessed himself that he fell and rose only to fall again.[15] Piette and Leger make conversion synonymous with moral resolve and aspiration, a term which expresses nothing more than a decision to form and to carry out a good resolution. Such a definition has no more significance than the usual New Year's resolution, and not much more chance of being carried out. If we accept such a concept of conversion, then we cannot limit Wesley's conversion to a date in the year 1725, or even 1738 for that matter, for he was continually making new reso-

[13] Piette, *John Wesley in the Evolution of Protestantism,* pp. 305-12. This view is set forth by A. Leger, from whom Piette derives most of his arguments. See Leger, *La Jeunesse de Wesley,* pp. 77-82, 350, 364.

[14] *Journal,* Tues., Jan. 24, 1738.

[15] *Ibid.,* Wed., May 24, 1738, sec. 10.

lutions up until the day he died. But if conversion be defined in the sense in which Wesley understood and defined it—God's own act in which a man is turned away from his former self, made to pass from darkness into light, delivered from the power of Satan unto God, made over in mind and spirit[16]—then the experience at Aldersgate on May 24, 1738, must stand without dispute as the date of Wesley's conversion. "In the evening I went very unwillingly to a society in Aldersgate-street, where one was reading Luther's preface to the Epistle to the Romans. About a quarter before nine, while he was describing the change which God works in the heart through faith in Christ, I felt my heart strangely warmed. I felt I did trust in Christ, Christ alone, for salvation; and an assurance was given me, that he had taken away my sins, even mine, and saved me from the law of sin and death."[17]

But the Aldersgate experience, the significance of which cannot be minimized in any consideration of Wesley's life and of the effect his preaching had upon the England of his day, is important to us here because a new theology gained Wesley's allegiance on the date of that experience and made a mighty contribution to the development of his thought. Aldersgate stands at the crisis of Wesley's thought as well as at the crisis of his religious experience and of his life. There he learned for the first time the true meaning of justification by faith. In this chapter, therefore, we must consider carefully those factors which made for the disintegration and collapse of Wesley's early concept of justification and final salvation, and likewise those precepts which he gained from the Moravians and which enabled him finally to arrive at his own doctrine of justification. Some have felt that assurance alone was the quest of Wesley's life, and that his contribution to theology can be understood only in the light of his discovery of experience as the center of salvation, the burning focus of faith. But this is to mistake the by-product of a phenomenon for the phenomenon itself. True, assurance did come; but it came along with, and as an aspect of, something else. What Wesley really learned at Aldersgate and in the events which preceded and led up to it was that man is justified by the grace of God alone, and that this grace is given only

[16] *Works*, IX, 92.
[17] *Journal*, May 24, 1738, sec. 14.

through faith.[18] Faith, given by God's grace, is that which enables a man to have assurance and to feel the power of Christ resting upon him.[19] Kill that faith through disobedience and a willful inclination to sin, and it follows as the night the day that intercourse with God is cut off [20] and the sense of assurance is no more.[21]

Factors in the Collapse of Wesley's Early View of Justification

The chief factor which made for the collapse of Wesley's early view of justification lay within himself and expressed itself in the form of uncertainty, doubt, and at times even ungarnished fear. Believing as he did that his own salvation was the most important thing in the world and that his eternal destiny lay completely within the range of his own action, the counsels of his own mind, and the power of his own will, he was forced to rest entirely on a self-confidence and self-dependence which could bear no reverses and could endure no moral setbacks, no spiritual defeats. In the light of such a belief, any diminution of the ideal, any failure in actual achievement, was disastrous, for it destroyed the very foundation on which salvation itself was believed to rest. It is no wonder, therefore, that such confidence had continually to be bolstered up and supported by acts of charity and services of devotion. Wesley had always to prove to himself that he was a saved individual, that he had fulfilled the conditions and merited the right to receive the gift of Christ's atonement. But this same Wesley had difficulty in convincing himself. He was afraid to die. How could he be sure that he had met all the requirements? How did he know that he would be received by Christ and accepted as his son?

It is only when we understand the significance of spiritual success and moral achievement in the thought of Wesley at this period prior to Aldersgate that we can begin to understand incidents which, seen apart from Wesley's religious convictions, appear either ridiculous or cowardly. Thus on board ship going to Georgia he was waked at eleven o'clock at night by a great noise; and, though the noise signi-

[18] Sermon I, intro.
[19] Sermon XIV, part ii, sec. 5.
[20] *Works*, VIII, 283.
[21] Sermon XIX, part iii, sec. 3.

fied no danger and disturbed none of the other passengers, the mere apprehension that there might have been danger caused him to be afraid and seriously to consider "what manner of men those ought to be, who are every moment on the brink of eternity." [22] Almost a month later he was waked by the tossing of the ship and the roaring of the wind, and he was then convinced that he was unfit because he was so unwilling to die.[23] In Georgia he refused to baptize a child because the child's parents would not consent to its being dipped, which was the law of the Church of England in all cases except those of physical weakness.[24] And even after he had fallen in love with a Savannah maiden and had desired to marry her, he carried his case before the elders of the Moravian Church; and, when they asked him whether or not he would abide by their decision, he answered, "I will," before he so much as knew what their decision would be.[25] Always Wesley was uncertain about his own spiritual status, and with an anxious cautiousness he guarded himself against anything which he thought in any way might jeopardize or hinder his spiritual success.

But another factor emerged and added its weight to Wesley's personal uncertainty. His public ministry in Georgia was a complete failure. At first sight this might appear of little consequence, for Wesley seemed to expect persecution and ill use.[26] But this failure did not come to him through that channel.[27] It came to him through another, one which beat against the very citadel of his faith and shook the foundation of all that he believed. Had not John Wesley been taught that a Christian is known by his fruits? Had he not expected to spread the gospel of Christ in the new world and to see converts added daily to the fold? Had he not left England, where he had achieved no mean success with his Oxford Club, because he had anticipated greater success in America? To be sure, when Wesley first arrived in Georgia, the people crowded into the church and with deep attention and serious expression received the word which he delivered unto them.[28] But

[22] *Journal*, Fri., Oct. 31, 1735.
[23] *Ibid.*, Sun., Nov. 23, 1735.
[24] *Ibid.*, Wed., May 5, 1736.
[25] H. Moore, *Life of Wesley*, I, 312.
[26] *Letters*, I, 113.
[27] *Works*, XII, 46.
[28] Journal, Sun., Mar. 7, 1736.

after Wesley became known, his influence dwindled and people came to have very little respect for him. One man frankly confessed to him, "All your sermons are satires upon particular persons, therefore I will never hear you more; and all the people are of my mind, for we won't hear ourselves abused." [29] Wesley could not accept such criticism with resignation; and he himself records how, in the face of a cold and heartless congregation at Frederica, before which he had "beaten the air" for twenty days, he gave up in despair and left the city.[30] People were unable to understand Wesley's religion, for they were repulsed by his personal behavior. "All the quarrels that have been here since you (Wesley) came. . . . Indeed there is neither man nor woman in the town, who minds a word you say. And so you may preach long enough; but nobody will come to hear you." [31] In fact on Ascension Day of the year 1736 only one family came to Holy Communion because of what Wesley called a "few words which a woman had inadvertently spoken." [32] It is not hard to see how failure of this sort but added to Wesley's personal uncertainty and doubt. Perhaps he did not appear to other people as a Christian simply because in truth he was no Christian. It was not as though he had been rejected and persecuted. Rather, it was that in the ordinary duties of a pastor and preacher he had failed to exercise any influence for the cause of Christ and had absolutely no fruits to show for his labor. Such ill success was not conducive to his spiritual and moral betterment, and we can well understand his confession: "How to attain to the being crucified with Christ, I find not, being in a condition I neither desired nor expected in America, in ease and honour and abundance." [33]

A third factor may be noted as having contributed to the dissolution of Wesley's early view of justification, and this factor has to do with what he thought about human nature and the self-adaptability of man to the conditions of salvation. Evidently he had gone to Georgia with a very high view of the American Indian, the "noble savage" of

[29] *Ibid.,* Tues., June 22, 1736.
[30] *Ibid.,* Wed., Jan. 26, 1737.
[31] *Ibid.,* Tues., June 22, 1736.
[32] *Ibid.,* Thurs., June 3, 1736.
[33] *Journal,* Sat., July 23, 1737.

Rousseau's philosophy, a creature untainted and unpolluted by the customs of civilized man.

I hope to learn the true sense of the gospel of Christ by preaching it to the heathen. They have no comments to construe away the text; no vain philosophy to corrupt it; no luxurious, sensual, covetous, ambitious expounders to soften its unpleasing truths, to reconcile earthly mindedness and faith, the Spirit of Christ and the spirit of the world. They have no party, no interest to serve, and are therefore fit to receive the gospel in simplicity. They are as little children, humble, willing to learn, and eager to do the will of God.[34]

This was written by Wesley to Dr. John Burton on October 10, 1735, four days before he set sail for Georgia.

Suffice it to say that when Wesley left Georgia he entertained quite a different concept of the noble savage. He had seen him in his own haunts and observed his behavior and his character. For the first time in his life Wesley began to understand empirically the meaning of original sin. "They know not what friendship or gratitude means; they show no inclination to learn anything, but least of all Christianity; being full as opinionated of their own parts and wisdom, as either modern Chinese, or ancient Romans."[35]

They are likewise all, except perhaps the Choctaws, gluttons, drunkards, thieves, dissemblers, liars. They are implacable, unmerciful; murderers of fathers, murderers of mothers, murderers of their own children; it being a common thing for a son to shoot his father or his mother, because they are old or past labour; and for a woman either to procure abortion, or to throw her child into the next river, because she will go with her husband to the war. . . . Whoredom they account no crime, and few instances appear of a young Indian woman's refusing any one. Nor have they any fixed punishment for adultery; only, if the husband take his wife with another man he will do what he can to both, unless speedily pacified by the present of a gun or a blanket.[36]

Gone was Wesley's view of the noble savage, innocent in his simplicity and eager to receive the gospel truth. He now saw human na-

[34] *Letters*, I, 188.
[35] *Journal*, Fri., Dec. 2, 1737, sec. 28.
[36] *Ibid.*, sec. 23.

ture in a different light—mean, selfish, sinful; ignorant of God and indifferent to saving truth.

The combination of these factors produced in Wesley the consciousness that, try as hard as he could, he was not able in himself to meet the conditions of justification and to achieve salvation of God. His voyage to America, his ministry in Georgia, and his contact with the redskins proved beyond doubt the inadequacy of the doctrines he held.

Behold I gave all my goods to feed the poor. . . . I have laboured more abundantly than they all. . . . I have thrown up my friends, reputation, ease, country; I have put my life in my hand, wandering into strange lands; I have given my body to be devoured by the deep, parched up with heat, consumed by toil and weariness, or whatsoever God should please to bring upon me. But does all this . . . make me acceptable to God? Does all I ever did or can know, say, give, do, or suffer, justify me in his sight? Yea, or the constant use of all the means of grace? . . . Or, that "I know nothing of myself;" that I am as touching outward, moral righteousness blameless? Or, (to come closer yet,) the having a rational conviction of all the truths of Christianity? Does all this give me a claim to the holy, heavenly, divine character of a Christian? By no means. If the oracles of God are true, if we are still to abide by the law and the testimony; all these things, though when ennobled by faith in Christ, they are holy and just and good, yet without it are dung and dross, meet only to be purged away by the fire that never shall be quenched.[37]

But if the way of salvation be not that of belief and works, then what is the true way? How is man justified before God?

Moravian Influence

On his journey across the Atlantic Ocean, Wesley came in contact with the Moravian Pietists for the first time. He observed the great seriousness of their behavior, their humility, their longsuffering and patience in abuse, and more especially their courage and complete freedom from fear.[38] After he reached Georgia he heard the story of Spangenberg's life from Spangenberg's own lips, heard him say, "But what God will do with me, I know not. I am blind. I am a child. My

[37] *Ibid.*, Wed., Feb. 1, 1738.
[38] *Ibid.*, Sun., Jan. 25, 1736.

father knows, and I am ready to go wherever he calls." [39] He saw the peace and joy with which the Moravians lived together,[40] the primitive simplicity of their church,[41] and the resignation and calm with which they greeted death.[42] In Georgia, Spangenberg asked him, "Have you the witness within yourself? Does the spirit of God bear witness with your spirit, that you are a child of God? Do you know Jesus Christ? Do you know he has saved you? Do you know yourself?" [43] At Oxford after his return to England, Peter Böhler told him, *"Mi frater, mi frater, excoquenda est ista tua philosophia."* [44] And about a fortnight later Böhler charged him, "Preach *faith till* you have it; and then, *because* you have it, you *will* preach faith." [45]

It is, therefore, at the point of faith, its nature and its function, that we note the radical change which took place in Wesley's thought concerning justification. The Moravians taught that man is saved by faith alone. "A man, who knows himself to be a poor sinner," writes Spangenberg, "cleaves by Faith to Jesus Christ." [46] Yes, and he writes also:

It is evident, that the sin, on account of which men are damned, consists in this, that they will not believe the divine and salutary truth; that God hath so loved them, as even to give his only begotten Son to be the Saviour of the world; that this Son of God, Jesus Christ, became a sacrifice for them, and hath shed his blood for the forgiveness of their sins.[47]

Anglicanism, too, taught that man is saved by the merits of Christ's death. But the Moravians saw this in a more personal light. Christ, they said, did die for the world as a whole,[48] but the important thing is that he died for you as a person.[49] So Böhler wrote to Wesley:

I love you greatly, and think much of you in my journey, wishing and praying that the tender mercies of Jesus Christ the Crucified, whose bowels

[39] *Ibid.*, Mon., Feb. 9, 1736.
[40] *Ibid.*, Tues., Feb. 24, 1736.
[41] *Ibid.*, Sat., Feb. 28, 1736.
[42] *Ibid.*, Sun., Mar. 7, 1736.
[43] *Ibid.*, Sat., Feb. 7, 1736.
[44] *Ibid.*, Sat., Feb. 18, 1738. Trans.: "My brother, my brother, that philosophy of yours must be purged away."
[45] *Ibid.*, Sat., Mar. 4, 1738.
[46] A. G. Spangenberg, *Exposition of Christian Doctrine*, p. 199.
[47] *Ibid.*, p. 196.
[48] *Ibid.*, pp. 99, 193, 195.
[49] *Ibid.*, p. 203.

were moved toward you . . . may be manifested to your soul; that you may taste and then see, how exceedingly the Son of God has loved you, and loves you still; and that so you may continually trust in him, and feel his life in yourself.[50]

The Moravian conception of faith is far from an intellectual assent to the truths of the gospel, far from a rational belief in the Christian way of life. It is not a human act. Faith itself is the gift of God. Thus writes Christian David, whom the founders of Hernhuth, with Count Zinzendorf at their head, recognized as the best exponent of Moravian doctrine,[51] and whose exact words Wesley himself translates:

This is the "word of reconciliation" (Christ's blood of propitiation is for you and for me) which we preach. This is the foundation which never can be moved. By faith we are built on this foundation: and this faith also is the gift of God. . . . But this gift of God lives in the heart, not in the head. The faith of the head, learned from men or books, is nothing worth. It brings neither remission of sins, nor peace with God.[52]

What, then, is the Moravian conception of justification? Count Zinzendorf tells us; and once again Wesley, who was present at the very conference at Frankfort where Zinzendorf spoke, records his definition: "Justification is the forgiveness of sins. The moment a man flies to Christ he is justified. . . . To be justified is the same thing as to be born of God." [53] Are good works necessary for justification? Is purity of life a condition? Decidedly not. Christian David cries:

See ye not that the foundation is nothing in us. Works, righteousness, contrition? No; ungodliness only. This then do, if you will lay a right foundation: Go straight to Christ with all your ungodliness. Tell him, thou whose eyes are as a flame of fire searching my heart, seest that I am ungodly. I plead nothing else. I do not say I am humble or contrite; but I am ungodly. Therefore bring me to him who justifieth the ungodly. Let thy blood be the propitiation for me. For there is nothing in me but ungodliness.[54]

---

[50] *Journal,* Wed., May 10, 1738.
[51] F. F. Hagen, *Old Landmarks,* p. 9.
[52] *Journal,* Wed. & Thurs., Aug. 9 & 10, 1738.
[53] *Ibid.,* Wed., July 12, 1738.
[54] *Ibid.,* Wed. & Thurs., Aug. 9 & 10, 1738.

Justification is more than a legal pronouncement that a man is accepted as righteous and is thus freed from guilt. Sin ceases to be that which divides men from God. "Sin is the only thing which unites them to God; i.e., the only thing which moves the Lamb of God to have compassion upon, and, by his blood, to give them access to the Father." [55] But immediately he justifies us and forgives us our sins; and, also, he sanctifies us and cleanses us from all unrighteousness. [56] Everything is God's own act upon us and in us, so that we do nothing of ourselves. Thus in a letter written by the Church of Hernhuth to the president of Upper Lusatia on January 24, 1732, we find this statement: "We have chiefly insisted on Christ given for us. This we urge as the principal thing: which if we rightly believe, Christ will surely be formed in us." [57]

The New Emphasis: Justification by Faith

Wesley, weary of himself and sick of asking what he was and what he ought to be, turned with enthusiasm to this doctrine of the Reformation as set forth by the Moravians, that God not only sets the conditions for man's salvation but actually works salvation in him. Wesley knew what Luther meant, as he listened to his introduction to Romans on the night of May 24, 1738. He understood from his own experience that a man cannot prepare himself for good by means of works, since he does no good works without displeasure and unwillingness of heart. [58] He must look somewhere else for justification, to a faith which is a divine work in him [59]—a living, daring confidence in God's grace, so sure and certain that a man will stake his life on it a thousand times. [60] Thus, on June 11, 1738, eighteen days after his conscious experience of the new life at Aldersgate, Wesley preached at Oxford his famous sermon on "Salvation by Faith"; and on Sunday, September 17, 1738, the very day after his arrival home from his pilgrimage to the Moravian center of Hernhuth, he began to declare in his own country

[55] *Ibid.*
[56] Spangenberg, *op. cit.*, p. 257.
[57] *Works*, I, 127.
[58] Luther, *Works* (Holman ed.) VI, 449.
[59] *Ibid.*, p. 451.
[60] *Ibid.*, p. 452.

the glad tidings of salvation and to call sinners to repentance.[61] This marks the beginning of the Methodist Revival; for, though the name "Methodist" was attached to Wesley and his Oxford Club followers as far back as 1729 [62] and though Wesley himself in later life set that year as the date of the origin of Methodism as a social phenomenon,[63] it did not find the secret of its power or rise above the status of a small club with an influence no wider than its membership until the year 1738 after Wesley began to preach justification by faith.[64] No longer satisfied by a selfish personal moralism, he turned, in gratitude for God's free gift of salvation to him, to the masses of sinful humanity.[65] He called with the authority of a prophet to the dirty colliers who worked in the coal mines of Bristol, to the filthy rakes who hid in the dens of London, and to the barbarous mobs who inhabited the wild moors of Northumberland.

The very first tenet which appears in this new emphasis in Wesley's preaching is that there is no character man can achieve and no act he can perform which can deserve the least thing at God's hands.[66] If sinful man finds favor with God, that favor is due to God's own act; and if God confers salvation upon him, the only thing he can say is, "Thanks be unto God for his unspeakable gift!" [67] For no man can atone for his own sins. His works in themselves are evil, for only corrupt fruit grows on a corrupt tree, and man's heart is altogether corrupt and abominable. Good works as such are God's and God's alone.[68]

But if man is saved by grace, what is the channel through which that grace comes, or what instrument puts it into operation on man's behalf? We are saved, says Wesley, by grace through faith. It is at this point that we must note carefully his doctrinal conversion, or the radical change of his thought in regard to faith. It is not enough that we simply state the fact that Wesley no longer thought of salvation in terms of good works, but we must likewise make clear that in his

---

[61] *Journal*, Sun., Sept. 17, 1738.
[62] *Works*, VIII, 339.
[63] Sermon CXXXII, part i, sec. 1.
[64] *Works*, VIII, 349.
[65] Sermon CXXXII, part i, sec. 5.
[66] Sermon I, intro., sec. 1.
[67] *Ibid.*, sec. 3.
[68] *Ibid.*, sec. 2.

mind the very faith which replaced works was of an entirely different nature from his old conception of faith as belief which accompanies works. Wesley in his sermon of June 11, 1738, before he so much as attempts to define faith, is careful to enumerate inadequate and incomplete definitions of it. To begin with, he says, saving faith is not just the faith of a heathen who believes in God. Such faith leads the heathen to give God thanks for all things, to attempt the practice of moral virtue—of justice, mercy, and truth toward all his fellow creatures. "A Greek or Roman," writes Wesley, "yea, a Scythian or Indian was without excuse if he did not believe thus much: the being and attributes of God, a future state of reward and punishment, and the obligatory nature of moral virtue." [69] Again, saving faith is not the faith of a devil, though this goes much further than that of a heathen. Here Wesley takes his stand against the Socratic notion that knowledge is virtue and that to know the good is to do the good. Devils are wise and know well the distinction between right and wrong. They even know that Jesus Christ is the Saviour of the world, and they believe in the validity of the Holy Scriptures. Yet devils are the enemies of God and man, and the extent of their faith is that they believe and tremble.[70] Finally, saving faith goes beyond even that which the apostles themselves possessed when Christ was with them on the earth. Though they so believed in him as to leave all and to follow him; though they possessed power to work miracles, to heal all manner of sickness and disease; though at times they had authority over devils; and though they were commissioned by their Master to preach the glad tidings of the Kingdom of God, they did not plumb the depths of the faith by which men are saved.[71]

But what is the nature of that faith by which men are saved? Its object is Christ, or rather God himself as he is seen in the face of the human Jesus. In this it is absolutely distinguished from the mere belief of a heathen. Yet it is distinguished from the faith of a devil in that it is not just "a speculative, rational thing, a cold, lifeless assent, a train of ideas in the head; but also a disposition of the heart." [72] As

[69] *Ibid.*, part i, sec. 1.
[70] *Ibid.*, sec. 2. See also, Sermon LXXII, part i.
[71] *Ibid.*, sec. 3.
[72] *Ibid.*, sec. 4.

Wesley wrote these words, perhaps he remembered his letter of July 29, 1725, written from Oxford home to his mother:

> I call faith an assent upon rational grounds, because I hold divine testimony to be the most reasonable of all evidence whatever. Faith must necessarily at length be resolved into reason. God is true; therefore what he says is true. When anyone can bring me more reasonable propositions than these, I am ready to assent to them: till then it will be highly unreasonable to change my opinion.[73]

With the heart, and the heart alone, does a man believe unto righteousness. How, we ask, does such faith differ from that which the apostles possessed while Christ remained with them on earth? In this, Wesley tells us,

> that it acknowledges the necessity and merit of his death, and the power of his resurrection. It acknowledges his death as the only sufficient means of redeeming man from death eternal, and his resurrection as the restoration of us all to life and to immortality; inasmuch as he "was delivered for our sins, and rose again for our justification." Christian faith is, then, not only an assent to the whole gospel of Christ, but also a full reliance on the blood of Christ; a trust in the merits of his life, death, and resurrection; a recumbency upon him as our atonement and our life, *as given for us,* and *living in us;* and in consequence hereof, a closing with him, and a cleaving to him, as our "wisdom, righteousness, sanctification, and redemption," or in one word, our salvation.[74]

If man is saved by grace through faith, what is the source of faith? We have seen that the nature of faith is a personal trust, confidence, complete reliance on the grace of God manifested in the life and death and resurrection of Christ, so that the individual who possesses it feels in his heart that Christ has died for him and has forgiven him of all his sins.[75] Is such faith the result of human effort? Is it the consequence of an act of man's intellect or will, so that man may be said to achieve trust or to make himself confident of the grace of God in Christ? In other words, does a man produce his own faith, so that we may say faith is the active human response to divine grace? No. Wesley is very

[73] *Letters,* I, 23.
[74] Sermon I, part i, sec. 5.
[75] Sermon II, part ii, sec. 5.

definite at this point. "Of yourselves," he writes, "cometh neither your faith nor your salvation: 'it is the gift of God;' the free, undeserved gift; the faith through which ye are saved, as well as the salvation which he of his own good pleasure, his mere favour annexes thereto. That ye believe, is one instance of his grace: that believing ye are saved, another." [76] For Wesley, grace is the source of salvation; faith, the condition.[77] But God is the sole cause of both, and each comes alone from him.

Under the influence of Moravian pietism and as the result of his own experience at Aldersgate, John Wesley was a new man; the center of his religion had shifted from an interest in self and an evaluation of all life in terms of his own spiritual self-aggrandizement to a love of God and to an appreciation of and care for humanity as the creation of God and the object of his love. With this came an entirely new conception of justification. He no longer thought of it as the hard struggle of man to achieve by means of good works his own salvation with fear and trembling and thus to merit the gift of Christ's atonement; rather, he saw it as God's act applied to man, the free gift of faith bestowed on man, the deliverance of a sinner from the power of his sin, and the remaking of a life after the fashion of the image of God in the face of Jesus Christ. Christ is so formed in a man's heart that "he who is justified, or saved by faith, is indeed *born again*. He is *born again of the Spirit* unto a new life, which is hid with Christ in God!" [78]

Such a doctrine makes its appeal to man as he actually is—selfish, weak, and mean—and it offers him the power to become what he would like to be.

[76] Sermon I, part iii, sec. 3.
[77] *Ibid.*, intro., sec. 3.
[78] *Ibid.*, part ii, sec. 7.

Chapter IV

WITHIN A HAIR'S BREADTH OF CALVINISM

Wesley's Mature Thought

PERSONAL EXPERIENCE IS A CONVINCING TEACHER, AND THE LESSONS learned in its classroom are seldom forgotten. The substance of the preceding chapter clearly indicates the central position which faith came to hold in John Wesley's conception of justification after his religious experience at Aldersgate and traces the origin of that faith to a divine act, to the grace of God wrought in the soul of man. Wesley always remained faithful to this new insight, and in the bitterest hours of his struggle with the Moravians he never forgot what they had taught him, nor ceased to be grateful.[1] In this concept, likewise, he recognized his kinship with Calvinism and on one occasion went so far as to say that he thought the same way on justification as John Calvin did.[2] Works never again intruded to make their claim as necessary precursors of the justifying act,[3] and the contemporary Anglican doctrine of justification by faith in the sense of *belief* and works in the sense of *moral achievement* was completely banished from his preaching.[4] The year 1738, therefore, saw the birth of the Wesleyan doctrine of justification. Thus in May, 1766, Mr. Wesley wrote:

I believe justification by faith alone, as much as I believe there is a God. I declared this in a sermon, preached before the University of Oxford, eight-and-twenty years ago. I declared it to all the world eighteen years ago, in a sermon written expressly on the subject. I have never varied from it, no, not a hair's breadth, from 1738 to this day.[5]

And again on March 26, 1790, one year prior to his death, Wesley wrote:

[1] *Works*, I, 244.
[2] *Journal,* Tues., May 14, 1765.
[3] "I believe no good works can be previous to justification; nor, consequently a condition of it. If a man could be holy before he were justified, it would set his justification aside."—*Works*, X, 389. See also *Works*, XII, 71.
[4] Sermon CXXXIV, part i, secs. 5-7.
[5] *Works*, X, 349.

About fifty years ago I had a clearer view than before of justification by faith; and in this, from that very hour, I never varied, no, not a hair's breadth. Nevertheless, an ingenious man has publicly accused me of a thousand variations. I pray God, not to lay this to his charge! I am now on the borders of the grave; but, by the grace of God, I still witness the same confession.[6]

Wesley gave his sermons and his *Notes on the New Testament* as the standard doctrine to be preached, taught, and kept by his followers and insisted that any preacher who did not conform to them should be replaced by another who believed them.[7] The task before us, therefore, is to set forth Wesley's mature doctrine of justification and to attempt to view it in the light of his other doctrines which helped to mold the theological pattern of the Revival.

The Nature of Justification

Already we have noted Wesley's assertion that man is justified by grace through faith, that faith is personal trust, and that the source of faith as well as grace is God. We have not, however, dealt with the nature of grace itself and with its operation in human life. We have said that a man does not produce his own faith, but we have not explained how that faith is actually produced in him, and why he calls it his very own. If man is impotent and cannot help himself, it is likewise true that he is sinful, devoid of righteousness, and stands in condemnation before God.[8] But God has prepared for man's salvation through the merits of his Son, who is the source of man's redemption.[9] Thus the foundation of justification rests on man's sinfulness and Christ's righteousness.[10]

But what does it mean for a man to be justified? John Wesley tells us at once that it is not the being made actually righteous or just.[11] This may be the immediate fruit of justification, but it is not the act itself. Neither can we say justification is the clearing us from any accusation brought against us by Satan, as if he had a place in our

[6] Sermon CXX, sec. 18.
[7] *Journal*, Fri., Sept. 5, 1783.
[8] Sermon V, part i, secs. 5-6.
[9] *Ibid.*, secs. 7-8.
[10] *Ibid.*, sec. 9.
[11] *Ibid.*, part ii, sec. 1.

trial or we owed him any recompense.[12] It is not the removal of any indictment laid on us by the law, though this may be taken for granted since violation of the law of God deserves death.[13] Least of all dare we to assert that justification implies that God is deceived in regard to the true character of those whom he justifies, that he thinks them to be what in fact they are not, or that he in any way accounts them to be otherwise than they are. God never judges contrary to the real nature of things; he never esteems anything better than it really is.[14]

The Wesleyan conception of justification must be understood as pardon, or the forgiveness of sins.[15] God, who is perfect wisdom, absolute truth, remains consistent in his omniscience; he sees man exactly as he is; and yet, despite what man is, he pardons him for the sake of Jesus Christ his Son. But if justification implies pardon or forgiveness, which is a negative term and signifies only the remission of past sins, it likewise implies acceptance, or the positive relationship of restoration to favor with God.[16] Pardon and acceptance, in the thought of Wesley, though perhaps they may be distinguished, can never be divided. In the very same moment, therefore, in which God forgives a sinner, he likewise restores him to the position of a son.[17] Justification, also, implies the acquittal from punishment for past sins,[18] so that God no longer holds a man accountable for wrong he has done.

According to Wesley, the justified are the ungodly, wicked people of every kind and degree. As they that are righteous need no repentance, so likewise they need no forgiveness. It is only sinners who must plead for pardon; it is only sin which admits of the possibility of being forgiven. "Forgiveness, therefore, has an immediate reference to sin, and, in this respect, to nothing else. It is our unrighteousness to which the pardoning God is *merciful*: it is our iniquity which he remembereth no more."[19] To those who affirm that holiness or obedience must precede justification, Wesley simply remarks, if such

[12] *Ibid.*, sec. 2.
[13] *Ibid.*, sec. 3.
[14] *Ibid.*, sec. 4.
[15] *Ibid.*, sec. 5; *Works*, VIII, 275, 281-82, 290; XII, 83.
[16] *Works*, VIII, 427.
[17] *Ibid.*, X, 323-24.
[18] Sermon V, part ii, sec. 5.
[19] *Ibid.*, part iii, sec. 1.

be the case, then it is absolutely impossible for a person to be justified. There can be no holiness apart from the love of God, and there is no love of God but from the sense of his having first loved us and forgiven us all our sins. But aside from this consideration the conception of justification through holiness and obedience is in itself contradictory and absurd. Thus Wesley tells us that it is not a saint who has reason to seek forgiveness but only a sinner; and, not only so, but when a man is actually pardoned of any wrong, he conceives of himself as a sinner and his act as sin. It is impossible for us to affirm that God justifies the holy or the righteous, for to assert this is simply to say that he takes away only those sins which were taken away before. How foolish it is to say that the good Shepherd seeks and saves only those sheep which are already found!

We have seen already that man can merit nothing at the hands of God, but now we must ask what is the significance of good works done before justification. A man can feed the hungry, clothe the naked, visit the sick, minister to those that are in prison, and engage in many works of charity and devotion; and Wesley tells us that these works are in one sense good. They are in themselves worth while and profitable. But in the true sense of the term they are not good works— that is, they are not acceptable in the sight of God. Only those works are acceptable which spring from a true faith in Christ. He says:

No works are good, which are not done as God hath willed and commanded them to be done:

But no works done before justification are done as God hath willed and commanded them to be done:

Therefore, no works done before justification are good.

The first proposition is self-evident; and the second—that no works done before justification are done as God hath willed and commanded them to be done—will appear equally plain and undeniable, if we only consider, God hath willed and commanded that all our works should be done in charity and in love, in that love to God which produces love to all mankind. But none of our works can be done in this love, while the love of the Father (of God as our Father) is not in us; and this love cannot be in us till we receive the "Spirit of adoption, crying in our hearts, Abba, Father." If, therefore, God doth not justify the ungodly, and him that (in this sense) worketh not, then hath Christ died in vain; then, notwithstanding his death can no flesh living be justified.[20]

Works, therefore, are irrelevant to justification; and deeds of merit and profit, together with all acts of charity, have no bearing on the forgiveness of sins. The single term of justification, the only necessary condition of pardon, is faith. To the ungodly man who worketh not, that faith which is given him by God is likewise counted to him for righteousness.[21]

The Wesleyan Doctrine of Justification in Relation to That of the Church of England

The Wesleyan doctrine of justification is a repudiation of those teachings concerning it which were predominant in the Church of England in Wesley's day. Wesley himself recognized that fact, and any attempt of scholarship to prove the basic unity between Wesleyan doctrinal standards on this issue and those of the English Church must slide over the theological literature of the seventeenth century and look for agreement in a period of Anglican theology far removed from Wesley's own.[22] Wesley says concerning his contemporaries that they adulterate the word of God and provide little wholesome food for the souls of their congregations and in the main supply them with an abundance of poison.[23] Or, again, he writes that he cannot honestly profess any veneration at all for those fellow pastors of the Church of England, men who solemnly subscribe to the Articles and Homilies and yet who do not believe them in their hearts or teach them from their pulpits.[24] The leaders of the Church of England likewise branded Wesley as a stranger and saw in his preaching a doctrine alien to their own. After the start of his new message, one by one the churches of the land closed their doors to him.[25] In his own home town of Ep-

[20] *Ibid.*, sec. 6.

[21] *Ibid.*, part iv, secs. 1, 5; *Notes on the New Testament*, pp. 369-72.

[22] E.g., D. Baines-Griffiths, *Wesley the Anglican*, pp. 93-132, seeks only to show that Wesley quoted the Prayer Book and the Homilies and gives no theological analysis of the distinction between his thought and that of his Anglican contemporaries.

[23] Sermon CXXXIV, part i, sec. 2.

[24] *Works*, XII, 64.

[25] *Journal*, Sun., Feb. 18, 1739.

worth, where he had been brought up, he was denied the use of the parish church and was compelled to announce his gospel to the people from his father's tombstone.[26] One need only glance at the polemical writings of Mr. Wesley in order to sense the tremendous pressure of attack leveled against his doctrine of justification by his contemporaries in the Anglican fold,[27] and Wesley himself writes over and over again that he can spare time to reply to only the more significant treatises of his opponents. No less a figure than the Lord Bishop of Gloucester said that in Wesley's teachings the symptoms of grace and perdition were interwoven and confounded with one another,[28] and Dr. Horne cried out that the heresy of antinomianism was rampant once again.[29]

The crux of the whole matter lies, of course, at the point of the Anglican emphasis on works as necessary precursors of the justifying act. Wesley frankly states that in this matter he is not taking issue with the deists, Arians, or Socinians, who are the first-born of Satan. No, he is drawing his sword against the orthodox leaders of his own Church, those "who are accounted the pillars of our Church, and the champions of our faith; who, indeed betray that Church, and sap the very foundations of the faith we are taught thereby." [30] He turns naturally to the thought of two men who helped to shape the Anglican theological position which was at that time predominant, and he specifically states that their teaching is erroneous at the point of justification. Thus no less a figure than John Tillotson, Archbishop of Canterbury, attempts in several of his sermons to prove that man is justified, not by faith alone, but by good works also, a fact so displeasing to Wesley that he refrains from quoting particular passages.[31] The other theologian is Bishop George Bull, whose work *Harmonia Apostolica,* as we saw in Chapter II, represents better than any other single work the normative Anglican position on the doctrine of justification during this period. Wesley expresses himself correctly when he says that

---

[26] *Ibid.,* Sun., June 6, 1742.
[27] *Works,* V, 12; VII, 454; VIII, 50-58, 275, 281, 291, 361-63, 366-69, 387-89, 402, 428-30, 508; IX, 110-17; X, 179, 349, 390, 432, 447; XIII, 499-500.
[28] *Ibid.,* IX, 121.
[29] *Ibid.,* p. 110.
[30] Sermon CXXXIV, part i, sec. 3.
[31] *Ibid.,* sec. 5.

Tillotson makes holiness the condition of justification and, therefore, prior to the justifying act;[32] but then immediately he turns from Tillotson to Bull with this statement:

> It may appear strange to some that an angel of the Church of God, (as the great Shepherd terms the overseers of it,) and one so highly esteemed both in our own and many other nations, should coolly and calmly thus speak. But O, what is he in comparison of the great Bishop Bull! Who shall be able to stand, if this eminent scholar, Christian, and Prelate, in his youth wrote and published to the world, and in his riper years defended, the positions that follow? . . .[33]

At this point Wesley proceeds to quote directly from the *Harmonia Apostolica,* where Bull expressly states that good works are set by the gospel covenant as requisite and necessary to a man's justification.[34]

But if the Wesleyan doctrine of justification is out of harmony with the teachings of the Church of England in the eighteenth century, one may ask why Wesley professes in his writings to be orthodox and to agree with the doctrines of the Church. The answer lies in the fact that he conceives of the true doctrine of the Church only in terms of the teachings of the Prayer Book and of the Homilies. To be sure, his opponents likewise profess their allegiance to the Prayer Book and the traditional standards of Anglicanism, but they reserve the right to interpret them. Bishop Bull, for instance, interprets the homilies on faith in the light of his own peculiar teachings.[35] And Wesley himself admits the ambiguity in the wording of the seventeenth article and frankly states that he imagines it was so worded on purpose. But then he claims that so far as possible he teaches the doctrines of the Articles and the Homilies in their plain, unforced, and grammatical meaning.[36]

The Wesleyan Doctrine of Justification in Relation to That of the Reformers

Now two facts stand out, it seems to me, in any consideration of Wesley's use of the Thirty-nine Articles and of the Homilies. The

[32] Sermon CXXXIV, part i, sec. 5.
[33] *Ibid.,* sec. 6.
[34] *Ibid.;* Bull, *Harmonia Apostolica,* p. 11.
[35] Bull, *ibid.,* pp. 206-15.
[36] *Works,* XII, 65.

first fact is that, as a matter of plain truth, the Thirty-nine Articles
and the Homilies were composed at a time when the Calvinistic emphasis was supreme in English theological thought, and they set forth
the cardinal doctrines of the Reformation.[37] The second fact is that two
months after his return to England from Hernhuth, John Wesley began "more narrowly to enquire what the doctrine of the Church of
England" was in regard to the "controverted point of justification by
Faith."[38] He began to study afresh both the Articles and the Homilies,
and he studied them from the point of view of the Moravian conception of justification by faith alone. These two facts stand together, and
on the basis of them it is not surprising at all that John Wesley claimed
that his teachings were true to the doctrines of the Church of England
while those of his opponents were false.

What can we say, then, of the Wesleyan doctrine of justification? In
its formulation does John Wesley but reassert a buried and yet not
forgotten precedent? Does he but turn back and accept unmodified the
doctrine of the Reformation? In regard to the justifying act itself,
Wesley is at one with Luther and with Calvin. At this point he does
not differ with Whitefield in the least. Luther conceives of justification
as the pardon and the acceptance of a sinner by God on the condition
of faith alone, as the inward righteousness which heals the malady of
the soul of man and which is itself the gift of God.[39] And Calvin

---

[37] Articles IX-XVIII, which deal with individual religion, are drawn largely from the
Confessions of the Continental Churches.—E. T. Green, *XXXIX Articles and the Age
of Reformation*, p. 18. The source of Article X is the *Article De Peccato* in the Wurtem-
burg Confession and agrees verbatim with the words of St. Augustine in his *De Gratia
et Libero Arbitrio*, chap. xvii. Article XI on Justification, though much briefer than the
Articles of the Continental Churches, still agrees with them and is set squarely over
against the teachings of the Council of Trent. See Session VI of *Canons and Decrees of
the Council of Trent; Augsburg Confession*, Article IV; *Saxon Confession*, Art III;
Confessio Variata, Art. *"De Fide," Second Helvetic Confession*, Art. XV; Calvin, *Institutes*,
III, xi, 2. Article XIII plainly states that works done before justification are not pleasing
to God, since they do not spring from faith. This is precisely the teachings of Calvin,
op. cit., III, xiv, 9; and of Luther, *Werke* (Weimar ed.) II, 513, 532; VI, 354. Cf. this
with the "Homily on Salvation," "Homily on Misery of Man" (part ii), "Homily on
Good Works," "Homily on Faith" in *Homilies of the Church of England*. The theology
of the Thirty-nine Articles, the Prayer Book, and the Homilies is Calvinistic. See J. R.
Green, *History of the English People*, II, 233-34.

[38] *Journal*, Sun., Nov. 12, 1738.

[39] Luther, *Werke* (Weimar ed.), II, 13-14, 427; VIII, 106, 111. (Erlangen ed.),
XXII, 138, 248; XIII, 238; XII, 89.

writes that we must think of justification simply as acceptance, whereby God receives us into his favor.[40] "Adieu, therefore, to the fanciful notion of those who imagine a righteousness compounded of faith and works."[41] Calvin insists on two points: first, there never was an action performed by man which, when scrutinized by divine justice, would not deserve condemnation; and, secondly, if such a work could be found, it would still be so contaminated and corrupted by the sins of which its performer is guilty that it would lose all its claim to divine favor.[42] George Whitefield writes that by justification "we are to understand" that we are "so acquitted in the sight of God as to be looked on as though we never had offended him at all."[43] Or, justification means the pardon for past sins;[44] and it comes to us, not through our works, but alone through the perfect obedience of Christ,[45] which is given us by faith.[46] To be sure, Wesley stands shoulder to shoulder with Whitefield and the Reformers in his conviction that man is justified by grace through faith and not by works; and it is interesting to note that in answering objections to his doctrine he follows Calvin almost exactly in his replies to similar objections in the *Institutes*.[47]

Wesley's Conception of Grace

Wesley is at one with Calvinism in regard to his conception of the act of justification, the means whereby man is accepted of God and forgiven of his past sins. He agrees also with the Calvinistic conception of the foundation on which justification rests or, as he himself calls it, the source from which the justifying act proceeds. God's grace is the source of justification in the thought of both Calvin and Wesley. But what is the nature of the operation of grace for the two men? It is at this point that we note the distinction between Wesleyan thought and historic Calvinism. The two are not the same; and any attempt to

[40] Calvin, *Institutes*, III, xi, 2.
[41] *Ibid.*, 13.
[42] *Ibid.*, xiv, 11.
[43] G. Whitefield, *Works*, VI, 216.
[44] *Ibid.*, p. 223.
[45] *Ibid.*, p. 224.
[46] *Ibid.*, p. 100.
[47] Wesley, Sermon I, part iii; and Calvin, *op. cit.*, III, xvi, 1-4; xvii, 1-2; xviii, 1-2, 4.

THE THEOLOGY OF JOHN WESLEY

equate them violates not only that movement in history in which
Wesleyanism recognized (with regret, it is true) its own incompati-
bility with the Calvinism of Whitefield, but also certain fundamental
principles which underlie each system and which give to each its
peculiar character.

Grace, for Calvin, though it does operate universally in one sense,
is in regard to justification restricted, limited, and particular. Grace
operates universally only in that, amidst the corruptions of human
nature, it intervenes to restrain evil operations, and thus to put limits
to man's uncontrolled fury. Good actions, or rather those actions which
appear good, are really just the products of the restraining grace of
God, which keeps men whose hearts are evil from breaking out into
acts of external violence.[48] But saving grace operates only in a particular sense and makes itself felt alone in the hearts and lives of those
whom God has chosen to receive it. Calvin believes that it is the result
of the divine will that salvation is freely offered to some, while others
are prevented from attaining it. This pushes us to a consideration of
the Calvinistic conception of election and predestination, for Calvin
himself says:

We shall never be clearly convinced as we ought to be, that our salvation
flows from the fountain of God's free mercy, till we are acquainted with
his eternal election, which illustrates the grace of God by this comparison,
that he adopts not all promiscuously to the hope of salvation, but gives to
some what he refuses to others.[49]

Predestination means, according to Calvin, that God has once for all
determined, by an immutable and eternal decree, all those whom he
will admit to salvation and whom he will condemn to destruction.
This decree, in so far as it concerns those whom God will save, is
founded on gratuitous mercy, totally irrespective of human merit; but
this decree, in so far as it concerns those whom God will damn, is
founded on a just and irreprehensible judgment. Thus in the elect
we consider calling as an evidence of election, and justification as a
token of its manifestation. Heaven, or eternal life in the presence of
the Saviour, constitutes its completion. But just as God seals his elect

[48] Calvin, *op. cit.*, II, iii, 3.
[49] *Ibid.*, III, xxi, 1.

90

by their calling and their justification, so likewise he serves the non-elect with an indication of his judgment by excluding them from the knowledge of his name and from the sanctification of his Spirit.[50] Not all men, therefore, are created with a similar destiny, but eternal life is foreordained for some and eternal damnation for others. Every man, before ever he comes into the world, is selected by God for either life or death, for either the rewards of heaven or the fires of hell.[51]

Now this discriminating election of God, which is ordinarily concealed within the counsels of the Godhead, is made manifest only by the calling, which may be termed the testification or evidence of the election. Thus Calvin writes:

> Though by choosing his people, the Lord has adopted them as his children, yet we see that they enter not on the possession of so great a blessing till they are called; on the other hand as soon as they are called, they immediately enjoy some communication of his election. . . . By connecting calling with election, the Scripture evidently suggests that nothing is requisite to it but the free mercy of God. For if we enquire whom he calls, and for what reason, the answer is, those whom he had elected. But when we come to election, we see nothing but mercy on every side.[52]

The validity of a man's election does not in any way depend on his own consent. According to such a notion, "the will of man is superior to the counsel of God." To be sure, the certainty of election is found in his embracing the gospel, but this has absolutely nothing to do with the fact of his election itself. The embracing of the gospel is merely God's means of disclosing his election to him.[53] In this he calls him as a soldier under the banner of his Son Jesus Christ. Thus, if any one wants to be certain whether God is concerned about his salvation or not, let him enquire whether he has committed him to Christ.[54]

But we ask the simple question: Why is it that some who appear to belong to Christ fall away from him again and again and finally sink into ruin? Calvin answers that in reality these people are not chosen by God at all; and if we must say that they are called, at the

[50] *Ibid.*, 7.
[51] *Ibid.*, 5.
[52] *Ibid.*, xxiv, 1.
[53] *Ibid.*, 3.
[54] *Ibid.*, 6.

same time we must remember that there are two kinds of calling. True, there is a universal call by which God invites through his word all people indiscriminately to come to him; but there is also a special call which he gives only to the elect, and it is this special call alone which is effective and which is accompanied by the inward illumination of God's Spirit. The universal call, therefore, has no meaning for salvation whatsoever; and when it is offered to the nonelect, even those whom God intends for damnation, it is given to them merely as "a savour of death" and "as an occasion of heavier condemnation." [55] "Observe, he directs his voice to them, but it is that they may become more deaf; he kindles a light, but it is that they may be more blind; he publishes a doctrine, but it is that they may be more besotted; he applies a remedy, but it is that they may not be healed." [56]

If, therefore, the election, effectual calling, and justification of those whom God has chosen stand as the expression of God's grace and the manifestation of his mercy, it is likewise true that the rejection, condemnation, and destruction of those whom God has not chosen stand as the demonstration of God's judgment and the expression of his wrath. Calvin teaches the stern doctrine of reprobation. The reprobates are "those, therefore, whom he has created to a life of shame and a death of destruction, that they might be the instruments of his wrath and examples of his severity." [57] Sometimes God deprives these creatures of the opportunity of hearing the word, as in the case of the heathen; sometimes he allows the word to be preached to them but only increases their blindness. Calvin himself raises the question why, in bestowing grace upon some, God passes others by. He tells us that St. Luke assigns as the reason for bestowing grace upon some that they were ordained to eternal life. Then Calvin says that the only conclusion which can be drawn is that the others were ordained for eternal death, that they were made as vessels of wrath for dishonor. Wherefore Calvin does not hesitate to say that God could convert to good the will of the wicked, because God is omnipotent. But it is evident that he does not do so. Why? Because he would not. The reason why he would not remains with himself, and we should ask no more. The

[55] Ibid., 7-8.
[56] Ibid., 13.
[57] Ibid., 12.

92

depths of the riches of the wisdom of God are beyond us; his judgments we cannot search out, and it does not become us to try.[58]

The Calvinistic conception of grace, therefore, rests squarely on the
conviction of the absolute sovereignty of God. God orders completely
everything that he has created; and all events of the universe, from
the highest to the lowest, are according to his will. Nothing happens
by accident or by any power not itself the instrument of the divine
choice. Saving grace is applied only where God chooses to apply it;
it is always effective, irresistible, and complete.

The Wesleyan conception of the nature of the operation of God's
grace is as far removed from the Calvinistic conception as the east is
from the west. Saving grace is not restricted; it is not particular; it
does not rest on the prior principle of election or predestination. "How
freely does God love the world! While we were yet sinners, 'Christ
died for the ungodly.' While we were 'dead in sin,' God 'spared not
his own Son,' but delivered him up for us all.' And how freely with
him does he 'give us all things!' Verily FREE GRACE is all in all!"[59] Yes,
and Wesley goes on to write in a sermon which Tyerman says "in
some respects was the most important sermon that he ever issued"[60]
that the grace or love of God, whence cometh our salvation, is "FREE
IN ALL, and FREE FOR ALL."[61] To be sure, it is free in all in the sense that
it is given without price, that it does not demand anything of us before
it is bestowed, and that it flows from the free mercy of God.[62] Here
Wesley is in fundamental agreement with the thought of Calvin and
of Whitefield. But note the change. Grace is free *for* all as well as free
in all. It is not free only for those whom God has ordained to life, but
it is like the air we breathe or like the wind that blows in our faces.
It is for every one who dwells upon the face of the earth.[63]

This brings us, therefore, to the Wesleyan consideration of the principle which underlies the Calvinistic conception of grace, the doctrine
of predestination. Wesley writes somewhere around the year 1764 that,
though he and his followers love many that are Calvinists, they do not

[58] *Ibid.*, 13.
[59] Sermon CXXVIII, sec. 1.
[60] Tyerman, *Life and Times of John Wesley*, I, 317.
[61] Sermon CXXVIII, sec. 2.
[62] *Ibid.*, sec. 3.
[63] *Ibid.*, sec. 4.

love their opinions.[64] Or again as late as September 9, 1772, he writes of Mr. Hill, the Calvinist:

What peace am I—or indeed any Arminian, to expect from him? Since any agreement with us would be "a covenant with death, and a conspiracy against the kingdom of Christ." I therefore give up all hope of peace with him, and with all that are thus minded. For I do not believe what he terms "the truths of God," the doctrine of absolute predestination. I never did believe it, nor the doctrines connected with it, no, not for an hour. In this I have been consistent with myself. I have never varied an hair's breadth.[65]

First of all, Wesley begins by a consideration of the various interpretations of the doctrine of predestination and attempts to show that fundamentally they are all the same and lead to the same consequences. Thus the notion of double predestination, which Calvin plainly teaches, in which the evil and the good alike are assigned to their respective ends by the absolute sovereign will which causes them to be exactly what they are, is really no more drastic or terrible than the milder concept of election, in which God chooses and calls those whom he desires to justify and to save and leaves the rest of mankind to themselves. It is not enough, thinks Wesley, just to say you do not hold the decree of reprobation or you do not believe that God actually hardens the hearts of men so that they cannot accept his grace. For, if God decrees that, all being dead in sin, he will say to some, Live, and to others he will not, the very fact that he refuses to offer life to some, that he does not give them an opportunity for salvation, is the same as actually to decree damnation for them or to predestinate them to eternal punishment.

Are any who are not thus elected saved? or were any, from the foundation of the world? Is it possible any man should be saved unless he be thus elected? If you say, "No," you are but where you was; you are not one hair's breadth farther; you still believe that, in consequence of an unchangeable, irresistible decree of God, the greater part of mankind abide in death, without any possibility of redemption; inasmuch as none can save them but God, and he will not save them. You believe he hath absolutely decreed not to save them; and what is this but decreeing to damn them?

64 *Works*, VIII, 350-51.
65 *Ibid.*, X, 378-79.

It is, in effect, neither more nor less; it comes to the same thing; for if you are dead, and altogether unable to make yourself alive, then, if God has absolutely decreed he will make only others alive, and not you, he hath absolutely decreed your everlasting death; you are absolutely consigned to damnation. So, then, though you use softer words than some, you mean the self-same thing; and God's decree concerning the election of grace, according to your account of it, amounts to neither more nor less than what others call God's decree of reprobation.[66]

"But what does such a doctrine do?" asks Wesley. Why, the most obvious thing is that it makes all preaching vain. Preaching is of no value to those who are elected; for, with or without it, they will be infallibly saved. And it is a mockery to those who are not elected; for, though they hear, they cannot understand and, though the word is proclaimed unto them, they cannot grasp or perceive its meaning.[67]

More than this, Wesley flatly affirms that the doctrine of predestination is no doctrine of God, for it directly tends to destroy holiness, which is the end of all the ordinances of God. It takes away those first motives of holiness, which are the hope of future reward and the fear of punishment. Immediately the Calvinist replies, "But man knows not whether he is assigned to life or death." Wesley answers that such knowledge is beside the point, and then makes this famous remark:

If a sick man knows that he must unavoidably die, or unavoidably recover, though he knows not which, it is unreasonable for him to take any physic at all. He might justly say, (and so I have heard some speak, both in bodily sickness and spiritual,) 'If I am ordained to life, I shall live; if to death, I shall die; so I need not trouble myself about it.'[68]

The doctrine of predestination closes the gate of holiness and prevents unholy men from ever approaching thereto or striving to enter thereat. At the same time such a doctrine tends to fill its adherents with pride, to stifle meekness and love within them, and to give them a sense of opposition to, yea, even of abhorrence of, those poor sinners whom God has hated from eternity.[69]

[66] Sermon CXXVIII, sec. 8.
[67] *Ibid.*, sec. 10.
[68] *Ibid.*, sec. 11.
[69] *Ibid.*, sec. 12.

Again, predestination tends, according to Wesley, to destroy the comfort of religion. Now it is interesting to note the way in which he puts the matter. He simply states that this is evident to all those either who believe themselves to be damned or who suspect or fear it. And then Wesley turns to those who believe themselves saved and asks them a question, which to say the least does not tend to inspire confidence or to engender hope. It seems almost like a subtle device on his part to evoke doubt and fear within them and to cause them to question the efficacy of their calling and the certainty of their election. "And as to you who believe yourselves the elect of God, what is your happiness? I hope, not a notion, a speculative belief, a bare opinion of any kind." [70] Are you possessed by a feeling, a compelling conviction that your past sins are forgiven and that you are a child of God? If you are possessed with such a conviction, can you be sure that it will always last? Is it given unto you to know the future and to say with confidence that you have the assurance of future perseverance? [71] St. Paul writes in I Corinthians 9:27 that after having preached the gospel to others he might even become a reprobate himself, and indeed he would actually have become such if he had not kept his body under subjection. [72] But can you say, between God and your own hearts, you have not had returns of doubts and fears concerning your own election and perseverance? [73] Or, if perchance you are genuinely saved yourselves, how can you, how can anyone who has put on Christ, endure the thought that thousands and millions of men, without any preceding offence of theirs, were unchangeably doomed to everlasting burnings? No, no, it is not possible. Those who are filled with the bowels of mercy, tenderness, and compassion would rather wish themselves accursed for their brethren's sake. [74]

Not only so, but such a doctrine tends to destroy zeal for good works. This is seen in two ways. It tends to destroy our love for the greater part of mankind—that is, for the evil and the reprobate. And whatever weakens love weakens likewise the desire to do good. It is impossible

[70] *Ibid.*, sec. 14.
[71] *Ibid.*
[72] *Notes on the New Testament*, p. 427.
[73] Sermon CXXVIII, sec. 15.
[74] *Ibid.*, sec. 17.

to serve those for whom we have no affection. Again, it cuts off the strongest motive for engaging in acts of charity and kindness—namely, the hope of saving souls from death. For what profit is there in relieving the temporal wants and in supplying the physical needs of those who are destined anyway for hell and who are dropping every day into the fire which is not quenched? Whether we know who is elected or not, our labor is still vain. For all our works of charity and kindness, not a single soul is rectified, not a single life is changed.[75]

After having said what the doctrine of predestination does, in his opinion, to certain aspects of the Christian life, Wesley comes now to assert that it has a direct and manifest tendency to overthrow the whole Christian revelation. At this point the defenders of the doctrine of predestination join hands with agnostics and deists, for in reality they maintain that the Christian revelation is not necessary. By affirming an eternal, unchangeable decree that part of mankind will be saved and part will be damned, they admit there is really no need in having a Christian revelation at all. The decree is prior to the revelation; and even though the Christian revelation were not in being, one part of mankind would inevitably be saved and the other part would inevitably be damned. Now, says Wesley, the wisest of the unbelievers labor most industriously to prove that the Christian revelation is not necessary; for they well know that it would follow without much difficulty that, if men were convinced of such a fact, they would likewise be easily persuaded that the Christian revelation is not true. No infidel could desire more. The Calvinist allows him all he asks. In making the Christian gospel unnecessary to all sorts of men, he gives up at the same time the whole Christian cause.[76] He makes the Scripture contradict itself and sets the oracles of God in array against one another.

True, all Calvinists claim that the doctrine of predestination rests firmly on a scriptural basis;[77] but in making such a claim they are forced to select certain passages of Scripture and interpret those passages in such a way that they flatly contradict other passages. For ex-

[75] *Ibid.*, sec. 18.
[76] *Ibid.*, sec. 19.
[77] E.g., Calvin, *op. cit.*, III, xxii, 1-11.

ample, says Wesley, the predestinarians interpret that text, "Jacob have I loved, but Esau have I hated," to mean that God in a literal sense hated Esau and all the damned from eternity. This is a flat contradiction of the whole scope of Scripture and especially of those particular texts which declare, "God is love."[78] This text does not relate to the persons of Jacob and of Esau at all, for Esau never did actually serve Jacob, and the preceding verse states, "The elder shall serve the younger." Rather, it relates to the tribes of Israel and of Edom, and it depends on the condition of their having accepted or refused God's grace. God thus has an indisputable right to reject those who will not accept the blessings on his own terms.[79] Or they infer from the words, "I will have mercy on whom I will have mercy," that God is love only to some men —the elect—and that he has mercy on them only. But this does violence to the words of Psalm 145:9: "The Lord is loving unto every man, and his mercy is over all his works."[80] Really, this text means nothing more than that God will have mercy on those who submit to his terms and who accept the way he has appointed.[81] Again, they take the words of Ephesians 1:4-7, "As he hath chosen us through him before the foundation of the world, that we might be holy and blameless before him in love: Having predestinated us by Jesus Christ, to the adoption of sons unto himself, according to the good pleasure of his will, To the praise of the glory of his grace, by which he hath freely accepted us through the Beloved," to mean that Christ died not for all but only for a few, whom God hath chosen out of the world. This interpretation of the text from Ephesians contradicts the whole spirit of the New Testament. "The same Lord over all is rich to all who call upon him" (Romans 10:12). "Destroy not him with thy meat, for whom Christ died" (Romans 14:15) is clear proof that Christ died not only for those that are saved but also for them that perish.[82] Therefore, Ephesians 1:4-7 can only be interpreted to mean that God, having chosen both Jews and Gentiles, foreordained that all who afterward believed should enjoy the dignity of being his sons and joint heirs with

[78] Sermon CXXVIII, sec. 20. Cf. Calvin, op. cit., III, xxii, 4-5.
[79] Notes on the New Testament, p. 388.
[80] Sermon CXXVIII, sec. 20. Cf. Calvin, op. cit., III, xxii, 6.
[81] Notes on the New Testament, p. 388.
[82] Sermon CXXVIII, sec. 21. Cf. Calvin, op. cit., III, xxii, 1.

Christ according to his free, fixed, unalterable purpose to confer this blessing on all those who should believe in Christ.[83]

Finally, the doctrine of predestination is full of blasphemy—"of such blasphemy," says Wesley, "as I should dread to mention, but that the honour of our gracious God, and the cause of truth will not suffer me to be silent." [84] To begin with, it makes Jesus Christ a hypocrite, a deceiver of men, and a leader without honesty or ordinary sincerity. For it cannot be denied that he everywhere speaks as if he is willing that all men should be saved. Listen to his plea to the Jews in Matthew 23:37: "O Jerusalem, Jerusalem, that killest the prophets, and stonest them that are sent unto thee, how often would I have gathered thy children together even as a bird gathereth her young under her wings: and ye would not!" [85] His words are full of invitations to sinners. "Come unto me, all ye that labour and are heavy laden, and I will give you rest" (Matthew 11:28).[86] If you say he did not intend to save all sinners, if you say he calls those that cannot come, then you represent the Son of God "as mocking his helpless creatures by offering what he never intends to give. You describe him as saying one thing, and meaning another: as pretending the love which he had not. Him, in 'whose mouth was no guile,' you make full of deceit, void of common sincerity." [87]

If such a doctrine makes a liar out of Jesus Christ, then likewise it overthrows the very attributes of God, corrupts his justice, his mercy, and his truth, and pictures the most Holy One as a very devil—false, cruel, and unjust. Yea, it pictures him as worse than the devil.

More *false;* because the devil, liar as he is, hath never said, "He willeth all men to be saved:" More *unjust;* because the devil cannot, if he would, be guilty of such injustice as you ascribe to God, when you say that God condemned millions of souls to everlasting fire, prepared for the devil and his angels, for continuing in sin for want of that grace *he will not* give them, they cannot avoid: and more *cruel;* because that unhappy spirit "seeketh rest and findeth none;" so that his own restless misery is a kind of temptation to him to tempt others. But God resteth in his high and holy

[83] *Notes on the New Testament,* p. 489.
[84] Sermon CXXVIII, sec. 23.
[85] *Notes on the New Testament,* p. 77.
[86] *Ibid.,* p. 42.
[87] Sermon CXXVIII, sec. 24.

place; so that to suppose him, of his own mere motion, of his pure will and pleasure, happy as he is, to doom his creatures, whether they will or no, to endless misery, is to impute such cruelty to him as we cannot impute even to the great enemy of God and man.[88]

Thus Wesley rests his case in regard to predestination. He is willing to go all the way with Whitefield and with Calvin in ascribing man's justification to the grace of God alone. He cannot, however, agree with them in their conception of the nature of the operation of God's grace. To make grace particular, restricted, special, is in the end to affirm that God himself is unjust. "This is the blasphemy clearly contained in *the horrible decree* of predestination! And here I fix my foot." [89]

Wesley finds such a view less compatible than the teachings of Rome.

And yet what are all the absurd opinions of all the Romanists in the world compared to this one, that the God of love, the wise, just, merciful Father of all spirits of all flesh, has, from all eternity, fixed an absolute, unchangeable, irresistible decree that part of mankind shall be saved, do what they will; and the rest damned, do what they can.[90]

In contradistinction to the Calvinistic conception of limited grace, Wesley proposes his doctrine of universal grace free for all and free in all. Now we have seen already that this grace is free in all in the sense that God gives it without price, that he confers it on a sinner in the very state of his sinfulness, and that the recipient does nothing to merit it. But there is another and a more profound meaning to Wesley's little phrase "free in all." If man is by nature sinful, conceived in iniquity, he is at the same time endued with the quality of what Wesley calls "preventing grace." There is something in him besides the attributes of his own nature. He is endowed with a spark of divinity. God works in him, not in the sense of momentary intervention or sudden, catastrophic possession, but rather in the sense of an abiding presence and a continual indwelling.

God worketh in you; therefore, you can work. . . . For allowing that all the souls of men are dead in sin by *nature,* this excuses none, seeing there is no man that is in a state of mere nature; there is no man, unless

[88] *Ibid.,* sec. 25.
[89] *Ibid.,* sec. 26.
[90] Sermon LV, sec. 1.

he has quenched the Spirit, that is wholly void of the grace of God. No man living is entirely destitute of what is vulgarly called *natural conscience*. But this is not natural: It is more properly termed, *preventing grace*. Every man has a greater or less measure of this, which waiteth not for the call of man. Every one has, sooner or later, good desires; although the generality of men stifle them before they can strike deep root, or produce any considerable fruit. Every one has some measure of that light, some glimmering ray, which, sooner or later, more or less, enlightens every man that cometh into the world.[91]

Grace can, therefore, be free *for* all; God's purpose of salvation can extend *to* all simply because grace already is operating *in* all. If God offers grace freely, it is likewise true that he freely makes good his offer and confers actually the gift which he promises. In short, the Wesleyan conception of grace is such that it is denied to no man. It is given to him as surely as is life; it is as much a part of him as if it were his inalienable birthright.

Wesley labels his view of grace as Arminian; and in a brief tract entitled *The Question, "What Is an Arminian?" Answered by a Lover of Free Grace*[92] he places himself within the tradition of the teachings of James Harmens, whose Latin name was Jacobus Arminius, a minister of Amsterdam, Holland, and later a professor of divinity at the University of Leyden.[93] Arminius began his career as a Calvinist, a convinced student of the theology of Geneva; but he ended with a modified form of Calvinism, and the modification of his former theology lay at this very point of grace. Like Wesley, Arminius reviews the theological conceptions of election and of predestination from the supralapsarian view to the milder concepts of preterition and single predestination only to find them all unsatisfactory.[94] True, God has decreed, according to Arminius, concerning man's salvation; but the nature of that decree is not such as to limit the offer of salvation but rather to extend the offer and to administer in a sufficient and effica-

[91] Sermon LXXXV, part iii, secs. 3, 4. Note how close Wesley comes in his conception of conscience to Joseph Butler. The only difference is that Wesley calls conscience "preventing grace" and separates it from mere human nature. See Butler, Sermon II, sec. 19; Sermon III, sec. 1; Sermon I, secs. 7, 8; Sermon II, secs. 2, 10, 12, 17, 18.

[92] *Works*, X, 358-61.

[93] *Ibid.*, p. 359.

[94] J. Arminius, *Works*, I, 550-83.

cious manner the means which are necessary to repentance and faith to all men. Such an administration of salvation is instituted according to divine wisdom, by which God knows what is proper and becoming both to his mercy and to his severity and, also, according to his divine justice, by which he is prepared to adopt whatever his wisdom may prescribe and to put it into execution.[95] Divine grace is that "gratuitous affection by which God is kindly affectioned towards a miserable sinner, by which he gives his Son, that whoever believeth in him might have eternal life, by which he justifies him in Christ Jesus and for his sake, and adopts him into the right of sons, unto salvation." Arminius ascribes to grace the commencement, continuance, and consummation of all good, and to such an extent that man can do nothing good without it.[96] But the big point is that man *can be without grace* and that the reason he is without it is due to himself and not to God. Though it is absolutely impossible for a man to win salvation or to perform acts which are genuinely good without grace, man does have the power to accept or to reject grace when it is offered to him.

The Arminian conception of grace is more cautious and guarded than the Wesleyan. Arminius, for instance, does not use the expression "free grace in all," as if grace existed in the same manner within the individual as any other natural endowment and was given him as soon as he came into the world. But the two men are one in their repudiation of predestination, or unconditional election, and in their abhorrence of the doctrine of reprobation. In regard to justification both recognize the merits of Calvinism, and in truth the Wesleyan doctrine comes, as John Wesley himself put it, "within a hair's breadth of Calvinism." [97] No one ever asserted man's absolute dependence on grace any more than John Wesley did, or preached justification by faith with more zeal or steadfastness. And yet, though Wesleyanism and Calvinism come in this instance so close together, they are in reality worlds apart. No man realized this any more than Wesley himself did; and he wrote concerning the Calvinists: "As to reprobation, seeing they have drawn the sword, I throw away the scabbard." [98]

[95] *Ibid.*, p. 589.
[96] *Ibid.*, pp. 597-98.
[97] *Works*, VIII, 284.
[98] *Ibid.*, XII, 137.

Chapter V

THE WAY TO THE KINGDOM

The Human Side of Justification

JUSTIFICATION, TO BE SURE, IS GOD'S OWN ACT; AND YET IT IS INTENDED for man's benefit and is performed in his behalf. The source, or ground, of justification is grace; and grace is universal and free. Like life itself, it is bestowed on all humanity; no person born into the world is denied a portion of it as his own possession. But the Wesleyan conception of justification, though it rests on the foundation of grace as its cause, depends likewise on faith as the instrument or condition of its being made effective. The issue before us, therefore, at this point resolves itself into a simple question: How is justifying grace either apportioned to or appropriated by individual human beings? The answer is made extremely difficult by the Wesleyan interpretation of faith. As we have seen in Chapter IV, faith is not the consequence of an act of man's intellect or will, so that it is legitimate to say that faith is the product of human effort or the response of man to grace. Rather, it springs from God, as grace does, and is equated with grace in that it is said to be God's àct also. Faith, for Wesley, is really nothing more than grace made conscious in the individual, or grace transformed from its latent stage into one of power and effectiveness. It is a divine, supernatural ἔλεγχοσ, evidence, or conviction, of things not seen. It is not discernible by bodily senses.[1] It is a work of God's omnipotence; no man is able to work it in himself.[2] It is far from a pious resolve or a fond conjecture;[3] it is a sure truth stamped on man by God.

Here Wesley is in fundamental agreement with Luther and with Calvin. But in any system of theology in which faith is thus associated with grace and the two are conceived to emerge from a single source, there is the problem of explaining the place of human response in the

[1] *Works,* VIII, 48, 428.
[2] *Ibid.,* p. 5.
[3] *Ibid.,* X, 299.

act of justification or of fitting man into a process which is ordained solely for his benefit.

Now of course there is the obvious solution to the problem. This is simply to confess that, though justification is executed in man's behalf, it is none the less independent of his responsiveness. It is an act performed *for* him and, to be sure, has its effects *in* him; and yet, as regards the precipitating cause of its execution, it is totally divorced *from* him. Man has, therefore, absolutely no part whatever in the act of his own justification. The grace of God which claims him is itself an irresistible force which conquers him, and the faith which emerges in him is the internal expression of that outward power which controls him. All that need be said is that God apportions grace to man and grants him the measure of faith needed to receive that grace. He is like a hollow vessel. He stands ready to be emptied and to be filled. And man can "assign no reason why God grants mercy to his people but because such is his pleasure"; neither can man find "any other cause but his will for the reprobation of others. For when God is said to harden or to show mercy to whom he pleases, men are taught by this declaration to seek no cause beside his will." [4] Yes, and it is the duty of the theologian, "not to please the ears with empty sounds, but to confirm the conscience by teaching things which are true, certain, and profitable." [5]

The Wesleyan Dilemma

Wesleyan theology cannot be understood in the light of such a solution. It rests on the conception of universal grace. Now if grace be *for all* and to a certain extent already present *in all,* it follows that, unless all men are said to be justified without exception, the justifying act must itself be conditioned by some other factor which lies outside the scope and bounds of divine grace. But here we are met by an almost insurmountable obstacle. Faith alone is said to be the condition of justification, and faith springs from the same source as grace does. Is it not reasonable, therefore, to suppose that God, who is the sole author of both grace and faith, confers faith just as freely and just as

[4] Calvin, *Institutes*, III, xxii, 11.
[5] *Ibid.*, I, xiv, 4.

universally as he confers grace? Why would he make any distinction? To say that he bestows the one and withholds the other is to throw us back into the predestinarian doctrine of Calvinism. For what difference is there? If a man is given a prize only to be denied the power of receiving that prize, what reward has he? Even so, if grace is offered to every man, then likewise every man must be given the power to receive it, else the offer itself is made null and void. God does not extend a gift with one hand only to withdraw it with the other.

The Key to the Solution: Free Human Responsiveness

The key to the solution of this difficulty must be sought in man himself, and the answer to what would otherwise be a meaningless riddle must be found in the free responsiveness of human nature. G. C. Cell, in his stimulating work *The Rediscovery of John Wesley,* attempts to show that the religious evaluation of human freedom, the liberty of the moral agent, and the spiritual nature and essential dignity of man do not hold an important place in Wesley's preaching and teaching of Christianity,[6] that Wesley's thought is even "more strictly monergistic" in regard to its expression of grace than some of the utterances of the later Calvinists,[7] that his disagreement with Calvinism in regard to predestination is of little consequence,[8] and that his rejection of predestination does not in the least give us the right to affirm that he assigns to man any place in his own justification.[9] "The Wesleyan doctrine of saving faith . . . is a complete renewal of the Luther-Calvin thesis that in the thought of salvation God is everything, man is nothing."[10] Wesley teaches that the true gospel not only comes to the very edge of Calvinism but also "touches the very edge of predestination."[11]

Now of course Cell's aim is to emphasize the inability of man to save himself and thus to demonstrate his absolute dependence on God's grace. But in doing this he goes too far. He is forced to admit on the basis of evidence, both from Wesley's doctrinal works and from the historical facts of the conflict with Whitefield, the Wesleyan repudia-

[6] G. C. Cell, *The Rediscovery of John Wesley*, p. 245.
[7] *Ibid.*, p. 256.
[8] *Ibid.*, p. 264.
[9] *Ibid.*, p. 270.
[10] *Ibid.*, p. 271.
[11] *Ibid.*, pp. 243-44.

tion of election in the predestinarian sense and of the Calvinistic doctrine of reprobation. But he interprets this solely in the light of its bearing on the righteousness of God and flatly denies that it has any relationship whatsoever to the positive appropriation of justifying grace on the part of man.[12] Yet he does not see that to deny predestination and to affirm free and universal grace is at once automatically to lift man into the picture and to make him an integral part, if not of the actual act of his own justification, at least of the conditions relative to its execution. Man does not justify himself; he does not merit his own justification by any positive works that he may perform or by any righteousness that he may acquire. But he does have an active part in the acquisition of faith, which is the sole condition of justification. Thus in the very act of man's willingness to receive the gift of faith he becomes an active factor in the fulfillment of the necessary conditions which God has set for his justification. The Wesleyan repudiation of predestination, therefore, ceases to be a factor of little concern in a study of the doctrine of justification. It is without doubt one of the most important issues with which we have to deal, for at once it shifts the balance from an emphasis in which irresistible grace is supreme to one in which human response comes to occupy the chief position. "If you ask," writes Wesley, " 'Why then are not all men saved?' the whole law and the testimony answer, First, Not because of any decree of God. . . . Whatsoever be the cause of their perishing, it cannot be his will. . . . And they, Secondly, declare what is the cause why all men are not saved, namely, that they will not be saved."[13]

Human freedom and liberty of the moral agent are of tremendous importance in Wesley's preaching and teaching of Christianity.

If God were to save men by his power alone, by his irresistible decree, this would imply no wisdom at all. But his wisdom is shown by his saving man in such a manner as not to destroy his nature, not to take away the liberty which he has given him.[14]

Without liberty there can be no moral good or evil, no virtue or vice. Fire burns us, yet it is not evil. There is no virtue except where an intelligent

[12] *Ibid.*, p. 270.
[13] Sermon CXXVIII, sec. 22.
[14] Sermon LXVIII, sec. 4.

106

being knows, loves, and chooses what is good, nor is there vice except where a being knows, loves, and chooses evil.[15]

He did not take away your understanding; but enlightened and strengthened it. He did not destroy any of your affections; rather they were more vigorous than before. Least of all did he take away your liberty; your power of choosing good and evil: He did not *force* you; but, being *assisted* by his grace, you, like Mary, *chose* the better part. Just so has he *assisted* five in one house to make that happy *choice;* fifty or five hundred in one city; and many thousand in a nation;—without depriving any of them of that liberty which is essential to a moral agent.[16]

Yea, I am persuaded every child of God has had, at some time, "life and death set before him," eternal life and eternal death; and has in himself the casting voice.[17]

Any doctrine of necessity destroys the valuable purpose of man's will and man's understanding and makes the human creature nothing more than a machine, a mere shadow of what in reality he is, a helpless toy in the hands of a tyrant.[18]

But what specifically is the nature of this human responsiveness? Is it to be conceived merely in a negative way as man's possessing the right not to exercise it, as when he is said to resist the gift of faith? Or is it to be conceived in a positive way as a power which exercises itself and which reaches out actively to claim the gift of faith? It seems to me that we must understand the Wesleyan conception in the second of these two ways provided that we do not separate it from the more basic context in which it is set. The basic context in which it is set, and from which we must not separate it, is this old notion of *preventing* grace, or God's grace *free in all.* Now this grace is the source of all active responsiveness, and all good desires spring solely from it. "God breathes into us every good desire, and brings every good desire to effect." [19] To be sure, we have nothing of ourselves and feel that the very first motion of good in us comes from above.[20] But the point is that this

[15] Sermon LXII, sec. 6.
[16] *Ibid.*, sec. 11.
[17] *Ibid.*, sec. 12.
[18] "Thoughts upon Necessity," *Works*, X, 468-69.
[19] Sermon LXXXV, part i, sec. 2.
[20] *Ibid.*, sec. 3.

preventing grace is not something to wait for, a gift that has been deferred until a future date, a bestowal that a man may patiently hope for and yet do nothing to achieve. It is already present in him; it is in his life even without his having asked for it. Therefore, says Wesley, if God works in you, then work yourself.[21] Since God works in you, it is possible for you to work; no excuse for not working can be given.[22] "You can do something, through Christ strengthening you. Stir up the spark of grace which is now in you, and he will give you more grace." [23]

Without doubt Wesley thought human responsiveness has this more active nature; and here he goes beyond Arminius, who says only that man can resist grace.[24] Wesley, recognizing that preventing grace exists in man even prior to man's ability to resist it and that no one living is without it,[25] is forced to ascribe to man, operating under its influence, some element of active responsiveness. Dr. Umphrey Lee goes so far as to say, "But for Wesley the *natural man* is a logical abstraction. Like the economic man or caricatures set up today by amateur psychologists, anthropologists, and theologians, the *natural man* does not exist." [26] Well, as we shall see later, no man is in a state of innocence; but certainly this illustrates the point in hand that every man is endowed with preventing grace and no man is denied the privilege of at least what is called "natural conscience."

But immediately the question arises, If there is such a thing as active human responsiveness, what form does it take? How does it express itself? In other words, if faith, which is the sole condition of justification, be the gift of God, what is there in man which enables him to receive that gift, or how actually does he respond to that offer? In the minutes of the very first session of the first Methodist conference, begun by Mr. Wesley and four other ordained clergymen and four lay preachers on Monday, June 25, 1744, the question is raised: "Is faith the condition of justification?" And the answer is immediately given: "Yes; for every one who believeth not is condemned; and every one

[21] *Ibid.,* part ii, sec. 1.
[22] *Ibid.,* part iii, sec. 3.
[23] *Ibid.,* part iii, sec. 6.
[24] Arminius, *Works,* I, 600.
[25] Sermon LXXXV, part iii, sec. 4.
[26] U. Lee, *John Wesley and Modern Religion,* p. 124.

who believes is justified." Then the following question is put: "But must not repentance and works meet for repentance go before faith?" Now note carefully this most significant answer: "Without doubt; if by repentance you mean conviction of sin; and by works meet for repentance, obeying God as far as we can, forgiving our brother, leaving off from evil, doing good, and using his ordinances, according to the power we have received." [27] There is before the bestowal of faith by God this urge within us, "this first wish to please God, this first dawn of light concerning his will," this first "slight transient conviction of having sinned against him." [28] Yes, and by it we are brought to desire faith and to wish fervently to be justified.

Thus Wesley writes that there is only one way to justification. This way leads, first of all, to repentance and then to positive belief. "And, first, *repent;* that is, know yourselves. This is the first repentance, previous to faith; even conviction, or self-knowledge. Awake then, thou that sleepest. Know thyself to be a sinner, and what manner of sinner thou art." [29] You must, first of all, see yourself as you actually are, devoid of good, imagining yourself to possess independence, and full of pride, lust, ambition, vanity, and covetousness. [30] You must be deeply sensible of how helpless you are to change your own life, to convert your heart from all sin to all holiness, and to quicken your body dead in corruption to the newness of life. To this you must add suitable affections, sorrow of heart, remorse, self-condemnation, shame even so much as to lift your eyes unto heaven, and fear of the wrath of God, which abides on you. You must feel the weight of his curse hanging over your head, the power of his fiery indignation ready to devour those who forget him and who do not obey his Christ. You must possess an earnest desire to escape from that indignation, to cease from evil, and to learn to do well. Then, and only then, are you truly repentant or in a position to enter the door of the kingdom of God. [31]

This way leads, in the next instance, to positive belief. *Believe the gospel.* What exactly does this mean? Wesley writes that the gospel,

[27] *Works,* VIII, 275-76.
[28] Sermon LXXXV, part ii, sec. 1.
[29] Sermon VII, part ii, sec. 1.
[30] *Ibid.,* secs. 2-3.
[31] *Ibid.,* secs. 6-7.

109

the good tidings, means, in the largest sense of the term, the whole revelation made to men by Jesus Christ. But the sum and substance of it is just that Jesus Christ came into the world to save sinners from their sins, that God so loved sinners that he sent his Son to them and permitted him to die on their behalf, that Christ actually suffered for the sins of others, and that by his suffering the wounds of sin are healed.[32] What Wesley is trying to express is that, over against the state of helplessness and corruption in which all men are found, is set this positive act of God for their deliverance and restoration. Or, to be even more exact, over against what man is not able to do for himself, is set what God is both able and willing to do for him. "*Believe* this, and the Kingdom of God is thine." [33] Then it is that faith comes, as the gift of God, to be sure, and only as his gift, but none the less as a gift most graciously received because first it has been most fervently desired. Faith may be the sole condition of man's justification, but repentance is his duty and must be actively fulfilled before ever faith will come.[34]

Yet is it not true to say that Wesley, in introducing this conception of repentance, repudiates his own Protestant teaching of *justification by grace through faith* and turns back to some hybrid concept of *justification by faith and works?* To say that repentance, accompanied of course by its fruits, or works, when there is opportunity, is merely a preceding disposition that prepares the sinner for the forgiveness of his sins but is not the actual condition by which forgiveness comes, is none the less to affirm, if it is impossible to effect the condition apart from that which prepares one for it, that repentance is essential to the act of forgiveness itself and may be said to participate in its fulfillment. Or, to put this in another way, if faith alone be the condition of justification (the forgiveness of sins) and if repentance plus its works be the condition of the granting of faith, then repentance, itself the condition of the condition, becomes a condition of justification. But repentance, as we have seen, implies some form of works when there is opportunity. Must we not say, then, that Wesley has introduced works as a prior condition of justification?

[32] *Ibid.,* sec. 8.
[33] *Ibid.,* sec. 9.
[34] *Works,* VIII, 389.

The answer lies in what we take works themselves to mean and the significance we attach to them. If we take them to mean, as Wesley did, the moral and charitable and ecclesiastical acts which a man performs and which demonstrate the righteousness and holiness of his nature, then works can be assigned no place whatever in the conditions necessary to man's justification. (For man is not by nature holy; he can perform no acts that are entirely good or, at least, that are not preceded and followed by other acts that are bad. If he could do this and if he did do it, he would be a saint by nature and would have no need for justification.) But if we take works to mean merely the outward acts produced by an inward disposition, then of course the works of repentance are essential, for they are nothing more than the signs of man's earnest desire for forgiveness and for pardon. (They are not good in themselves; they remain the products of a nature which, though dissatisfied with its corruptness, yet is corrupt—which, though despising its sinfulness, still is the victim of sin.) Wesley, in his great stress on the practical aspects of repentance, was less interested in theological consistency of expression than in driving home the lesson that, if a man is sincerely sorry for his sins, that sorrow will express itself in deeds of contrition and rectitude. Let me summarize the matter in Wesleyan language.

Question. We affirm, faith in Christ is the sole condition of justification. But does not repentance go before that faith? yea, and supposing there be opportunity for them, fruits or works meet for repentance?

Answer. Without doubt they do.

Question. How then can we deny them to be conditions of justification? Is not this a mere strife of words? But is it worth while to continue a dispute on the term condition?

Answer. It seems not, though it has been grievously abused. But so the abuse cease, let the use remain.[35]

This brings us to the consideration of another question. If repentance and works meet for repentance always go before faith, what is there that causes a man to be repentant; what makes him sorry for what he is; what gives him the vision of what he ought to be? It would

[35] "Minutes of Some Late Conversations," Bristol, Thurs., Aug. 1, 1745, *Works*, VIII, 281-82.

seem, on the face of it, that faith should itself precede repentance; for, except a man have complete confidence in the gospel of Christ and sincerely believe that Christ alone is sufficient for his every need, he is not apt to grieve over sin, to detest it, and to desire the power to overcome it and to be set on the way of a better life. Is it not one of the elements of sin that it blinds the eyes of the sinner, that it gives him a sense of false security, that it causes him to assert his complete independence, as if he were his own master and his own god? Wesley himself is aware of this, and he likens the state of the natural man to one of sleep. "For his soul is in a deep sleep: his spiritual senses are not awake: they discern neither spiritual good nor evil." [36] Yes, and he also recognizes that because man is asleep to his eternal good, he is likewise at rest, perfectly satisfied with the state in which he finds himself and totally oblivious to his fate.

The darkness which covers him on every side, keeps him in a kind of peace. . . . He sees not that he stands on the edge of the pit; therefore he fears it not. He cannot tremble at the danger he does not know. . . . Why is it that he is in no dread of God? Because he is totally ignorant of him: if not saying in his heart, "There is no God;" . . . yet satisfying himself as well, to all Epicurean intents and purposes, by saying, "God is merciful;" confounding and swallowing up all at once in that unwieldy idea of mercy all his holiness and essential hatred of sin; all his justice, wisdom, and truth.[37]

Wesley goes on to say that man even remains in a sort of self-created joy of congratulating himself upon his own wisdom and goodness and of indulging in the pleasures of the finite and the temporal.[38]

Thus, he remains a willing servant of sin, content with the bondage of corruption; inwardly and outwardly unholy, and satisfied therewith; not only not conquering sin, but not striving to conquer, particularly that sin which doth so easily beset him.[39]

But, though Wesley both recognizes and acknowledges the blindness of man's natural state prior to repentance, he does not ascribe to faith the sight-restoring power which enables man to see his own con-

[36] Sermon IX, part i, sec. 1.
[37] Ibid., sec. 2.
[38] Ibid., sec. 5.
[39] Ibid., sec. 7.

dition and realize his own fate. At least, he does not teach that justifying faith, the faith of personal trust in Christ, is the agent that produces repentance. At this point we meet with an obvious difficulty in his thought. He is forced to admit that man must be aroused from his slumber, that he must actually become concerned over himself, even to the point of producing works meet for repentance, and yet he is not willing to say that man possesses faith without which he cannot possibly have confidence in the efficacy of his works or be certain that his concern over himself is genuine. All Wesley will say is that, by some awful providence or by God's word applied with power, a man's heart is touched and he is made to see his real state.[40] Or he says that a man, on hearing a sermon on repentance and the remission of sins, is pricked to the heart and is convinced of sin and becomes truly repentant.[41] But it does not seem possible that he can become truly repentant unless first he is convinced of the validity of what he hears, of the truth of those standards against which his life is set and by which his character is measured and appraised. Yes, and Wesley admits this; for he says that the spiritual meaning of the law of God must begin to glare upon him.[42] But notice that for Wesley man recognizes this standard and confesses his impotence in the face of it before ever he possesses saving faith.

What does this mean? It means simply this: that the common grace of God given unto all men alike is sufficient to bring men to see the light of the gospel truth and to lead them to repentance and to the performance of acts meet for repentance. Thus preventing grace implies some "tendency toward life; some degree of salvation; the beginning of a deliverance from a blind, unfeeling heart, quite insensible to God and the things of God."[43] And it leads directly to "convincing grace," which is repentance.[44]

The Problem of Synergism

We are now face to face with the problem of synergism in Wesleyan thought. Can we, on the basis of Wesley's own conception of active

[40] Ibid., part ii, sec. 1.
[41] Sermon IV, part i, sec. 1.
[42] Sermon IX, part ii, sec. 2.
[43] Sermon LXXXV, part ii, sec. 1.
[44] Ibid.

responsiveness, ascribe to man as man an actual co-operation with the grace of God in making possible the conditions necessary for his own justification? Now note carefully that this question is raised prior to any discussion of regeneration and of conversion. Our aim is not in this instance to examine human responsiveness at the time of or immediately after the justifying act but rather to determine the extent of its effectiveness and the significance of its operation in making possible the justifying act itself. If, as we have already seen, active human responsiveness in the form of man's willingness to receive the gift of faith is an important factor in the fulfillment of the conditions necessary for justification, is it correct also to say that man, the agent of such responsiveness, is himself a co-operator with God? At first sight, the answer seems obvious. Why of course man is a co-operator with God. The very use of the term active human responsiveness implies as much; and, if the term stands, so likewise must its implication. But to say this too glibly is to forget another factor of no small consequence. It is to forget the basic context in which human responsiveness is set; and that is the prevenient grace of God. Thus, though man is active in his response to justifying faith, he is active not because of any inherent natural ability or willingness of his own but merely as the instrument of the grace of God housed within him. Wesley, therefore, in his insistence on grace discards, it seems, any notion of mere human co-operation.

And yet, even at this point, the solution of the problem has not been completely attained. There is a negative factor which thrusts itself into the picture and which, in the light of a careful consideration of its implications, comes to have positive significance. Man is able, not just to resist the grace of God in the Arminian sense of the term, but actually to kill the grace of God which is already housed within him.[45] In this sense, therefore, in making himself immune to the promptings of what some call natural conscience and what others call divine grace, he steels himself against the power of the gospel, stifles the first urges to repentance, and dulls himself forever to the raptures of faith. In this negative way man is the absolute master of his fate and the captain of his own salvation. And though Wesley in his sermon on "The General

[45] Sermon LXXXV, part iii, sec. 4.

Spread of the Gospel" does not deny that there are exempt cases in which the overwhelming power of saving grace does, for a time, work as irresistibly as lightning falling from heaven, he flatly denies that this is God's usual method of operation and goes on at once to say that, even in these cases, such grace will operate irresistibly only for a time but not at all times unless man wills it.[46]

Granting, therefore, man's ability to stifle and to kill the grace of God within him, have we the right to ascribe to him the positive role of a co-operator with God? We have. For in the very act of not killing grace and of listening to the voice of natural conscience, even though at times very inattentively, man is actually co-operating with God in God's efforts in behalf of his salvation. This must be the case; it cannot be otherwise. Once you grant to man a power great enough to make itself felt as a deciding factor in the acceptance or rejection of the means necessary for the bestowal of saving faith, you lift him, whether you will or not, out of a state of mere passivity into one of activity and of co-operation or non-co-operation with the grace of God. In the same sense in which Jesus said, "He that is not against us is for us," so he who does not stifle and kill divine grace really nourishes and preserves it and thus co-operates with God to make it effective within him. Wesleyan thought, therefore, is decidedly synergistic in its description of the operations prior to justification and essential to the bestowal of saving faith. There is a genuine co-operation of man with God. "Even St. Augustine, who is generally supposed to favour the contrary doctrine, makes that just remark, *Qui fecit nos sine nobis, non salvabit nos sine nobis*: 'He that made us without ourselves, will not save us without ourselves.' "[47]

Human Initiative and Divine Response

This brings us, on the basis of the foregoing analysis, to a final statement in regard to the appropriation by man of the means necessary to his justification, and the actual bestowal of justifying grace, or faith, on man by God. In answer to the question raised at the very beginning of this chapter—How is justifying grace either apportioned to or

[46] Sermon LXIII, sec. 12.
[47] Sermon LXXXV, part iii, sec. 7; Sermon LXIII, sec. 12.

appropriated by human beings?—the Wesleyan reply is that it is done through the agency of God acting in co-operation with, and not in violation of, free human response. There is in the Wesleyan conception, therefore, neither merely an apportionment of justifying grace to man by God nor simply an appropriation of that same grace by man from God but *both* divine apportionment and human appropriation standing together in a single process. By denying to man the inherent, natural ability to generate his own faith and by his own act to claim and to lay hold of justifying grace, Wesley ascribes to God alone the power and the glory manifested in the wondrous act of man's justification. But by affirming the doctrine of free and universal grace in defiance of Calvinistic predestination, Wesley likewise ascribes to man alone the right of decision as to whether he will accept or reject God's offer. The usual conception of divine initiative and human response is of course descriptive of Wesley's teaching; but, if understood properly, the conception of *human* initiative and *divine* response is likewise descriptive of his teaching and is not alien to his theology. Why? Simply because divine initiative in bestowing common or "preventing" grace is taken for granted.

Thus Wesley, in those very sermons in which divine initiative is most poignantly stressed and which are said most clearly to demonstrate his affinity with Calvinism [48] and which are called quite aptly by one interpreter "bugle calls to reformation," [49] stresses at the same time human initiative and assures man of divine response:

"Whosoever believeth on him shall not be ashamed: . . . the same Lord over all is rich unto all that call upon him:" here is comfort, high as heaven, stronger than death! What? Mercy for all? For Zacchaeus, a public robber? For Mary Magdalene, a common harlot? Methinks I hear one say, "Then I, even I, may hope for mercy!" And so thou mayest, thou afflicted one, whom none hath comforted! God will not cast out thy prayer. . . . O glad tidings! tidings of great joy, which are sent unto all people! "Ho, every one that thirsteth, come ye to the waters: come ye, and buy, without money and without price." Whatsoever your sins be, "though red like crimson," though more than the hairs of your head, "return ye unto the

[48] G. C. Cell, *op. cit.*, pp. 38-39, 195 ff., 271-72.
[49] *Ibid.*, p. xv.

Lord, and he will have mercy upon you; and to our God, for he will abundantly pardon." [50]

Let no man persuade thee, by vain words, to rest short of this prize of thy high calling. But cry unto him day and night, who, "while we were without strength, died for the ungodly," until thou knowest in whom thou hast believed, and canst say, "My Lord and my God!" [51]

Thou ungodly one, who hearest or readest these words! thou vile, helpless, miserable sinner! I charge thee before God, the Judge of all, go straight unto him with all thy ungodliness. . . . Go as altogether ungodly, guilty, lost, destroyed, deserving and dropping into hell; and thou shalt then find favour in his sight, and know that he justifieth the ungodly. . . . The Lord hath need of thee. . . . Oh, come quickly! believe in the Lord Jesus, and thou, even thou, art reconciled to God. [52]

Then delay not. All things are now ready. "Arise, and wash away thy sins." The fountain is open. Now is the time to wash thee white in the blood of the Lamb. [53]

Now cast thyself on the Lamb of God, with all thy sins, how many soever they be; and "an entrance shall" now "be ministered unto thee into the kingdom of our Lord and Saviour Jesus Christ!" [54]

In conclusion, therefore, we cannot say that the "Wesleyan doctrine of saving faith . . . is a complete renewal of the Luther-Calvin thesis that in the thought of salvation God is everything, man is nothing." Quite the contrary seems actually to be the case—not, of course, in the sense that man is everything and God is nothing; not in the sense that Wesley believed man could in any degree save himself by moral and ecclesiastical works or by any inherent goodness; but simply in this sense, and in this sense alone, that man is the sole determinative factor in the decision of his own justification. Faith as the one condition of justification is offered unto him as a free gift by a gracious God, but then he must actively respond to that offer and reach out with the arms of true repentance to receive the gift.

[50] Sermon I, part iii, sec. 6.
[51] Sermon II, part ii, sec. 10.
[52] Sermon V, part iv, sec. 9.
[53] Sermon VI, part iii, sec. 2.
[54] Sermon VII, part ii, sec. 13.

No clearer illustration can be given of the importance of man in the fulfillment of the conditions necessary to the bestowal of saving faith than the Wesleyan hymn "Wrestling Jacob." That hymn can be best understood if it is set in contrast to Francis Thompson's "Hound of Heaven." In the "Hound of Heaven" God pursues man and finally overtakes and captures him. But always man resists God's love and tries to escape from divine goodness. In the Wesleyan hymn "Wrestling Jacob" the two roles, the human and the divine, are reversed. God's justifying grace comes to man as the angel came to Jacob, but in the struggle man has the active role and will not let his opponent go until he promises to bless him:

> Come, O Thou Traveller unknown,
>   Whom still I hold but cannot see;
> My company before is gone,
>   And I am left alone with Thee;
> With thee all night I mean to stay,
> And wrestle till the break of day.
>
> What though my shrinking flesh complain,
>   And murmur to contend so long,
> I rise superior to my pain;
>   When I am weak then I am strong;
> And, when my all of strength shall fail,
> I shall with the God-Man prevail.
>
> Yield to me now, for I am weak,
>   But confident in self-despair;
> Speak to my heart, in blessings speak;
>   Be conquered by my instant prayer.
> Speak, or Thou never hence shalt move,
> And tell me if Thy name is Love.
>
> 'Tis Love! 'tis Love! Thou diedst for me!
>   I hear Thy whisper in my heart;
> The morning breaks, the shadows flee;
>   Pure universal Love Thou art;
> To me, to all, Thy mercies move;
> Thy nature and Thy name is Love.[55]

[55] *The Poetical Works of John and Charles Wesley*, II, 173-76.

Chapter VI

THE MEANS TO GOD'S END

The Relationship of Justification to Salvation

As BIRTH IS RELATED TO LIFE, SO JUSTIFICATION, IN WESLEYAN THOUGHT, is related to salvation. Just as birth starts man on his earthly pilgrimage, even so justification starts him on his heavenly; just as birth marks the beginning of an individual's activity in the kingdom of this world, even so justification marks the beginning of a similar activity in the Kingdom of God. Salvation can no more be separated from justification than life can be separated from birth. And yet salvation is not the same as justification. It is far broader, far more inclusive. It is no more confined to the single instance of its beginning than life is confined to birth. Salvation is synonymous with the whole of a man's spiritual activity; it extends from the very moment of its inception until either its extinction in sin and death or else its final culmination and glorification in that which lies beyond this world of sense and time. It is God's present, continuing, and full possession of a man's life.

Salvation, therefore, can never be isolated from ethics, or the works of moral endeavor. Forgiveness is incomplete; it must be matched by holiness and Christian perfection. Thus Wesley in his work entitled *The Character of a Methodist* writes:

Nor, lastly, is he [a Methodist] distinguished by laying the whole stress of religion on any single part of it. If you say, "Yes, he is; for he thinks we are saved through faith alone:" I answer, You do not understand the terms. By salvation he means holiness of heart and life. And this he affirms to spring from true faith alone. Can even a nominal Christian deny it? Is this placing a part of religion for the whole? "Do we then make void the law through faith? God forbid! Yea, we establish the law." We do not place the whole of religion (as too many do, God knoweth) either in doing no harm, or in doing good, or in using the ordinances of God. No, not in all of them together; wherein we know by experience a man may labour many years, and at the end have no religion at all, no more than he had at the beginning. Much less in any one of these; or, it may be,

119

in a scrap of one of them: Like her who fancies herself a virtuous woman, only because she is not a prostitute; or him who dreams he is an honest man, merely because he does not rob or steal. May the Lord God of my fathers preserve me from such a poor, starved religion as this! Were this the mark of a Methodist, I would sooner choose to be a sincere Jew, Turk, or Pagan.[1]

Or, as Wesley writes in a letter to Mr. Church, justification is by faith alone, but salvation is righteousness, peace, and joy—holiness in the sight of God.[2] Salvation, therefore, embraces the concept of sanctification as well as justification. As soon as a man has been pardoned by God and accepted as righteous, the Spirit of God begins to operate within him and to prepare his life to bring forth fruits worthy of his calling.[3] In sanctification he actually becomes renewed in the image of God, in righteousness, and in true holiness.[4]

The Concomitants of Justification

In this chapter, therefore, we must examine the actual effects of justification on man and view the benefits derived from God's act of pardon and forgiveness in the light of the general purpose which underlies the entire conception of salvation and of the Christian life. If the doctrine of justification is itself partial and does not embrace the whole of Wesleyan theology, it is none the less fundamental and furnishes the basis on which all the other doctrines are built. In the first instance, therefore, it is necessary for us to consider certain benefits which are themselves concomitant with justification. These benefits are described by Wesley as adoption [5] and conversion, or regeneration.[6] Adoption is the more primary of the two, for that really cannot be distinguished from the justifying act itself in that it is but the carrying into effect of what God has actually pronounced in justification. Man is both pardoned and accepted; and, because he is accepted, he is adopted into the fellowship of God's children and made an heir of God and a joint heir with Jesus Christ. Wesley expresses this in legal terms. He pictures

[1] *Works*, VIII, 341.
[2] *Ibid.*, p. 391.
[3] Sermon V, part ii, sec. 1.
[4] *Works*, VIII, 279.
[5] Sermon IX, intro. sec. 1.
[6] Sermon XLV, intro. sec. 1.

120

man in the bonds of sin; and thus, when he comes to write of adoption, he portrays it as that state in which the miserable bondage ends and man is no more under a law which he finds impossible to obey but rather under the favor of God, or under grace.[7] His sins are laid on Christ;[8] the wrath of God is allayed;[9] and he is set at liberty, free from guilt because he is free from sin and the heavy yoke which sin imposes. He is made by God to be a partaker of the blessings of precious faith and is given "the glorious liberty of the sons of God."[10] Or, as Wesley puts the matter in another sermon, if God goes so far as to pronounce a man righteous and to account him worthy to be a partaker of the inheritance of the saints in light, then likewise he accepts him into that Kingdom which was prepared for him and for all true believers before the world began, and also glorifies him.[11] This Wesleyan conception is synonymous with restoration to favor and with the bestowal of the privileges of sonship. If looked at from the standpoint of the renewal of a broken friendship, it may be called reconciliation;[12] if seen in the light of the renewal of the soul's true relation to God as a father, it may be called adoption.[13] Adoption and reconciliation automatically follow justification and are never divorced from it.

The second benefit concomitant with justification is conversion, or regeneration. It is called by Wesley the new birth and relates specifically "to the great work which God does in us, in renewing our fallen nature."[14] In order of time, neither justification nor regeneration goes before the other. In the very moment in which a person is justified by the grace of God through the redemption that is in Christ Jesus, he is likewise born of the Spirit; but in the order of thinking—that is, in terms of intellectual sequence—justification precedes the new birth. We first conceive of God's wrath as having been turned away from us and then of his Spirit as coming to do his positive work in our lives.[15]

[7] Sermon IX, part iii, sec. 1.
[8] *Ibid.*, sec. 3.
[9] *Ibid.*, sec. 4.
[10] *Ibid.*, sec. 6.
[11] Sermon LVIII, sec. 10.
[12] *Notes on the New Testament*, pp. 374-75.
[13] *Ibid.*, pp. 213, 481.
[14] Sermon XLV, intro. sec. 1.
[15] *Ibid.*

The Nature of the New Birth

Wesley says that it is of the utmost importance for every child of God thoroughly to understand the meaning of the new birth, for it is fundamental to a knowledge of true religion.[16] It is necessary, therefore, for us to give careful attention to the Wesleyan analysis of the new birth and to its place in the Christian life. We shall consider, first of all, the nature of the new birth and attempt to answer Nicodemus' question, "How can a man be born again?" Wesley tells us at the outset that we can expect no minute or philosophical account of the manner in which the new birth takes place. Christ cautions us against desiring any such explanation by saying: "The wind bloweth where it listeth, and thou hearest the sound thereof, but canst not tell whence it cometh, and whither it goeth." Then he adds, "So is every one that is born of the Spirit."[17] In other words, one may be as absolutely assured of the fact of the new birth as of the blowing of the wind and yet be unable to give an account of the exact manner in which this work is performed in human life.[18]

Wesley tells us that the expression used by Jesus, "Ye must be born again," was not first coined by him in his conversation with Nicodemus but was rather a phrase in common use among the Jews before ever Jesus was born or ever Nicodemus thought of raising his question. It referred to the old custom of proselyting. When a non-Jew was convinced of the truth of the Jewish religion and made known his desire to be included among the chosen people of Israel, the Jewish custom was to baptize him before admitting him to circumcision, the physical mark and sign of God's covenant with Abraham and his children forever. As soon as he was baptized, he was said to have been born again; for in very truth he had died to his old life of paganism and had taken on the new life of another religion and another nationality. The Jews meant, says Wesley, "that he who was before a child of the devil was now adopted into the family of God, and accounted one of his children."[19] In this sense, then, our Lord spoke to Nicodemus;

---

[16] *Ibid.*, sec. 2.
[17] *Notes on the New Testament*, p. 218; and Sermon XLV, part ii, sec. 2.
[18] Sermon XLV, part ii, sec. 2.
[19] *Ibid.*

122

and he, a teacher of Israel, ought well to have known what our Lord meant.

Moreover, Wesley writes that this new birth which brings a man into the world of spiritual life bears a very close analogy to the natural birth. A child in his mother's womb has eyes, but he sees not; he has ears, but he hears not. The use of his other senses is very imperfectly developed, and he has no knowledge of any of the things of the world and no natural understanding whatsoever. To the existence of the child in the womb, we do not so much as assign the name of life. It is only when he is born into the world that we say he really begins to live.

This parallels in most instances man's spiritual and religious state. "How exactly does this parallel hold in all these instances!" [20] Thus, while a man is enclosed in the womb of his natural state, before he has experienced the new birth, he has, in a spiritual sense, eyes, and yet he sees not; he has ears, and yet he hears not. His other spiritual senses are dormant; for, though he is by creation in possession of them and is endued with preventing grace even in the womb of nature, these spiritual senses are "locked up" and man lives as if he did not have them. "He has no true knowledge of the things of God, either of spiritual or of eternal things; therefore, though he is a living man, he is a dead Christian." [21] But as soon as he is born of God, this is all changed. At the very moment of new birth, what God does *for* man, the objective deed which God performs when he forgives man of his sins and pardons him from guilt and punishment and accepts him as a son, is united with what God does *in* man; and the process of sanctification is actually begun in man's life. [22] As we saw, Wesley does not separate justification and the new birth in point of time; and, indeed, he dare not separate them. Why? Simply because justification, as an objective act of pardon pronounced by God in total disregard of any requirements of goodness or moral works, if it be not matched at once by another act of purification effected in man and simultaneous with justification, would indicate that divine mercy operates in defiance of divine justice, that God forgives man of sin and yet permits him to remain a sinner. We dare not equate justification with paternal indul-

[20] Sermon XLV, part ii, sec. 4.
[21] *Ibid*.
[22] Sermon V, part ii, sec. 1.

gence. If God pardons sin, at the same time he washes and purifies the sinner. In one sermon, therefore, Wesley does not even make the distinction between justification and the new birth, but actually uses the word justification to include both the pardon and acceptance of a sinner by God and also purification and the beginning of the new life in Christ.[23]

Let us note the actual changes in man as they manifest themselves in the particular aspects of his life. Wesley writes:

The "eyes of his understanding are opened;" (such is the language of the great apostle;) and He who of old "commanded light to shine out of darkness, shining on his heart, he sees the light of the glory of God," his glorious love, "in the face of Jesus Christ." His ears being opened, he is now capable of hearing the inward voice of God saying, "Be of good cheer; thy sins are forgiven thee;" "Go, and sin no more." This is the purport of what God speaks to his heart; although not perhaps in these very words. He is now ready to hear whatsoever "He that teacheth man knowledge" is pleased from time to time, to reveal to him. He "feels in his heart," to use the language of our church, "the mighty workings of the Spirit of God;" not in a gross, carnal sense, as men of the world stupidly and willfully misunderstand the expression; though they have been told again and again, we mean thereby neither more nor less than this: He feels, is inwardly sensible of, the graces which the Spirit of God works in his heart. He feels, he is conscious of, "a peace which passeth all understanding." He many times feels such a joy in God as is "unspeakable and full of glory." He feels "the love of God shed abroad in his heart by the Holy Ghost which is given unto him;" and all his spiritual senses are then exercised to discern spiritual good and evil. By the use of these, he is daily increasing in the knowledge of God, of Jesus Christ whom he hath sent, and of all the things pertaining to his inward kingdom. And now he may be properly said to live: God having quickened him by his Spirit, he is alive to God through Jesus Christ. He lives a life which the world knoweth not of, a life "which is hid with Christ in God." God is continually breathing, as it were, upon the soul; and his soul is breathing unto God. Grace is descending into his heart; and prayer and praise ascending to heaven: and by this intercourse between God and man, this fellowship with the Father and the Son, as by a kind of spiritual respiration, the life of God in the soul is sustained; and

[23] Sermon I, part ii, sec. 7.

124

the child of God grows up, till he comes to the "full measure of the stature of Christ." [24]

In this passage, more than anywhere else in the whole of Wesleyan literature, we find the clearest expression of the nature of the new birth and catch the brightest reflection of the moral and spiritual aspects of justification shining in human life. If justification, says Wesley, implies only a relative change, one in which our outward relationship to God is altered "so that of enemies we become children," then the new birth implies a *real* change, not external but internal, "so that of sinners we become saints" [25] and start our journey on the road to perfection. [26]

From hence it manifestly appears, what is the nature of the new birth. It is that great change which God works in the soul when he brings it into life, when he raises it from the death of sin to the life of righteousness. It is the change wrought in the whole soul by the almighty Spirit of God when it is "created anew in Christ Jesus;" when it is "renewed after the image of God, in righteousness and true holiness;" when the love of the world is changed into the love of God; pride into humility; passion into meekness; hatred, envy, malice, into a sincere, tender, disinterested love for all mankind. In a word, it is that change whereby the earthly, sensual, devilish mind is turned into the mind which was in Christ Jesus. [27]

The Relationship of the New Birth to Baptism

If the new birth implies a complete change of heart and life, then how is it related to the sacrament of baptism, and what place does this sacrament hold in Wesleyan thought? Wesley frankly avows that baptism and the new birth are not one and the same thing. Though many imagine they are the same thing and feel that, because they have been baptized, they are also regenerate, this is not Wesley's opinion; and he finds no grounds for such an opinion among the teachings of either the Church of England or the Dissenters. Wesley quotes from the Church of England Catechism. " '*Q.* What meanest thou by this word, sacrament? *A.* I mean an outward and visible sign of an inward and

[24] Sermon XLV, part ii, sec. 4. Also, Sermon XIX, part i, secs. 8-10.
[25] Sermon XIX, intro. sec. 2.
[26] Sermon LXXVI, intro.
[27] Sermon XLV, part ii, sec. 5.

spiritual grace. *Q.* What is the outward part or form in baptism? *A.* Water, wherein the person is baptized, in the name of the Father, Son, and Holy Ghost. *Q.* What is the inward part, or thing signified? *A.* A death unto sin, and a new birth unto righteousness.' " [28] On the basis of this second quotation Wesley interprets the position of his Church in regard to baptism and states that it is manifest that baptism, the sign, is distinct from regeneration, the thing signified. He says that the one is an external and visible work, while the other is an internal and invisible thing. Baptism applies only to an act of man, purifying the body. Regeneration (conversion or new birth) applies to an act of God, cleansing the soul. The two acts are just as distinguishable from one another as the soul is distinguishable from the body, or water from the Holy Ghost.[29] In this Wesley denies that the Church of England teaches baptismal regeneration.

Though it is true that the Church of England teaches that baptism is but the sign of regeneration,[30] it is likewise true that it teaches that baptism is a genuine sign and that regeneration is not divorced from the ecclesiastical act which signifies it. The Anglican Church believes, as one of its divines expresses it, that spiritual regeneration is that which the gospel has set forth to be the "principal correlative of Baptism," and through the waters of baptism we receive the new birth of the Holy Ghost.[31] Thus, though baptism and regeneration are distinguishable perhaps, and water is not the same as Spirit, yet both are united in one act and stand together.

At this point Wesley breaks with the teachings of the Church of England. Of course, he does not emphasize his disagreement with the traditions of his Church; and, by attempting to point out that the Church of England recognizes a distinction between the sign and the thing signified, he tries to appear in accord with the Anglican doctrine. But he does not call attention to the fact of the concomitant relationship that exists in Anglican thought between baptism and regenera-

---

[28] These quotations are made by Wesley in his sermon on the "New Birth" (Sermon XLV, part iv, sec. 1). The first quotation is taken from the *Larger Catechism,* completed by Westminster Assembly on April 14, 1648, Questions 163, 165. The second quotation is taken from Church of England Catechism, 1662.

[29] Sermon XLV, part iv, sec. 1.

[30] *Thirty-nine Articles,* art. xxvii.

[31] J. Taylor, *Works,* I, 155.

tion. Thus, by failing to state one of the necessary aspects of the Anglican doctrine, he does violence to it and gives only a partial picture of what in reality it is. After clearly distinguishing the internal change wrought in man by the Holy Ghost from the act in which water is applied to him as a sign of purification, he immediately affirms that, on the basis of such a distinction, we may observe that the new birth is not the same thing as baptism, and so does not always accompany it.[32] But note carefully that Wesley is not willing for such an inference to be drawn from his own teaching in regard to regeneration, or conversion, and justification. It is just as legitimate for us to say, for instance, that, since there is a distinction between the subjective act of purification, in which a man's life is changed, and the objective act of pardon and acceptance, in which he is restored to favor with God, we may observe that regeneration, or conversion, is not the same as justification, and so does not always accompany it. But Wesley tells us that regeneration always accompanies justification and is simultaneous with it.[33] If such be the case in one instance, it might just as well be the same in another. Even though the new birth is not the same as baptism, it might be conceived always to accompany it; and this precisely is the Anglican position. At this point, therefore, whether Wesley admits it or not, he does depart from the teachings of his Church.

And yet, simply because Wesley deliberately attempts to harmonize his conception with that of the Anglican Church, we receive at his hands no clear-cut and definitive statement in regard to baptism; and what he has written on the subject serves more to confuse than to clarify the issue. In his sermon on "The Marks of the New Birth," for instance, he goes so far as to say that the privileges of sonship and adoption "are ordinarily annexed to baptism;"[34] and in the very sermon in which he tells us that the new birth does not always accompany baptism and that a man may be born of water and not be born of the Spirit, he hedges at the point of infant baptism and writes:

[32] Sermon XLV, part iv, sec. 2. Wesley struck out the word "regenerate" from the "Exhortation to Thankful Prayer" when revising the baptismal office of the Church of England for American Methodism. See Nolan B. Harmon, *The Rites and Ritual of Episcopal Methodism,* p. 184.

[33] Sermon XIX, intro. sec. 2; Sermon XLV, intro. sec. 1.

[34] Sermon XVIII, intro. sec. 1.

127

I do not now speak with regard to infants: it is certain our Church supposes that all who are baptized in their infancy are at the same time born again; and it is allowed that the whole office for the baptism of infants proceeds upon this supposition. Nor is it an objection of any weight against this, that we cannot comprehend how this work can be wrought in infants. For neither can we comprehend how it is wrought in a person of riper years.[35]

In addition to this Wesley published, in November, 1756, a work entitled *Treatise on Baptism;*[36] and when one reads and compares this work with the writings of Wesley's father, he finds, much to his surprise, that, in form and substance, the *Treatise on Baptism* is identical with the section on baptism included in Samuel Wesley's *The Pious Communicant Rightly Prepar'd.*[37] In this work he calls baptism "the ordinary instrument of our justification."[38] By it we enter into an everlasting covenant with God, we are admitted into the Church, and consequently we are made members of Christ, its Head. Note the strong language employed:

By baptism, we who were "by nature children of wrath" are made the children of God. And this regeneration which our Church in so many places ascribes to baptism is more than barely being admitted into the Church. . . . Nor does she ascribe it [baptism] to outward washing, but to inward grace, which, added thereto, makes it a sacrament. Herein a principle of grace is infused, which will not be wholly taken away, unless we quench the Holy Spirit of God by long continued wickedness.[39]

Here, you see, baptism is made concomitant with the new birth, while in the sermon on the "New Birth" the two are said not always to accompany one another. In that sermon Wesley says:

Whatever be the case with infants, it is sure all of riper years who are baptized are not at the same time born again. "The tree is known by its fruits." And hereby it appears too plain to be denied that divers of those who were children of the devil before they were baptized continue the

[35] Sermon XLV, part iv, sec. 2.
[36] *Works,* X, 188-201.
[37] Samuel Wesley, "Short Discourse on Baptism," in *Pious Communicant Rightly Prepar'd,* pp. 189-249.
[38] *Works,* X, 191.
[39] *Ibid.,* pp. 191-92.

same after baptism; "for the works of their father they do:" they continue servants of sin, without any pretence either to inward or outward holiness.[40]

This means that for Wesley the important thing is not the ecclesiastical rite of baptism as such but the spiritual act, of which that rite is the symbol. It means that his one concern is not that a man has been baptized and is a member of the Church but, rather, that he has been converted from pride and selfishness and renewed in the moral and spiritual image of God. If baptism signifies a real and genuine change of heart and life, then, well and good, it is the concomitant of regeneration, or the new birth. But if baptism is merely a formal act and is separated from spiritual change and moral renewal, then it is not accompanied by the new birth and has no part in man's salvation. In the *Treatise on Baptism* even we find these words: "Baptism doth now save us, if we live answerable thereto; if we repent, believe, and obey the gospel." [41]

But how is the Wesleyan doctrine of the new birth to be reconciled with Wesley's acceptance of the efficacy of infant baptism? It must be understood, it seems to me, that Wesley's acceptance of the efficacy of infant baptism is just an acceptance, and nothing more. He affirms it as a teaching of the Church.[42] Nowhere does he stress it as a fundamental tenet of his own doctrine; and, though he repeats his father's arguments for it in his *Treatise on Baptism,*[43] he gives it no emphasis in his preaching and refuses to accept it as the sign and seal of true faith. But, we ask, if a child has been made regenerate in baptism, what is the use or the necessity of the new birth for him? Wesley's only reply is that he must display the moral and spiritual marks of regeneration else his baptism is of no effect.

Baptism is the outward sign of this inward grace, which is supposed by our Church to be given with and through that sign to all infants, and to those of riper years, if they repent and believe the gospel. But how extremely idle are the common disputes on this head! I tell a sinner, "You must be born again." "No," say you: "He was born again in baptism. Therefore he cannot be born again now." Alas, what trifling is this! What,

[40] Sermon XLV, part iv, sec. 2.
[41] *Works,* X, 192.
[42] Sermon XLV, part iv, sec. 2.
[43] *Works,* X, 193-201.

if he was then a child of God? He is now manifestly a child of the devil; for the works of his father he doeth. Therefore, do not play upon words. He must go through an entire change of heart. In one not yet baptized, you yourself would call that change, the new birth. In him call it what you will; but remember, meantime, that if either he or you die without it, your baptism will be so far from profiting you, that it will greatly increase your damnation.[44]

To say, then, that you cannot be born again, that there is no new birth but in baptism, is to seal your own damnation, to consign you to hell, without help, without hope. . . . Lean no more on the staff of that broken reed, that ye *were* born again in baptism. Who denies that ye were then made children of God, and heirs of the kingdom of heaven? But, notwithstanding this, ye are now children of the devil. Therefore, ye must be born again.[45]

The Marks of the New Birth

If baptism cannot be relied upon as the sure sign of the new birth, what, then, are the marks of a man's conversion, the indications of his having been made regenerate by the Spirit of God? It is not enough merely to define the nature of the new birth and to label it as that great change wrought in the whole soul by God. It is not enough just to say that in the act of regeneration man is renewed in the moral image of God. No, from this point we must go on to examine the immediate results of the new birth in the light of man's character; or, as Wesley says, we must consider the "first fruits of the Spirit." [46] Note carefully that before Wesley enters into any consideration of man's new character, he reminds us of St. Paul's words in Philippians 3: 8-9, where the Apostle exclaims that he counts all things loss for the excellency of the knowledge of Christ Jesus, his Lord, and at the same

---

[44] "A Farther Appeal to Men of Reason and Religion," *Works,* VIII, 48-49.

[45] Sermon XVIII, part iv, secs. 4-5. Wesley conceives the form of baptism apart from the spiritual change in a man's life to be actually harmful. He calls the sacramental regeneration in baptism of the Church of Rome "a form of conjuration."—*Works,* X, 115. See also pp. 114, 116. He cannot conceive the majesty of baptism to lie in a ceremony in which the priest blows in the face of a child three times, saying, "Get thee out, Satan," and ending with the phrase, "Peace be with thee." And yet Wesley will not give up the outward sign of baptism, since it is employed in the Bible, or accept just the "inward seed of life" of the Quakers.—*Ibid.,* p. 184.

[46] The title of Sermon VIII.

time expresses his one desire to be found in him, not having his own righteousness, which is by the law, but that which is by faith in Christ, the righteousness of God by faith.[47] But then Wesley proceeds to give his interpretation of the Apostle's words, and this interpretation is of the utmost importance. Though he does admit that there is a righteousness of faith which, before we are made regenerate, comes to us only by way of promise [48] and brings no moral demands or ethical requirements,[49] he declares that what the Apostle means here is of a more positive nature; it is the righteousness that comes to us because we are found in God, actually "ingrafted in Him." Faith, therefore, has no longer the meaning of promise but signifies such a close bond between him who possesses it and God who gives it that the righteousness which is in him "can flow from no other fountain." [50] Wesley does not interpret the Apostle to mean that man, forsaking all attempts to be righteous himself, appeals to God for mercy on the claim of Christ's righteousness alone. Rather, he conceives the Apostle to mean that man is himself righteous, because a portion of Christ's righteousness abides within him. Immediately after regeneration, therefore, a harmonious moral and spiritual unity exists between the human and the divine, an interaction of spirit in which Christ is said to dwell in man and man to dwell in Christ.[51] This unity rests on the bond of faith.[52]

The very first effect of the new birth on human character is that God enables whoever has experienced it to avoid committing sin.[53] What does this mean? Does it mean that man is set on the road to righteousness so that little by little he is given power over sin? No, it means, in Wesley's own words, that "even babes in Christ are so far perfect as not to commit sin." [54]

An immediate and constant fruit of this faith whereby we are born of God, a fruit which can in no wise be separated from it, no, not for an hour, is power over sin;—power over outward sin of every kind; over every evil

[47] Sermon VIII, part i, sec. 1.
[48] Sermon VI, part i, secs. 7-9.
[49] *Ibid.*, secs. 12, 14; part ii, secs. 7-8; part iii, secs. 2-4.
[50] *Notes on the New Testament*, pp. 511-12.
[51] Sermon VIII, part i, sec. 1.
[52] *Notes on the New Testament*, p. 258.
[53] Sermon VIII, part i.
[54] *Works*, XI, 375.

word and work; for wheresoever the blood of Christ is thus applied, "it purgeth the conscience from dead works;"—and over inward sin; for it purifieth the heart from every unholy desire and temper.[55]

This new power expresses itself, first of all, in a negative way: the converted man refuses to do wrong, or to commit evil. He does not give way to his affections and lusts. He is not guilty of adultery, fornication, uncleanness, lasciviousness, idolatry, witchcraft, hatred, variance. He is free from emulations, wrath, strife, sedition, heresies, envyings, murders, drunkenness, revelings—from every design, word, and work to which the corruption of nature leads. Although he feels the pull of temptation, he is endued with the power to withstand and master it. Further, this power expresses itself in a positive way: he who walks by the Spirit is led into all holiness of conversation. He not only refuses to engage in corrupt communications, but speaks also that which is good. He attempts in his dealings with his neighbor to do justly, to display mercy and truth, and in all actions to glorify God.[56] Thus the righteousness which is of faith is not an illusion but a real force operating in human life, restraining man from sin, and both enabling him and prompting him to do good. Wesley firmly believes that if a man is in Christ, who is sinless, he himself will commit no sin.[57]

To those who say that regeneration takes away man's habit of sinning so that he no longer finds pleasure in sin and does not sin habitually, but who refuse to admit that the regenerate man commits no sin at all, Wesley replies by quoting I John 3:9: "Whosoever is born of God doth not commit sin." He then asks them their authority for the word "habitually" and in doing so gives without equivocation his own view:

Habitually! Whence is that? I read it not. It is not written in the Book. God plainly saith, "He doth not commit sin;" and thou addest *habitually!* Who art thou that mendest the oracles of God?—that "addest to the words of this book?" Beware, I beseech thee, lest God, "add to thee all the plagues that are written therein!" [58]

[55] Sermon XVIII, part i, sec. 4.
[56] Sermon VIII, part i, secs. 3, 5.
[57] Sermon XVIII, part i, sec. 6.
[58] *Ibid.,* sec. 5.

132

The second effect of the new birth on human character is that God gives whoever has experienced it a new motive for life. That motive is the motive of love. Wesley tells us that the love of God is shed abroad in the heart of him who has been converted.[59] That little phrase "shed abroad in the heart," scriptural in origin[60] and yet so hackneyed and worn that to many it has become mere cant, is none the less central to Wesley's message. For Wesley, as I interpret him, the love of God is not alone human love directed toward and fixed upon the divine object. It is not just human affection given in response to divine mercy, so that man may be said to love God because God first loved him. To be sure, that is the cause of love, the only cause; and so Wesley tells us that love is born of faith alone.[61] But this love of God is at the same time *shed abroad in the heart.* It becomes not alone the bond of affection that ties man to God but also a disposition of character that marks man's life. In a very real sense the quality as well as the object of man's love has been altered. We do not mean by this that love, like faith, is given man as a divine gift, so that it may be called a supernatural grace operating in human life. But rather that love partakes of the nature of its object, and man becomes like that on which his affection is placed. Man loves what God loves, and the desire of his soul is to do God's will.[62]

The necessary fruit of this love of God shed abroad in man's heart is the love of the neighbor. And the term "neighbor" is all inclusive. If man really loves God, he will at the same time love every soul that God has created.[63] Thus Wesley tells us that we must love every man just as we love ourselves.

Nay, our Lord has expressed it still more strongly, teaching us to "love one another even as He hath loved us." Accordingly, the commandment written in the hearts of those that love God is no other than this, "As I have loved you, so love ye one another." Now, "herein perceive we the love of God, in that he laid down his life for us." "We ought," then, as the

[59] *Ibid.,* part iii, sec. 1.
[60] Rom. 5:5.
[61] Sermon XCI, part i, sec. 2.
[62] Sermon XVIII, part iv. sec. 1.
[63] *Ibid.,* sec. 3.

133

apostle justly infers, "to lay down our lives for the brethren." If we feel ourselves ready to do this, then do we truly love our neighbour.[64]

Now this love of the neighbor must be genuine. It must be a real affection of the soul, not feigned outward works in his behalf or deeds of charity done for his benefit but not accompanied by real love. True love is not a duty but a pleasure. A lover joyously serves his love.[65]

New Birth and the Potentiality of Evil

This new birth, or the experience of conversion, Wesley conceives to be instantaneous; it happens in the twinkling of an eye.[66] Does that mean, then, that, immediately after man has been born of the Spirit and has been given the new mind of Christ, he is at once free from sin and motivated by love? From the preceding description of the marks of the new birth and of its first effects on human life, it would seem that such is Wesley's position. Man, a sinner, is immediately converted; instantaneously he is transformed into a saint.[67] But note carefully what such a position necessarily implies. It implies that all the functions of human life are motivated by a single principle, that this principle is itself capable of immediate transformation, and that such a transformation of principle issues at once in a new set of functions. It implies that life itself is simple and unified, that it consists alone in the choice of an ideal, or end, and that merely to choose the end is at once to effect its realization. But is such a picture of conversion true to life? After man has experienced the regenerative power of God's grace, is he entirely clean; is his every action motivated by love? Wesleyan theology is forced to face this issue, and Wesley himself reconsiders his doctrine of the new birth time and time again in the light of the hard facts of Christian living. We have seen that Wesley teaches that God enables the converted man to avoid committing sin. Now we must face the issue that, as a matter of plain fact, converted men have sinned; and perhaps we can best approach the problem of why they have sinned by first asking the general question, In what sense is there sin in believers? Wesley approaches the problem in a little different

[64] *Ibid.*
[65] *Ibid.*, sec. 4.
[66] *Works,* VIII, 48; IX, 171.
[67] Sermon XIX, intro. sec. 2.

way; for he does not ask the question, In what sense is there sin in believers? but rather, Is there sin in believers? He tells us that the ancient Christians, the Church of England, the Roman Catholic and Greek Orthodox churches all give substantially the same answers and say that believers are still inclined to evil and are driven by the lusts of the flesh against the prompting of the Spirit.[68] In this the churches of the Reformation agree. Indeed, some of the Reformation churches go so far as to describe the corruption in the heart of believers in such a way that the believers appear still to remain actually in the bonds of sin. Such churches hardly make any distinction between believers and unbelievers.[69] To avoid this extreme, the followers of Count Zinzendorf affirm that all true believers are not only saved from the dominion of sin but from the *being* of inward as well as outward sin, so that sin no longer remains in them.[70]

Wesley himself is not prepared to take the extreme view of the Moravians. Yet he maintains his position that man does not commit sin after he has been converted.[71] He has a conscience void of offence toward God and man and has power over both outward and inward sin. But he is not free from all sin, so that there is not any left in his heart. The regenerate man is still the victim of inward sin.[72] And Wesley tells us that he understands inward sin to mean any sinful temper, passion, or affection, such as pride, self-will, love of the world, anger, peevishness, or any other disposition contrary to the perfect mind of Christ.[73] Thus he accepts the Pauline principle and applies it even to believers, or the regenerate: that there are two contrary forces, or tendencies, that still continue to operate—nature and grace, flesh and spirit. Believers are exhorted continually to fight with the evil tendencies by the power of faith which is within them.

But isn't it true that if a man abstains from the appearance of evil, he automatically cleanses himself from all evil tendencies? Wesley thinks not. He says that if a man reviles a believer, it is but natural for the believer to feel resentment, which is an evil tendency. Yet the believer

[68] Sermon XIII, part i, secs. 2-4.
[69] *Ibid.*, sec. 4.
[70] *Ibid.*, sec. 5.
[71] *Ibid.*, part ii, sec. 1.
[72] *Ibid.*, part iii, sec. 1.
[73] *Ibid.*, part ii, sec. 2.

does not show that resentment; he says not a word.[74] Thus the Wesleyan position that God enables the regenerate man to avoid committing sin cannot be interpreted to mean, as it at first appears, that God eradicates from his nature all evil tendencies and suggestions so that he is totally immune to temptation. "Christ indeed cannot reign where sin reigns; neither will he dwell where sin is allowed. But he is and dwells in the heart of every believer, who is fighting against all sin; although it be not yet purified, according to the purification of the sanctuary." [75]

Is not this in flat contradiction to the doctrine of the new birth in which it is affirmed that man is completely changed, that his devilish mind is turned into the mind which was in Christ Jesus? How can a man be sanctified, clean, holy and at the same time be unsanctified, unclean, unholy? Wesley, when faced with this issue, replies that, strange and contradictory as it may seem, these two opposites do exist side by side in a single life so that a man is a new creature and an old creature at one and the same time.[76] His old judgment concerning truth, holiness, happiness, and all the things of God is completely altered, so that he may be said to have a new mind. And yet, though he has a new mind and is, indeed, a new creature, he has not forgotten his old self. He still remembers what he was; yes, and to his shame and sorrow he continues to feel the remains of his old self, the pull of his former desires and affections; and he is haunted by the possibility that these may once again creep to ascendency and regain the mastery of his life.[77] So, for Wesley, in regeneration a man's heart is renewed and yet not entirely renewed; his carnal mind is "nailed to the cross," yet it is "not wholly destroyed." [78]

Yet note carefully that sin has no power over the regenerate man. It exists merely as a tendency, or, even more accurately, as a possibility. Perhaps the matter may be more clearly grasped if we set the regenerate state of man in contrast with his unregenerate state. In unregenerate nature man is a creature of selfish desire and idolatrous pride. There

[74] *Ibid.*, part iii, sec. 6.
[75] *Ibid.*, sec. 8.
[76] *Ibid.*, part iv, sec. 2.
[77] *Ibid.*
[78] *Ibid.*, sec. 1.

is no health in him. And yet man, even in this state, is possessed of preventing grace. He has latent within him a tendency toward salvation, or, even more accurately, a possibility of salvation. In regeneration man's status is exactly reversed. He is the creature of God, and he has absolute mastery over sin through God's grace. And yet he is possessed of carnal desire. He has latent within him the urge to return to his former self. But man is delivered from the power of sin, and consequently from its guilt.[79]

The supposing sin is in us, does not imply that it has the possession of our strength; no more than a man crucified has the possession of those that crucify him. As little as does it imply that "sin maintains its usurpation of our hearts." The usurper is dethroned. He remains, indeed, where he once reigned; but remains in chains. So that he does, in some sense, "prosecute the war" yet he grows weaker and weaker; while the believer goes on from strength to strength, conquering and to conquer.[80]

New Birth and Sin in Believers

Now we are in a position to inquire why converted men have as a matter of fact sinned. In this sense we mean by sin an actual, voluntary transgression of the law, of the revealed, written law of God, of any commandment of God, acknowledged to be such at the very time of its transgression.[81] The fact that converted men have committed such sins is a common observation of experience. This no man can deny.[82] King David, for example, was said to have been a man after God's own heart; and yet he committed sins, even the horrible sins of adultery and murder.[83] And even Peter, "the aged, the zealous, the first of the apostles, one of the three most highly favoured by his Lord," after he had been taught by God that he should not call anyone common or unclean, separated himself from the Gentiles because he was afraid of the criticism which he might receive from the followers of James.[84] Here, then, are two examples, taken from the Bible, of men who were unquestionably converted and yet who committed actual sin. Because

[79] *Ibid.*, sec. 10.
[80] *Ibid.*, sec. 11.
[81] Sermon XIX, part ii, sec. 2.
[82] *Ibid.*, sec. 3.
[83] *Ibid.*, sec. 4.
[84] *Ibid.*, sec. 6.

these men did commit sin, however, we need not affirm that all Christians must commit sin, or that evil deeds are the necessary accompaniment of life. It is at this point that we note one of the profound convictions of Wesley's life and one of the cardinal tenets of his theology. Regenerative grace keeps man so long as man keeps it.

So long as he thus believeth in God through Christ, and loves him, and is pouring out his heart before him, he cannot voluntarily transgress any command of God, either by speaking or acting what he knows God hath forbidden: so long as that seed which remaineth in him, that loving, praying, thankful faith, compels him to refrain from whatsoever he knoweth to be an abomination in the sight of God.[85]

Here, then, is the Wesleyan affirmation of synergism after justification. Man must willingly co-operate with God in order to preserve the fruits of his own conversion and remain on the heavenly road through life. "I answer," writes Wesley, "What has been long observed is this: so long as 'he that is born of God keepeth himself,' (which he is able to do by the grace of God,) 'the wicked one toucheth him not;' but if he keepeth not himself, if he abideth not in the faith, he may commit sin even as another man."[86]

The reason why converted men, therefore, have sinned is not that they have been forced to do wrong, not that any necessity of nature has compelled them to violate God's law, but rather that they themselves have not remained steadfast, that they have deliberately chosen to give up the grace which keeps man from all sin. Let us note carefully the Wesleyan analysis of the steps that lead to sin. First of all, temptation arises; and it has a tremendous effect on man, for, as we have seen, human nature is not immune to its appeal. But the normal response of the Christian is to resist sin. The Spirit of God gives him warning, and calls on him actively to exercise his faith and to watch and pray. Secondly, he does not listen to the voice of God, but gives way in some degree to temptation, which now begins to grow pleasing to him. Thirdly, in doing this his faith in God is weakened and his love of God grows cold. But the Spirit of God reproves him and struggles with him to keep him from sin. Fourthly, he turns away completely from

[85] *Ibid.*, sec. 2.
[86] *Ibid.*, sec. 7.

the voice of God and listens to the pleasing voice of the tempter. Finally, evil desire begins and spreads in his soul, till faith and love vanish away. He is then, and only then, capable of committing outward sin, the power of the Lord having departed from him.[87] Consider what this means. It means that in Wesleyan thought an evil deed is of such profound significance and is considered with such horror that, for a man actually to be able to commit it, he must strangle the faith that is in him and drive the love of God from his breast. It means that old nature must rise again to master his affections and that human lust must become superior to grace. An act of sin is not a mark of weakness which is branded upon all men, even the children of God; rather, an act of sin is a mark of the devil and is more to be feared by a regenerate Christian than death or hell. It makes shipwreck of faith and renders the grace of God of no effect.[88]

New Birth and Repentance of Believers

But if it is not normal for a converted man to commit sin, and if the open violation of divine law is the effect of the loss of faith, not its cause, what is the relevance of the Wesleyan doctrine of *repentance of believers?* How does it fit into a system in which evil deeds are eradicated by the purification of conversion? The answer to these questions lies in an appreciation of the significance of two major principles. First of all, there is the principle of the abiding potentiality of evil, the old sinful nature, which remains latent in regenerate man. Secondly, there is the principle of man's absolute dependence on grace. Even after he has been converted he can do no good of himself but must rely completely on the Spirit of God, which performs the good in and through him. These two principles define the Wesleyan conception of *repentance of believers,* and apart from them it has no meaning. Thus repentance, in the first instance, means self-knowledge, or rather that particular kind of self-knowledge in which we know ourselves for exactly what we are.[89] A child of God after he has experienced conversion dare not imagine himself to be immune to sin, to have attained such a degree of moral and spiritual security that he need no longer

[87] *Ibid.*, sec. 9.
[88] *Ibid.*, part iii, sec. 4.
[89] Sermon XIV, part i, sec. 1.

take heed lest he fall. There is no room for spiritual pride and moral
self-satisfaction. Man is always in danger—in danger of becoming
himself again and of turning back as a dog to his vomit. But more than
this, there are the sins of omission, those thousand instances, not
recognized at the time, wherein he might have done good to brethren,
to strangers, to enemies, in regard to their bodies or even their souls,
and yet did not.[90] The danger of returning into open sin, matched by
the consciousness of having failed to do all the good possible in behalf
of other people, leads at once to a sense of *guiltiness,* or spiritual condemnation.[91] Now this is a peculiar concept in Wesley's thought, and
one that bears careful consideration. He does not mean by this that
guilt actually attaches itself to the converted man's acts so that, weighed
in the scale of justice, those acts are no better than the sins of an un-
believer. He does not mean by this that the deeds of a converted man
are prompted by the urges and cravings of his own nature in the same
sense and degree as are the deeds of an unconverted man. Not at all!
And yet he does mean that the deeds of a converted man are, objec-
tively considered, not perfect. He does mean that, weighed in the
scales of divine justice, those deeds will be found not without flaw.
He means that although the motives which prompt the action of the
regenerate man are good, for he is guided by the love of God and man,
yet he himself realizes that what he does is still tainted by the evil and
corruption of his former self. If his conscience is awake, he finds sin
cleaving to his actions, so that in doing God's will as he sees it, he is
doing his own will at the same time and seeking to please himself as
much as God.[92] Though love is the motive of the converted man's life,
it is not the only motive; alongside it still remain the inordinate desires of a former affection.[93] Love must control in so far as the converted man's actions affect the welfare of other people. But who can be
sure, or say with certainty, that all he does is prompted by love alone?
The regenerate man is always conscious of *inward defects* and realizes
he is a "ground overrun with thorns." [94]

[90] *Ibid.,* sec. 14.
[91] *Ibid.,* sec. 16.
[92] *Ibid.,* sec. 13.
[93] *Ibid.,* sec. 5.
[94] *Ibid.,* sec. 15.

If repentance, in the first instance, means self-knowledge, then, in the second instance, it means utter *helplessness.* Now Wesley tells us that he means by helplessness two things: first of all (and this is directly based on the principle of man's absolute dependence on grace), that the regenerate man is no more able now than he was before regeneration to think one good thought, to form one good desire, to speak one good word, or to do one good work of himself alone. He has still no strength of his own, no power either to do good or to resist evil, no ability to conquer or even to withstand the world, the devil, or his own old nature. He can, it is certain, do all these things; but it is not by his own strength. He has power to overcome all these enemies; but this power is the mere gift of God, a gift not given all at once, as if a man had stock laid up in advance for many years, but rather given from moment to moment as needs arise.[95] Secondly, the regenerate man is unable to deliver himself from the *guiltiness,* or spiritual condemnation, of which he is conscious.[96] Even in his redeemed state he is not all spiritually that he would like to be.

Indeed, this is so evident a truth, that well-nigh all the children of God scattered abroad, however they differ in other points, yet generally agree in this;—that although we may "by the Spirit mortify the deeds of the body;" resist and conquer both outward and inward sin; although we may *weaken* our enemies day by day; yet we cannot *drive them out.* By all the grace which is given at justification we cannot extirpate them. Though we watch and pray ever so much, we cannot wholly cleanse either our hearts or our hands.[97]

The old desires of man's former nature are still with him.

The sum and substance of the Wesleyan doctrine of repentance of believers, therefore, is nothing more than a profound recognition of human weakness, of man's utter dependence on God's grace, and a sincere consciousness of humility and of gratitude—humility engendered by the thought of what man was and what he might yet return to, gratitude engendered by the thought of what he is and what he hopes yet to become.

[95] *Ibid.,* sec. 17.
[96] *Ibid.,* sec. 18.
[97] *Ibid.,* sec. 20.

New Birth and the Danger of Falling from Grace

If there is the possibility of evil latent in human nature, and if there is always the danger of man's returning into open sin, is it true also that man, after he has been regenerated and has experienced the new birth, may completely forsake the ways of righteousness and deny the faith by which he was claimed? In other words, is it possible for a man who has been justified to return to the state of nature prior to justification and to erase forever the effects of the justifying act on his own life? Wesley considers this question very carefully in his work entitled the *Perseverance of the Saints,* and he admits that to answer it in either one way or the other is to subject oneself to great difficulties, perhaps dangers. These difficulties reason alone can never remove; and so he says that we must go "to the law and to the testimony" for our answer. "Let the living oracles decide: And if these speak for us, we neither seek nor want farther witness." [98] Consider, therefore, that on the authority of the Bible, a man who is righteous in the judgment of God himself may "nevertheless so fall from God as to perish everlastingly." Thus in Ezekiel 18:24 we receive the word of the Lord: "When the righteous turneth away from his righteousness, and committeth iniquity, . . . in his trespass that he hath trespassed, and in his sin that he hath sinned, in them shall he die." And this means eternal death, as appears from the twenty-sixth verse: "When a righteous man turneth away from his righteousness, and committeth iniquity, and dieth in them" (Wesley calls this temporal death, which is obvious), "for his iniquity that he hath done shall he die" (Wesley reminds us that this refers to death eternal). Now this is not inconsistent, says Wesley, with God's covenant with David and with the House of Israel. That covenant itself was conditional; it was conditioned on the Israelites' keeping God's law and repenting for all their failures and mistakes. When they did not do this, God in turn "failed David" and broke "the covenant of his servant and cast his crown to the ground." [99]

The fact that a man endued with faith and a good conscience may

[98] *Works,* X, 285.
[99] *Ibid.,* pp. 266, 287.

fall forever is brought out by the words of the Apostle in I Timothy 1:18-19: "War a good warfare; holding faith, and a good conscience; which some having put away concerning faith have made shipwreck." [100] Wesley tells us that the use of the phrase "made shipwreck" implies total and final loss, for a vessel once wrecked can never be recovered.[101] But how, we ask, can this be reconciled with the words of the Master himself when he says, "He that believeth . . . shall be saved"? This does not mean that a man shall be saved at the very moment of his belief, that is, saved *certainly* and *inevitably*. For, if such were the case, then, by all the rules of speech, the other part of the Master's statement, "He" that does "not believe" at this very moment "shall," *certainly* and *inevitably,* "be damned." The plain meaning of the whole statement, according to Wesley, is that, "He that believeth," if he continue in faith, "shall be saved; he that believeth not," if he continue in unbelief, "shall be damned." [102] Now it is true that to believe is to possess the chance of everlasting life, for belief implies the love of God, which is everlasting life. But man must endure therein in order to convert this chance into a reality.[103] Wesley pursues his argument through one stage after another of the Christian life and shows in one instance after another that man may fall and perish everlastingly.[104]

This doctrine must of course be set in contrast with the Calvinistic teaching of the perseverance of the saints, and in doing so we see at once another mark of divergence which distinguishes Wesleyan Arminianism from the precepts of the School of Geneva. Calvin teaches that if a man is once saved, he is always saved. Thus Calvin writes that man's first entrance into the Church, or the Kingdom of God, is characterized by the remission of his sins, without which he could have

[100] *Notes on the New Testament*, p. 539.

[101] *Ibid.,* p. 540; *Works,* X, 288.

[102] *Works,* X, 288.

[103] *Notes on the New Testament,* p. 221; *Works,* X, 288.

[104] Wesley goes on to show, from Scripture, how those who have been taken into the fellowship of the invisible Church may fall and perish (*Works,* X, 289); also, those that have become united with Christ as a branch with the vine (p. 291), those who have escaped the thought of the pollutions of the world (p. 292), those who see the light of the glory of God and live by faith alone (pp. 293, 295), those who have been sanctified (p. 296).

no covenant with God.[105] But then he goes on to say that not only does God pardon man of his former offences but he likewise preserves and keeps him by the power of his divine mercy. "For to what purpose would it be, if we obtained a pardon which would afterwards be of no use?"[106] If, in the light of the teaching of the irresistibility of God's grace, man is drawn by God to repentance and to faith, it

incontrovertibly follows . . . that the hearts of the pious are divinely governed with such effect that they follow with an affection which nothing can alter. . . . For we see that the neutral, inefficacious impulse imagined by the sophists, which every one would be at liberty to obey or resist is evidently excluded, where it is asserted that God gives a constancy that is effectual to perseverance.[107]

Perseverance, therefore, like justifying grace, is to be esteemed the gratuitous gift of God. Thus man is not vainly to imagine that, by his own industry, he can render the grace of God efficacious in himself or add thereby grace to grace in his own life.

Calvin realizes at the same time that man remains guilty of sin after he has been converted, that he carries the relics of his evil nature with him as long as he lives, and that he is in constant need of pardon and of forgiveness. But God grants him pardon at all times, for "that divine mercy would be vain and delusive if it were only granted for once."[108] But, come what may, no man who has been claimed by God will ever be lost.

[The] Lord has called his people to eternal salvation; they ought, therefore, to believe that his grace is always ready to pardon their sins. Wherefore it ought to be held as a certain conclusion, that from the Divine liberality, by the intervention of the merit of Christ, through the sanctification of the Spirit, pardon of sins has been, and is daily, bestowed upon us, who have been admitted and ingrafted into the body of the Church.[109]

The stress in Calvinistic thought is always on God; in the perseverance of the saints God is everything, man is nothing. The stress in

105 Calvin, *Institutes*, IV, i, 20.
106 *Ibid.*, 21.
107 *Ibid.*, II, iii, 10.
108 *Ibid.*, IV, 1, 21.
109 *Ibid.*

Wesleyan thought is quite the contrary. Always the emphasis is laid on man. To be sure, man can do no good of himself and is always dependent on the grace of God, even after justification; and yet man is given the power to kill the grace that is within him and to destroy the work of God in his own life. Thus the Calvinists of Wesley's day stood in horror at Wesley's teaching of man's ability to fall from grace. They said: "What, can the blood of Christ burn in hell? Or can the purchase of the blood of Christ go thither? . . . Can a child of God then go to hell? Or can a man be a child of God to-day, and a child of the devil to-morrow? If God is our Father once, is he not our Father always?" [110] Wesley replies: "God is the Father of them that believe so long as they believe. But the devil is the father of them that believe not, whether they did once believe or no." [111]

The Relationship of Justification to Sanctification

But, though the new birth does not free man from the potentiality of evil or rescue him from the possibility of falling completely from grace and of annihilating the effects of divine goodness in his character, it none the less affords him power over sin if he will exercise it and releases a new force of positive goodness in his life. It is to this new force of positive goodness that we turn now as we attempt to examine the relationship between regeneration, the mark of justification on man, and sanctification, the process of man's purification. To be sure, regeneration is itself a part of sanctification; for as soon as a man is born again his actual purification is begun and he is set on the road to holiness.[112] Just as a child is born of a woman in a very short time and yet afterward grows gradually and slowly until he attains the stature of a man, even so a sinner is born of God in a very short time, and yet it is by slow degrees that he grows up unto the measure of the stature of Christ. Thus there exists in Wesleyan thought the same relationship between man's natural birth and his growth and man's spiritual birth and sanctification. Only one point must always be kept in mind; and that, of course, is that regeneration itself has purified man to such a degree that he does not commit acts of sin and that love has already become the

[110] Quoted by Wesley, *Works*, X, 297. Cf. Whitefield, *Works*, IV, 64-65, 72, 290.
[111] *Works*, X, 298.
[112] Sermon XLV, part iv, sec. 3.

145

chief motive of his life. Any development, or growth, therefore, must of necessity have to do with man's internal disposition, with the control of those forces of his old nature which make war on the Spirit and which constitute a target whereon temptations can strike. Wesley tells us that as a man grows in grace the new power which animates his life manifests itself and he is recognized as a child of God. It is, therefore, as the manifestation of this power of God in the soul of man that we understand the Wesleyan emphasis on good works and the insistence that without them no man can attain final salvation.

Wesley reports that certain of the Moravians in England taught that there is no commandment in the New Testament but to believe, and that when a man does believe, he is not bound or obliged to do anything which is commanded in the Bible—he need not pray, read the Scripture, feed the poor, obey the moral law, or engage in any exercises which aid in the promotion of righteousness and purity of life.[113] The whole work of man's salvation was accomplished once and for all by Jesus Christ on the cross.[114] Christ's blood and man's sins went away together.[115] To believe that Christ suffered death for him is enough; man needs no more. He is justified and saved by his submitting in his judgments to the truth of God's grace in Jesus Christ. It is not necessary for him to do any works that he may be saved. God does not require man to do anything. Nay, works are absolutely forbidden. Man need not bother about holiness. Let him live as the Spirit leads him. To look for inherent righteousness is to deny the Spirit and to trample under foot the blood of the covenant. Believers have no inherent righteousness. They trust alone in the imputation of the righteousness of Christ.[116]

Such a doctrine Wesley never embraced, and his emphasis on justification by faith alone was never at the expense of good works after justification or holiness of heart and life as the supreme condition of final salvation. Thus, while he lived, he set himself steadfastly against all antinomian tendencies and decried any teaching which compromised with sin or which failed to exalt righteousness as the essential

[113] *Journal*, Fri., June 20, 1740.
[114] *Works*, X, 266.
[115] *Ibid.*, p. 267.
[116] *Ibid.*, p. 272.

requirement of man's salvation. Thus Wesley writes in his famous
reply to Mr. Church that, to be sure, faith is the sole requirement of
justification, but all obedience must follow the moment after a man
believes.[117] Or, he goes on to say, good works cannot be the condition
of justification because it is impossible to render them; but it is possible
to render them after justification, and they are the condition of final
salvation.[118]

He went so far as to enumerate the differences between his thought
and that of the Moravian Brethren. In this enumeration he says that
the Brethren's use of the statement that Christ has done all that is
necessary for man's salvation, is ambiguous and, therefore, worthless.
A man must do more than believe in Christ. He must exercise his belief through love. The Moravian teaching that there is but one duty
or command, namely, to believe in Christ, is proved false by almost
every page of the New Testament. To assert that Christ has taken
away all commands and duties and has wholly abolished the law is
to make Christ contradict himself: "Think not that I am come to
destroy the law, or the prophets: I am not come to destroy, but to
fulfil. . . . One jot or one tittle shall in no wise pass from the law, till
all be fulfilled." A believer is free from the curse of the law and from
the power of sin and death, but nowhere is it written that he is free
from the law of God and from the eternal standards of holiness. To
say that we are no more sanctified at the end of our Christian life than
we were at its beginning is to do violence both to the tenor of God's
word and to the experience of God's children. To claim that if a man
regards prayer or the reading of the Bible or Communion as a matter
of duty and feels obliged to do them, he is in bondage and has no faith
is to make obedience a proof of unbelief and disobedience a proof of
faith, to put darkness for light and light for darkness.[119]
Thus Wesley writes in regard to Martin Luther, from the reading of
whose Preface to the Epistle of Romans he had at one time gained
such strength:

[117] *Ibid.*, VIII, 289.
[118] *Ibid.*, p. 290.
[119] These thoughts are condensations of Wesley's tract on "An Extract from 'A Short
View of the Difference between the Moravian Brethren, (so called,) and the Rev. Mr.
John and Charles Wesley,'" *Works,* X, 201-4.

I . . . read over . . . that celebrated book, Martin Luther's Comment on the Epistle to the Galatians. I was utterly ashamed. How have I esteemed this book, only because I heard it so commended by others! Or, at best, because I had read some excellent sentences occasionally quoted from it! But what shall I say, now I judge for myself? Now I see with my own eyes? Why, not only that the author makes nothing out, clears up not one considerable difficulty; that he is quite shallow in his remarks on many passages, and muddy and confused almost on all; but that he is deeply tinctured with mysticism throughout, and hence often dangerously wrong. To instance only one or two points: How does he (almost in the words of Tauler) decry reason, right or wrong, as an irreconcilable enemy to the Gospel of Christ? Whereas, what is reason, (the faculty so called,) but the power of apprehending, judging, and discoursing? Which power is no more to be condemned in the gross, than seeing, hearing, or feeling. Again, how blasphemously does he speak of good works and of the law of God; constantly coupling the law with sin, death, hell, or the Devil! and teaching that Christ delivers us from them all alike. Whereas, it can no more be proved by Scripture, that "Christ delivers us from the law of God," than he delivers us "from holiness or from heaven." Here (I apprehend) is the real spring of the ground of the error of the Moravians. They follow Luther for better or for worse. Hence their, "No works; no law; no commandments." But who art thou that "speakest evil of the law, and judgest the law?" [120]

He goes on to say that in London, in the course of his sermon on Galatians 5:6, he thought it his bounden duty to warn the congregation against that dangerous treatise of Martin Luther's on the subject and openly to retract whatever recommendation he might ignorantly have given to it.[121] In another reference to Luther, Wesley tells us that he must have been a man highly favored of God and a blessed instrument in God's hands, and yet he was rough, possessed of an untractable spirit, and driven by a bitter zeal for opinions, all of which greatly obstructed the work of God.[122] Finally, in the *Large Minutes,* which contain the plan of discipline as practiced in the Methodist Connection during the life of Mr. Wesley, we find these questions and answers, probably taken from the conversation between Wesley and his preachers in the year 1789:

[120] *Journal,* Mon., June 15, 1741.
[121] *Ibid.,* Tues., June 16, 1741.
[122] *Ibid.,* Wed., July 19, 1747.

THE MEANS TO GOD'S END

Question. What is the direct antidote to Methodism, the doctrine of heart-holiness?

Answer. Calvinism: All the devices of Satan, for these fifty years, have done far less toward stopping this work of God, than that single doctrine. It strikes at the root of salvation from sin, previous to glory, putting the matter on quite another issue.

Question. But wherein lie the charms of this doctrine? What makes men swallow it so greedily?

Answer. (1) It seems to magnify Christ; although in reality it supposes him to have died in vain. For the absolutely elect must have been saved without him; and the non-elect cannot be saved by him. (2) It is highly pleasing to flesh and blood, final perseverance in particular.[123]

From these quotations we see what Wesley thought of any tendency in religion to exclude works and moral goodness from their rightful place among the requirements of salvation.

But what does all this mean? At long last, after all the facts are in, is it true that the Aldersgate experience was just an illusion, that faith given freely by God was all a mistake, and that man's hope fixed on the everlasting mercy of a heavenly Father was as insubstantial as a dream? Is it true that works have pushed their way again to the fore-front of Wesley's thought and that divine grace has been nailed to the cross by human piety and holiness? No, such is not the case. That great truth that man is saved by faith will never be worn out; sanctification as well as justification, Wesley tells us, is the free gift of God.[124] God alone is the author of salvation. It is he that works in us both to will and to do. He is the sole giver of every good gift and the sole author of every good work.[125] But the fact remains that God does give good gifts and God does perform good works. Works as the expression of grace are absolutely essential to man's salvation;[126] and without holiness no man can see God.[127] Grace and works in the Wesleyan conception of salvation, like form and matter in Aristotelian philosophy,

[123] *Works*, VIII, 336. This obviously refers to a brand of Calvinism practiced in Wesley's day, and the mark of condemnation falls in this instance on the antinomianism practiced by its adherents. But it clearly indicates that Wesley thought Calvinistic theology, as well as Lutheran and Moravian, endangered morality and led toward antinomianism.

[124] *Works*, XII, 333.

[125] *Ibid.*, VIII, 49.

[126] *Ibid.*, X, 432.

[127] *Ibid.*. p. 364.

stand together. They cannot be isolated or separated in an individual. A man's works are the living portrait of God's grace. But, in the last analysis, does salvation come by faith or works? Why must men insist on the use of the conjunction "or"? Why must they speak as if faith excluded works, or works drove faith, cold and dying, from the human breast? The man who is finally accepted of God is he who believes in Christ with a loving and obedient heart [128] and exercises that belief in deeds of kindness and love.[129] If faith produces works, then works in turn support faith, yea, even bring it to glorious fruition in human life.[130] Our Lord expressly commands us to *work for life*. "*Labour,* literally *'work,* for the meat that endureth to everlasting life.' And in fact every believer, till he comes to glory, works *for* as well as *from* life." [131]

Is not this salvation by works? Not by the merits of works, but by works as a condition.

What have we then been disputing about for these thirty years? I am afraid about words, namely, in some of the foregoing instances.

As to merit itself, of which we have been so dreadfully afraid: We are rewarded according to our works, yea, because of our works. How does this differ from, 'for the sake of our works?' And how differs this from *secundum merita operum?* which is no more than, 'as our works deserve.' Can you split this hair? I doubt I cannot.[132]

Justification, in the final analysis, is the gate of religion; [133] but religion itself is the love of God and of all mankind.[134] Even faith is not an end in itself but only a means; the end of all things is love. "Let this love be attained, by whatever means, and I am content; I desire no more. All is well if we love God with all our heart, and our neighbour as ourselves." [135]

[128] *Ibid.,* VIII, 337.
[129] *Ibid.,* p. 57; X, 432.
[130] Sermon XCIX, part i, sec. 6.
[131] *Works,* VIII, 337.
[132] *Ibid.,* pp. 337-38. Note, also, that those who have never heard of Christ are justified according to the light that they have, according to their fear of God and works of righteousness.—*Ibid.* These quotations are taken from the famous "Minutes of the Conference of 1770."
[133] *Ibid.,* p. 473.
[134] *Ibid.,* p. 474.
[135] *Ibid.,* XII, 79.

Part Two

THEOLOGICAL AND ETHICAL CONCEPTS ARISING
FROM THE DOCTRINE OF JUSTIFICATION

Chapter VII

GOD AND PROVIDENCE

IT IS OBVIOUSLY IMPOSSIBLE TO MAKE A THOROUGH EXAMINATION OF THE doctrine of justification without considering its implications and its relationship to other fundamental concepts. To try to isolate justification from the other major concepts of theology would not only distort the general theological pattern but also do violence to the concept of justification itself and render almost useless any attempt to understand its essential nature. Albrecht Ritschl reminds us that justification is comprised within the general scheme of God's operation on men.[1] It can therefore never be separated from the more ultimate conception of the nature of God. What God does is determined by what God is; and justification, if it is an act of divine pardon, has as its ultimate ground the very nature and character of God. God is the author, or the subject, of justification, while man is its object. But the purpose of the justifying act and the end of its execution stem from the character of him who performs it. In this chapter, therefore, we are brought to consider the Wesleyan conception of God.

Eighteenth-Century Approach to a Knowledge of God

Now it must be said in all fairness to the rationalistic temper of eighteenth-century thought that it had not dispensed with the concept of God. Indeed, deism affirmed God's existence on the basis both of nature and of conscience. If man was taught to use his reason and with it to look on nature, he was taught at the same time to look through nature and to behold nature's God.[2] The writings of the deists were not intended to strike a blow at the root of religion itself but rather to prune the religious vine of the dead branches of supernaturalism and biblical literalism in the hopes that it might yield a better crop of spiritual fruit. Revelation, or the disclosure of the nature of God, must,

[1] *Justification and Reconciliation*, III, 27.
[2] B. Willey, *Eighteenth Century Background*, p. 76.

they thought, be found in the world about them rather than in the dusty pages of some old book. The champions of orthodoxy, on the other hand, though they respected reason and employed it as a tool of supreme importance in matters of religion, did not dispense with supernatural revelation and insisted that revealed religion must exist as an essential adjunct to natural religion. God's nature and character, they taught, cannot be adequately set forth in natural phenomena; it remains for God himself to speak and to set forth his own truth.

Bishop Butler stands as the representative of eighteenth-century Christian apologetics. He does not deny that there are difficulties involved in the concept of revelation, which concept he attempts to defend. And yet these difficulties offer no legitimate excuse for abandoning revelation and turning back to a religion of nature alone. The very same difficulties which are found in revelation are equally apparent in the notion of natural religion. Thus Butler, quoting from Origen, writes: "He who believes the Scripture to have proceeded from him who is the Author of nature, may well expect to find the same sort of difficulties in it, as are found in the constitution of nature."[3] There is in Butler's argument a close analogy between natural and revealed religion, so that any factor of incomprehensibility in the natural government of the universe should lead us to expect similar factors of incomprehensibility in the moral government of the universe.[4] But, in spite of all that is incomprehensible, writes Butler, there is still no need of abstruse reasonings and distinctions to convince an unprejudiced mind that there is a God who made and governs the world.[5] It is intuitively manifest that creatures ought to live under the highest standards set for them by their Maker. And, indeed, it is their duty to do so; for the very fact that Christianity may be true lays persons under the strictest obligations to pay due regard to its precepts.[6] No revelation would have been given had the light of nature been sufficient to render one needless and useless. But the point is that the light of nature has not been sufficient, and any serious man can see this by comparing religion in the heathen world prior to revelation with religion as it exists

[3] *Works*, I, 9.
[4] *Ibid.*, pp. 246-47.
[5] *Ibid.*, p. 371.
[6] *Ibid.*, p. 382.

in the Christian tradition.[7] To inquire into the importance of Christianity alone is to furnish an introduction to its credibility.[8] Natural religion is the foundation and perhaps the chief part of Christianity, but it is not the whole of it.[9] If Christianity is a republication of natural religion in that it instructs mankind in the moral system, shows that virtue is law, and that all mankind must be judged according to their works,[10] it at the same time goes beyond nature and discloses truths which unaided reason could never have discovered alone.[11] It proclaims, not only the truths of general providence in which God is disclosed as the righteous governor of the universe, but also a particular dispensation of providence in which God seeks the recovery and salvation of mankind through his Son and his Spirit.[12] Thus we find the true meaning of religion by searching the Scripture, for the Scripture contains a doctrine which the light of nature cannot discover.[13] Butler, therefore, as the apologist for the Anglican position, goes beyond the deists' naturalistic and rationalistic approach to God and affirms divine revelation as the final basis of the Christian faith. Reason is not discredited by Butler, but its limits are frankly confessed. Revelation does not contradict reason, nor does it deny to reason her natural right to judge of the evidence which is presented.[14] The evidence itself, however, comes from another source; it is from God and, as such, is incapable of human discovery.

To be sure, Butler's argument is negative; it rests on the fact that man cannot know the whole course of nature and, therefore, cannot tell what God will do in every circumstance of human history. It assumes the existence of the Divine Being and, on the basis of analogy between revelation and the evidences of God in nature, it attempts to show that revealed religion is as credible as natural religion and as worthy of man's allegiance and devotion. The significant fact for us to note, however, is the conclusion which Butler reaches: namely, that

[7] *Ibid.*, pp. 185-86.
[8] *Ibid.*, p. 187.
[9] *Ibid.*, p. 188.
[10] *Ibid.*, p. 189.
[11] *Ibid.*, p. 196.
[12] *Ibid.*, p. 197.
[13] *Ibid.*, p. 209.
[14] *Ibid.*, p. 238.

revelation defines the concepts of theology and that through it truths from God and about God are disclosed to man, truths which man could never have reached—or at least did not reach—through the faculties of his own reason. In this Butler, the apologist, is not far removed from Wesley, the evangelist; and as we study the Wesleyan approach to a knowledge of the nature and character of God, we see the close similarity in thought between the founder of Methodism and the Anglican theologians of his day. The fact that a man is in disagreement with his contemporaries over certain issues does not mean that he has nothing in common with them whatever, or that there are not other issues on which he and they fundamentally agree. It is a point of no small importance that Wesley read Bishop Butler's *Analogy* and that, though he found it difficult to read and expressed some misgivings as to its adaptability to the understanding of the readers for whom it was intended, he did not criticize its arguments or list any disagreements with its conclusions but went so far as to call it a "fine book."[15]

Wesley's Approach to a Knowledge of God

The Wesleyan consideration of the problem of religious knowledge, the object of which is God, starts with an empirical estimate of knowledge itself; and at the outset Wesley frankly admits that the desire for knowledge is a universal principle of human nature, that as such it exists for excellent purposes, and that its very intention is to prevent man's taking rest in anything here below. The object, as well as the source of all knowledge, is the all-gracious Creator.[16] But though man's desire for knowledge is without limits, knowledge itself is partial and incomplete.[17] To be sure, Wesley thinks that it is sufficient for man's present needs. But to say that man knows enough about certain things to use them and to get along in the world is not to say that he knows everything about all the phenomena with which he comes into daily contact. We see the stars far off in the heavens, and they inspire wonder and awe. But can we say how far the universe extends, or what is the measure of the distance between its bounds? Can we de-

[15] *Journal*, Tues., Jan. 21, 1746; Fri., May 20, 1768.
[16] Sermon LXIX, intro. sec. 1.
[17] *Ibid.*, sec. 2.

termine the use of the fixed stars or the substance of which they are composed?[18] What is light, and how is it communicated to us? Does light flow in a continued stream from the sun, or does the sun "impel the particles next his orb, and so on and on, to the extremity of his system?" Does light attract or repel bodies?[19] What about the air we breathe? By what power do dew, rain, and other vapors rise and fall in the air?[20] Is the earth itself any more understandable? We know what lies immediately below the earth's surface; but who can inform us what "lies beneath the region of stones, metals, minerals, and other fossils?"[21] Not only so, but who can explain all the details of the functions of vegetable and animal life about us;[22] who knows all the intricacies of insects and of fish? Can we say with Descartes that beasts are mere machines? If so, who among us can account for their display of different qualities and tempers?[23] But bringing the lesson closer home, we do not know ourselves. What is our soul? Where is it lodged? Is it "in the pineal gland, in the whole brain, in the heart, in the blood, in any single part of the body, or (if any one can understand those terms) 'all in all, and all in every part'"?[24] To the argument of the deists that we know God through nature, through the works of his creation, Wesley replies: To be sure;[25] but when we know him thus, consider how little we really know, for even the works of creation present us with mystery and the simple things about us are far from being wholly understood.[26]

If knowledge itself is partial and incomplete, what can we say for reason, which is the organ of knowledge? Here once again Wesley is in fundamental agreement with Bishop Butler. Reason is not to be discredited or despised. Reason is not to be driven from the temple of religion as if it had no place in the service of God. It is a true observation of experience, says Wesley, that "if reason be against a man, a

---

[18] *Ibid.*, part i, sec. 5.
[19] *Ibid.*, sec. 6.
[20] *Ibid.*, sec. 7.
[21] *Ibid.*, sec. 8.
[22] *Ibid.*, sec. 10-11.
[23] *Ibid.*, sec. 12.
[24] *Ibid.*, sec. 13.
[25] *Ibid.*, sec. 4.
[26] *Ibid.*, sec. 5.

man will always be against reason." [27] Thus you get examples of well-meaning but foolish Christians who vilify reason, substitute for it dreams of their own fancy, and say that it has no place in the apprehension of divine truth. [28] But on the other hand reason itself is not to be exalted to the throne of God. Some men overvalue it, say that it is the highest gift of God, describe it as very nearly infallible, and look upon it "as the all-sufficient director of all the children of men." [29] These men do not see the need of divine revelation and, therefore, do not receive the Bible as the oracle of God. [30] Really, there is a medium between these two extremes, and this is the place reason must occupy in any sensible approach to a knowledge of God. [31] Now Wesley is very careful to give a clear statement of what he takes reason itself to be. It is not just argument, nor is it the relation of things to one another. [32] Rather, reason is that faculty of the human soul which performs three important functions. Those functions are apprehension, judgment, discourse. By "apprehension" Wesley means the act of conceiving a thing in the mind. By "judgment" he means "the determining that the things before conceived either agree with or differ from each other;" while by "discourse" he means "the motion or progress of the mind from one judgment to another." [33] On the basis of his conception of its nature, we must now consider what reason can do and also what it cannot do.

It is not our purpose here to consider what reason does in the ordinary course of human life, [34] but rather to ask at once what it is that it can do in the realm of religion. Note Wesley's reply at this point. He

[27] Sermon LXX, intro. sec. 1.

[28] *Ibid.*, sec. 2.

[29] *Ibid.*, sec. 3.

[30] *Ibid.*, sec. 4.

[31] *Ibid.*, sec. 5.

[32] *Ibid.*, part i, sec. 1.

[33] *Ibid.*, sec. 2. In epistemology Wesley agrees with Locke that man has no innate ideas, but that all ideas come from sensation and reflection. See Wesley's "Remarks on Mr. Locke's 'Essay on Human Understanding,'" *Works,* XIII, 455-64. If God had impressed any idea of himself upon man, that idea would not have been either false or imperfect; but the point is that we have no innate idea of God. What we know of him must be gathered from his works or be given us through revelation.—Sermon LXIX, part i, sec. 4.

[34] Of course, Wesley himself does enumerate the virtues of reason as it is employed apart from philosophy and religion in the ordinary duties of life. See Sermon LXX, part i, secs. 3-4.

says with Butler that reason is the ordinary channel by which revelation makes its contact with man. Religion is built on the Bible, and reason is that which enables man to understand the Bible, to grasp its statement of the truths concerning God and his relation to the universe, "and to comprehend his method of dealing with the children of men." Reason is that which makes possible an understanding of the precepts of the Christian life: repentance, faith, the new birth, holiness, final salvation. "In all respects . . . God has given us our reason for a guide. And it is only by acting up to the dictates of it, by using all the understanding which God hath given us, that we have a conscience void of offence towards God and towards man." [35] But reason cannot supply the content of Christian truth; it cannot produce faith,[36] give a clear or satisfactory evidence of the invisible world,[37] or produce the hope which maketh not ashamed but which inspires confidence and trust.[38] It is the will of God that man should be guided by his reason so far as it can go, but in many cases it gives very little light, and in some cases it gives no light at all.[39] Reason must be willing to become once again the handmaid of faith, the servant of revelation.

Wesley, in turning to revelation itself, recognizes, as Butler, that through it not everything is explained, and that the works of grace are beset with mystery just as are the works of nature.[40] Wesley says, if this be used as an objection, though it applies as much to natural religion as to revealed religion, there is still no way of man's answering the objection except only to say that there are many things of which he is ignorant.[41] Why did God keep his Son for so long a time apart from the world; and, when he came, why did he come only to the Jews? [42] Why is the New Zealander or the Hottentot cut off from the truths of the gospel? [43] These problems we cannot solve, for the answer to them lies in the unsearchable wisdom of God.[44] But rather than

[35] *Ibid.*, secs. 6-7.
[36] *Ibid.*, part ii, sec. 1.
[37] *Ibid.*, sec. 3.
[38] *Ibid.*, sec. 5.
[39] *Works*, XIII, 66.
[40] Sermon LXIX, part iii, sec. 1.
[41] *Ibid.*, sec. 2.
[42] *Ibid.*, sec. 3.
[43] *Ibid.*, sec. 1.
[44] *Ibid.*, sec. 2.

raise these problems as objections to the Christian revelation, we should accept them as lessons of humility, trust, and patience.[45]

In turning to the Bible as the oracle of God's revelation, however, Wesley is more positive. He seems not to have sensed the objections which the deists raised against it or to have recognized any inconsistencies in its content. In fact, he offers what he calls an indisputable argument for its validity. This argument is threefold. Wesley tells us that the Bible must have been the invention of good men or angels, bad men or devils, or God himself. It is impossible for the Bible to have been the invention of good men or angels because they neither would nor could tell lies about it, saying, "Thus saith the Lord." It is impossible for the Bible to have been the invention of bad men or devils, for they would not make a book which "commands all duty, forbids all sin, and condemns their souls to hell to all eternity." Therefore, if the Bible was not the invention of either of the former groups, it must have been given by the inspiration of God, and that is the Wesleyan conclusion.[46] In the last analysis, therefore, the Bible is for Wesley the way to religious knowledge and to a comprehension of truth concerning God and God's relation to men.[47] To be sure, reason is an essential tool for the interpretation of the Bible, and Wesley writes that he builds all his religious opinions on Scripture as he interprets it through the means of common sense.[48]

The Nature of God

The Wesleyan doctrine of God is fashioned out of the teachings of the Bible, and it draws very little on the principles of metaphysics or the demonstrations of philosophy. Indeed, it seems as if Wesley shies away from metaphysical questions in regard to the nature of God and contents himself with an affirmation of the most obvious facts which come to him through the channel of religious needs. Thus on the basis of the words in I John 5:7—"There are three that bear record in heaven, the Father, the Word, and the Holy Spirit: and these three are

[45] *Ibid.*, part iv.
[46] *Works*, XI, 484.
[47] *Ibid.*, VI, 354, 390; VIII, 6, 108, 206; X, 133-34, 142, 511; XI, 450, 466; XIV, 252.
[48] *Ibid.*, VIII, 248; XII, 476-77.

160

one"—Wesley prepared his sermon on the Trinity. But this sermon is almost apologetic in character and lacks the positive assertiveness of most of the Wesleyan writings. In it Wesley frankly admits that he personally can require no one to use the word "Trinity" or "person" as if the refusal to do so were blasphemous and worthy of death at the stake.[49] Nor will he say that it is of importance to believe any particular explication of the doctrine of the Trinity. He does not think that any well-judging man ought to attempt to explain it at all, for he agrees with Dean Swift that those who have endeavored to explain it have utterly lost their way and "have, above all other persons, hurt the cause which they intended to promote; having only, as Job speaks, 'darkened counsel by words without knowledge.' "[50] On the basis of the divine testimony alone, he believes the fact of the Trinity, but he has no idea of its *manner*. God has not revealed this to men; but it is foolish to reject what God has revealed merely because we do not comprehend what he has not revealed.[51] The significant thing in this revelation is that Jesus Christ is God, the Holy Spirit is God, and the Father is God. What matters is not an explanation of this but that all men honor the Son, the Holy Spirit, and the Father as One God.[52] Wesley's doctrine of God is not alien to the other principles of his theology; all rest on religious insights alone. For him there could be no such thing as a "philosophical religion."[53]

And yet in limiting his doctrine of God to religious considerations alone and employing only the materials of revelation in its construction, Wesley does not free himself from the necessity of attempting to explain God's relationship to the universe and his control over all his works. True, he makes no attempt to prove God's existence; but, having assumed his existence and having accepted as a matter of faith both his power and his goodness, he is still under obligation to consider his manner of dealing with his creatures and the nature of his purposes as they express themselves in his positive commands to the children of men. If Wesley tells us that there are two attributes which are insepa-

[49] Sermon LV, sec. 4.
[50] *Ibid.*, sec. 3.
[51] *Ibid.*, sec. 15.
[52] *Ibid.*, sec. 17.
[53] *Works*, IX, 467.

rable from the very idea of God, namely, justice and goodness,[54] and that no factor in the universe can mean that God is not love or that his mercy is not over all his works,[55] he goes on to say also that God possesses infinite wisdom to conceive his designs and infinite power to bring them to positive realization.[56] God's goodness is not limited by his nature; his power is sufficient to execute the dictates of his character and to give adequate expression to the promptings of his wisdom, his justice, and his love.[57]

The Nature of God in the Light of Creation

At the same time, in considering any of the attributes of God we are dependent on the manner in which God himself discloses them to us. Wesley tells us that God reveals himself under a "two-fold character." He reveals himself as a Creator and as a Governor. Now these two aspects of God's character, though they are in no way inconsistent with one another, are yet totally different and manifest distinct attributes of the one divine nature.[58] As Creator, God has acted in all things according to his own *sovereign will.* He has acted to please himself, and no other consideration has been brought to bear on his divine counsel. Thus we cannot say that justice has any place whatsoever in a consideration of the creative act, for nothing is due to what has no being. In the most absolute sense, therefore, we must say that in this act God may do what he will with his own. Wesley says that he created the heavens and the earth and all things therein "in every conceivable respect according to his own good pleasure." Thus there is no point in raising the question why creation came when it did. God began creation at that particular point in eternity which seemed good to him. He determined, also, the duration of the universe; decided whether it should last seven thousand, seven hundred thousand, or numberless millions of years. He appointed, also, the place of the universe in the immensity of space and determined the number of stars, all the components of the world, even the magnitude of the atom and of every-

[54] *Ibid.,* VIII, 7.
[55] Sermon CXXVIII, sec. 26; Sermon LX, sec. 1.
[56] *Works,* X, 70.
[57] *Ibid.,* pp. 232-34.
[58] *Ibid.,* p. 361.

thing that exists.[59] God decided on the quality and fashioned the substance of all the furniture of nature, both animate and inanimate, and gave to all things such properties as he desired them to possess. Man himself was no exception to God's action. He made him also according to his divine pleasure, gave him an embodied spirit and a spiritual nature, and endued him with will, understanding, and freedom. More than this, God determined the times for every nation to come into existence and set the bounds of its habitation. Likewise, he foreknew the time, the place, and the circumstance of every particular person's birth. But does this mean that God planned the body of everyone born into the world? Wesley answers that in a sense he did, for he saw in advance the nature of every child of man and he provided this power by which all things, even the weak or imperfect, are produced. This implies that God considered the understanding of men, that he gave men various degrees of understanding and of knowledge, diversified by numberless circumstances. It is difficult, however, to be certain how far this extends; and Wesley recognizes the amazing difference, in comprehension and the ability to improve one's understanding, between one born in England, for instance, and one born and reared in a family of Hottentots. The things of the universe, the products of God's hand, display alone his power as Creator and as Sovereign.[60] Thus Wesley writes, after having expressed his belief in one infinite and independent Being, that the Father of all, who is that Being, is not only able to do whatsoever pleases him but possesses, also, the eternal right to make "what and when and how he pleases" and to dispose of all that he has made in any manner he may desire.[61] "As Creator, God could not but act according to his sovereign will." [62]

What does this mean? It means precisely this: that everything inasmuch as it is the product of God's hand expresses in its nature his design and his purpose. Nothing, therefore, in itself is evil. Thus Wesley reminds us that when God had finished his creation of the heavens and the earth, it pleased him to pass sentence upon it and to say, in

[59] *Ibid.*, p. 235, 361.
[60] *Ibid.*, p. 362.
[61] *Ibid.*, p. 81.
[62] *Journal*, Sat., June 15, 1777.

regard to every particular object, that it was good.[63] It is necessary for us, therefore, to examine the Wesleyan conception of God's creative act and to view the nature of those works as they stood in the day of divine approval. Wesley tells us that, first of all, God created the matter of the heavens and the earth, the four elements out of which the whole universe was composed: earth, water, air, and fire, all mingled together in a common mass. Into these God infused a principle of motion, commanded the air to move upon the face of the waters, brought light into existence, and gave separate being to these four original and simple elements out of which all compound bodies are made.[64] God, then, adorned the earth with flowers, caused trees and plants to spring forth, and made the land fertile as well as beautiful. He added variety to his work, and we can readily believe that it was for the sake of variety that he created the mountains; and yet these did not furnish obstacles as they do today, with their abrupt sides and their steep slopes which are so difficult of ascent. The earth was in no way deformed by rough and ragged rocks; "it did not shock the view with horrid precipices, huge chasms, or dreary caverns; with deep, impassable morasses, or deserts of barren sand." [65] There was perfect harmony, even in the bowels of the earth, no violent convulsions, no earthquakes, no volcanoes, and no burning mountains.[66] Water was confined to the great abyss, and it is probable that there was no external sea, and certainly there were no putrid lakes or stagnant waters.[67] The element of air was healthful and calm. There were no tempests and no heat waves, only "cool and gentle breezes."

But if inanimate nature was so wonderful and glorious that the ground of the earth was free from any poisonous weeds or useless plants,[68] animate nature was no less splendid; and animals were made to set forth their Creator's praise. To be sure, some creatures possessed less understanding than others and were endowed with fewer senses. The bivalved shellfish, for example, seems to have had no sense but that of feeling, perhaps a small measure of taste. Water creatures in

[63] Sermon LVI, intro. sec. 1.
[64] *Ibid.*, part i, sec. 1.
[65] *Ibid.*, sec. 2.
[66] *Ibid.*, sec. 3.
[67] *Ibid.*, sec. 4.
[68] *Ibid.*, secs. 7-10.

general were the lowest in the scale of animal life, and yet each tended to fulfill his end in creation perfectly, and none attempted to devour or hurt another.[69] Next in the scale of animal life came the insects. None of them had any need or temptation to prey on any other living thing for sustenance. The spider was as "harmless as the fly." Birds came next in the scale, and they were endowed with considerably more understanding than the fish or the reptiles. At the top of the scale—with the exception, of course, of the angels [70]—stood man, and he too was good, perfect after his kind.

Such was the state of the creation, according to the scanty ideas which we can now form concerning it, when its great Author, surveying the whole system at one view, pronounced it "very good." It was good in the highest degree whereof it was capable, and without any mixture of evil. Every part was exactly suited to the others, and conducive to the good of the whole. There was a "golden chain" (to use the expression of Plato) "let down from the throne of God;" an exactly connected series of beings, from the highest to the lowest; from dead earth, through fossils, vegetables, animals, to man, created in the image of God, and designed to know, to love, and enjoy his Creator to all eternity.[71]

Wesley, in his doctrine of creation, draws on the current thought of his day and affirms his belief in the conception of the "great chain of being." God, who by nature is good, communicates his own goodness to all created things. Addison said that if the scale of being rises in a regular progress as high as man, we may by a parity of reason suppose that it continues on through those beings which are superior to man until it reaches God himself.[72] And Soame Jenyns in his *Free Enquiry into the Nature and Origin of Evil* writes that man is but one link in that vast chain descending by insensible degrees from God, who is absolute perfection, to nothing. If we look downward, he reminds us, we see innumerable species of inferior beings, whose happiness and lives are dependent on man's will; we see man "clothed by their spoils, and fed by their miseries and destruction, enslaving some, tormenting

[69] *Ibid.*, sec. 11.
[70] Sermon LXXI, part i.
[71] Sermon LVI, part i, sec. 14.
[72] Addison, *Spectator*, 519.

others, and murdering millions for his luxury and diversion." [73] The lower in the scale of creation, in good Thomistic fashion, serve the higher until all fulfill God's end.

What does this do with evil? How is the problem of physical evil to be explained? Here we note the difference between Wesley's thought and that of most of his contemporaries. Basil Willey tells us that in the eighteenth century the perfections of the universe were taken for granted and the philosopher conceived his task to be merely that of vindicating the existing order of nature against all subversive criticism. The Christian doctrine of the Fall, in which the fact of evil is recognized, was in the mental climate of that century no longer acceptable. The Newtonian world scheme seemed to work perfectly, and scholars felt that all things, even in their present state, were in perfect order. [74] What appears as evil to us is not really evil; in the words of Jenyns, "there is something in the abstract nature of pain conducive to pleasure," and "the sufferings of individuals are absolutely necessary to universal happiness." [75] Basil Willey calls the thought of this period "Cosmic Toryism," the projection of the thought patterns of a particular class on the universe as a whole. Thus the *status quo* represented divine wisdom in expression. The scale of being was conceived to be fixed, incapable of improvement and hence unchangeable. It was thought to be the business of man to content himself with the station, both in the cosmical and social scale, in which he had been placed. [76] In the last analysis, the wisdom and goodness of God in creation were defended on the basis of the existing order of things; and the problem of evil was solved by a flat denial of its existence. Thus Bishop Butler tells us that the natural government of the world is carried on by general laws, and that these laws have for the basis of their establishment wise and good reasons. [77] Our ignorance in the possibilities of things and in all the uses of the functions of nature render us incompetent judges of the works of providence. [78] Evil is used by God for his own inscrutable purposes. Why any hazard or danger should be put upon

[73] S. Jenyns, *Free Enquiry into the Nature and Origin of Evil* (1790 ed.), pp. 71-72.
[74] Willey, *op. cit.*, p. 46.
[75] Jenyns, *op. cit.*, pp. 67, 68.
[76] Willey, *op. cit.*, p. 55.
[77] J. Butler, *op. cit.*, I, 170.
[78] *Ibid.*, p. 175.

such frail creatures as we are may be a difficulty for speculation, but let us confess that we do not comprehend the whole.[79]

> All Nature is but Art, unknown to thee;
> All chance, direction, which thou canst not see;
> All discord, harmony, not understood;
> All partial evil, Universal Good;
>
> . . . .
>
> One truth is clear, Whatever is, is right.[80]

The Wesleyan doctrine is not so optimistic. It admits the existence of physical as well as moral evil in the present state of the universe. How is this to be reconciled with the goodness of God, which Wesley accepts as a matter of religious faith? The answer to this question lies in the fact that Wesleyan thought does not recognize the physical world in its present state as identical in all respects with the world which emerged as the product of the creative act of God. To be sure, the world as God made it was good, with each particular perfect after its kind. Each thing was good inasmuch as it fulfilled its own nature, realized its own end in creation.[81] Wesley shows his familiarity with the thought of Thomas Burnet in his *Sacred Theory of the Earth,* John Ray in his *Wisdom of God in Creation,* and William Derham in his *Physico-Theology, or a Demonstration of the Being and Attributes of God from His Works of Creation.* Indeed, Ray was especially influential on the thought of the time; his work became somewhat of a classic in the eighteenth century, and he has been called "the Aristotle of England and the Linnaeus of his age."[82] His work was published in 1691, and Wesley probably studied it while he was a student at Oxford. But as regards the creative act itself, Wesley depended almost entirely on the *Sacred Theory of the Earth* by Thomas Burnet, for in this work we find the exact pattern which Wesley employed in his own statement of the perfection of God's works in creation. Burnet describes a paradise which existed as a result of the creative act (the description is almost parallel to the Wesleyan) and then, after charg-

---

[79] *Ibid.,* p. 104.
[80] Pope, *Essay on Man,* epistle i, ll. 277-82.
[81] Sermon LVI, intro. sec. 1.
[82] Willey, *op. cit.,* p. 34.

ing his readers not to think this unnatural, he says: " 'Tis we that have left the tract of Nature, that are wrought and screw'd up into artifices, that have disguis'd our selves; and 'tis in our world that the Scenes are chang'd, and become more strange and fantastical." [83] Marks of disorder which characterize the present structure of the universe are not the signs of what it once was as the product of God's hand. Take the sea, for example. If it were drawn around the earth in regular figures and borders, it might be of great beauty and wonder and display the glory of God's hand; but as it is, disordered and disproportioned, we can only conclude that it does not belong to the first order of things, but to something "succedaneous." [84] And Wesley writes that those philosophers who have reason to find fault with God's wisdom and his goodness because of the defects of nature rest their argument on a fundamental mistake. They think that the world is now in the same state that it was in at the beginning. The world in the beginning was in a totally different state from that wherein we now find it. [85] If the common eighteenth-century answer to the problem of evil is that evil as it exemplifies itself in those processes of nature whose author is God is really not evil at all but good misunderstood, the Wesleyan answer is that in the original state of creation physical evil as such did not exist, and that God's work in every particular displayed the power and the goodness of its author. [86]

In conclusion, therefore, we learn from a study of God's revelation of himself as Creator that his sovereign power is the sole source of existence; that all things received their nature and their function and their goal, or end, from the design of God's will; and that, since God's will is absolutely good and his counsel is absolutely perfect, all things as he made them were good. If God is the *Cause* of all things, he is the *End* of all things. Thus, according to the words of the Apostle, " 'Of him, and through him, and to him, are all things!' (Romans xi: 36) *Of him,* as the Creator,—*through him,* as the Sustainer and Preserver, —and *to him,* as the ultimate End of all." [87] In Wesley's writings we

[83] T. Burnet, *Sacred Theory of the Earth*, p. 249.
[84] *Ibid.*, p. 129.
[85] Sermon LVI, part ii, sec. 1.
[86] *Ibid.*, sec. 2.
[87] Sermon LXXVII, part i, sec. 10.

find positive affirmations and explications of the metaphysical attributes of God: his eternity, or his existence which had no beginning and will have no end;[88] his wisdom and his knowledge, by which he appoints the ends of all things and directs the means which are conducive to their realization;[89] his omnipotence, or his power, by which he is able to carry into execution the designs of his will;[90] his omnipresence, which signifies his existence throughout infinite space so that the whole universe is filled with his presence;[91] his omniscience, by which he knows everything that is happening in every corner of his universe at the time of its occurrence;[92] his foreknowledge, by which he knows every future action, not as possibility, but as actuality;[93] and his unity, which expresses the harmony of his nature as well as the oneness of his being so that there is no other God beside him.[94]

The Nature of God in the Light of Providence

But God reveals himself not only as the sovereign Creator of the universe but also as its Governor. Wesley's religion led him to the conviction that God is never absent from the world which he has made and that his hand sustains its process and his power is always available for the needs of his creatures. In a letter to his sister dated January 2, 1781, Wesley writes:

It is a great step towards Christian resignation, to be thoroughly convinced of that great truth, that there is no such thing as chance in the world; that fortune is only another name for Providence. An event, the cause of which does not appear, we commonly say, comes by chance. O no; it is guided by an unerring hand; it is the result of infinite wisdom and goodness.[95]

Divine providence, therefore, applies to all aspects of human existence. Nature, though it is no longer the perfect product of the creative act of God, is none the less under his absolute control, and all its forces

[88] Sermon LIV, sec. 3.
[89] Sermon LXVIII, sec. 1.
[90] Sermon CXIV, sec. 5.
[91] *Ibid.*, sec. 3.
[92] *Ibid.*, sec. 6.
[93] Sermon LVIII, sec. 5.
[94] Sermon CXIV, sec. 1.
[95] *Works*, XII, 484.

are manifestations of the divine will. Thus, in a brief treatise entitled *Serious Thoughts Occasioned by the Late Earthquake at Lisbon,* Wesley says the fact that thousands of houses were destroyed, many more lives were lost, and a fair city was left in "ruinous heaps" indicates an act of God and proves that he is still alive in his universe and that he judges the world.[96] "True philosophy ascribes everything to God."[97] Even the sufferings and afflictions which accompany the life of a particular individual are expressions of his purpose. Wesley reminded his sister, in whose life one "afflictive circumstance" had followed another "in a constant succession" almost from her childhood, that God himself was acting through her trouble in order to teach her patience and obedience and to make her perfect through the things which she suffered.[98] In the present state of the universe God uses evil as well as good in the realization of his ends, and man should praise him in affliction as well as in health and rest always in the confidence that God does all things well.[99]

It is necessary, however, to understand the manner in which God governs the universe, to set forth the operations of divine providence. The heathen have had some conception of it, for Cicero reminds us that all things, all events in this world, are under the management of God.[100] And when the chief of the Paustoobee Indians in North America was asked, "Why do you think the Beloved Ones take care of you?" he replied, "I was in battle with the French; and a bullet went on this side, and a bullet went on that side; and this man died, and that man died; but I am alive still; and by this I know that the Beloved Ones take care of me."[101] But, though men everywhere have expressed some notion of divine providence, only God himself can give a clear, perfect, consistent account of his manner of governing the world; and this account we find in the Bible, which in literal truth is the "history of God."[102] Here we are taught that nothing is so small or insignifi-

[96] *Ibid.,* XI, 1.
[97] *Ibid.,* p. 7.
[98] *Ibid.,* XII, 484.
[99] Sermon LVI, part ii, sec. 3.
[100] Sermon LXVII, sec. 1.
[101] *Journal,* Tues., July 20, 1736.
[102] Sermon LXVII, sec. 4.

cant as not to be the object of God's care,[103] and that everything that is he preserves from moment to moment, else it could not remain in existence.[104] God sees the inmost essence of everything,[105] knows all the properties of the beings that he has made, sees all the connections, dependencies, and relations, and understands all the ways wherein one of them can affect another.[106]

Perhaps what the ancient philosopher speaks of the soul, in regard to its residence in the body, that it is *tota in toto, et tota in qualibet parte,* might, in some sense, be spoken of the omnipresent Spirit, in regard to the universe: That he is not only "All in the whole," but "All in every part." Be this as it may, it cannot be doubted but He sees every atom of his creation, and that a thousand times more clearly than we see the things that are close to us.[107]

But note carefully this point: in the manner of divine providence, though God has sufficient wisdom and power to manage all things well, he cannot deny himself; he cannot contradict his nature; he cannot counteract what he has done or oppose his own work.[108] Wesley, though he recognizes the two aspects of God's character which express themselves as Creator and as Governor, is certain there is no contradiction between them, and that each is in harmony with the other. Therefore, what God has called into existence and has given a nature through the power of his sovereign will must likewise be supported and preserved through the power of his governing providence. God, says Wesley, would like to eradicate sin, to abolish wickedness out of his whole creation, and to suffer no trace of it to remain.[109] But this God cannot do. As a sovereign act of creation he made man in his own image, endowed him with understanding, will, and freedom, or liberty. Therefore, he must respect the creation which he has made. It is a part of man's God-given nature that he is free to disobey his Maker. If God were to exert his power to destroy man's liberty, he

[103] *Ibid.,* sec. 6.
[104] *Ibid.,* sec. 9.
[105] *Ibid.,* sec. 12.
[106] *Ibid.,* sec. 11.
[107] *Ibid.,* sec. 10.
[108] *Ibid.,* sec. 15.
[109] *Ibid.*

171

would at the same time destroy the very quality which makes him man. Without liberty, or freedom, "neither man's understanding nor his affections could have been of any use, neither would he have been capable either of vice or of virtue. He could not be a moral agent any more than a tree or a stone." [110] In the Wesleyan conception, creation as the sovereign act of God has prior claim to providence, or the process of divine government. A thing is what it is: that is to say, it possesses the nature that it has, because of the creative act of God. And God remains always faithful to that which he has created. Thus in his government of the universe he is free to use inanimate objects as he pleases simply because inanimate creation is by nature passive in his hands.[111] The same is true of animal life. The fish of the sea and the beasts of the field possess no liberty. By nature they, too, were created solely to obey. But such is not the case with man. By creation man was made more than just a clod of earth, or a bundle of animal flesh with no sense or understanding.[112] He can oppose God's will and so create numberless irregularities in God's government.[113]

Does this mean that God is limited, that his power is not complete, and that his control over his universe is partial? To an extent it does. God has limited himself in the very act of creation. Before things came into existence God was free to create what he would and to endow all things with the natures he wished them to possess. But once God performed the creative act and called things into existence, he obligated himself to respect the creation which he had made and to remain faithful to the works of his own hand. "Therefore, (with reverence be it spoken,) the Almighty himself cannot do this thing. He cannot thus contradict himself, or undo what he has done. He cannot destroy out of the soul of man that image of himself wherein he made him: And without doing this he cannot abolish sin and pain out of the world." [114] God's government of the universe is absolute in every particular save only in the activity of free men; and God's providence displays itself, not in overriding human freedom, but rather in affording help to man

[110] *Ibid.*
[111] Sermon LXVIII, sec. 4.
[112] Sermon LVII, sec. 1.
[113] Sermon LXVIII, sec. 4.
[114] Sermon LXVII, sec. 15.

and assistance in working out his salvation, so far as such assistance can be given without compulsion, without overruling his liberty. To those who say that God has been dethroned as sovereign by man's freedom, that at best he is but a limited monarch and that, since man possesses genuine liberty, he is free to rebel, Wesley's one reply is that such is the way God has made us; he has foreseen all eventualities and knows in advance all future actualities; his power consists in his ability to deal with the wickedness and folly of men and to counteract all the subtlety of Satan rather than in any act of power which takes away the liberty of men.[115]

In the last analysis, keeping in mind always God's inviolable regard for human freedom, we may say the manner of divine providence is such that God manages all the affairs of his creation for the good of his creatures.[116] Man, of course, holds the highest place in the divine interest, and the inanimate world and the brute creation are subservient to his needs.[117] In regard to man himself, there is a threefold circle of divine providence. The outmost circle includes all the races of men, even those peoples who have never heard the name of Christ. God's love is as free as the air, and his mercies are as diffusive as the beams of sunshine.[118] And yet we must admit that God exercises more particular care over a smaller circle of people, and this circle includes all who are called Christians. God has provided them with the light of his gospel, and in their midst the forces of darkness do not reign in the same sense or degree as they do over the heathen world.[119] The third, or innermost, circle is composed of those people who are genuinely Christian, who love God, fear him, and work righteousness.

Nothing relative to these is too great, nothing too little for His attention. He has his eye continually, as upon every individual person that is a member of this his family, so upon every circumstance that relates either to their souls or bodies; either to their inward or outward state; wherein either their present or eternal happiness is in any degree concerned.[120]

[115] Sermon LXVIII, sec. 4.
[116] Sermon LXVII, sec. 14.
[117] *Ibid.*, sec. 15.
[118] *Ibid.*, sec. 16.
[119] *Ibid.*, sec. 17.
[120] *Ibid.*, sec. 18.

The most precious form of providence is that which supervises and strengthens the lives of the saints.[121]

Wesley affirms particular providence; yes, he goes so far as to say that a providence which is not particular is no providence at all.[122] But does this mean that God deviates from the general laws of the universe in favor of particular persons? Such a concept was totally out of fashion in the eighteenth century, and this Wesley knew.[123] And yet he affirmed it most vigorously, because the Bible taught it.[124] Wesley writes that if it pleases God to continue the life of any of his servants, he will suspend any law of nature for that purpose.[125] Inanimate nature is still under God's direct control, and gravitation shall cease to operate whenever it pleases the Author of it to halt its force.[126] Indeed, general providence has no meaning for Wesley apart from particular providence. He asks the question: Is not every general made up of its several particulars? You can, he says, instance no general that is not. Every whole must be made up of parts; and if there be no parts, there can be no whole.[127] The providence of God furnishes no exception.

The Character of God: Holiness

This brings us finally to a consideration of the Wesleyan conception of God's character, for it is the moral character of God which underlies the government of the universe and which defines the operations of providence. If it is true that Wesley was not a child of the eighteenth century in the sense that he did not hold with his contemporaries that the laws of nature are inexorable and incapable of modification or change, he was none the less in harmony with his age and with all ages in his firm insistence on the inexorability of the moral law and on the unchangeableness of God's nature. The law, Wesley tells us, is

an incorruptible picture of the High and Holy One that inhabiteth eternity. It is He whom, in his essence, no man hath seen or can see, made visible to men and angels. It is the face of God unveiled; God manifested to his

121 *Ibid.*, sec. 19.
122 *Journal*, Fri., July 6, 1781.
123 *Ibid.*
124 Sermon LXVII, sec. 20.
125 *Ibid.*, sec. 21.
126 *Ibid.*, sec. 22.
127 *Ibid.*, sec. 23.

creatures as they are able to bear it; manifested to give, and not to destroy, life,—that they may see God and live. It is the heart of God disclosed to man.[128]

Wesley agrees with his age when he says that moral law is supreme, unchangeable reason, "unalterable rectitude." [129] Thus, as a copy of the eternal mind, or a transcript of the divine nature,[130] it is holy, just, and good.[131] But we ask the question: Is a thing right because God wills it, or does God will it because it is right? What constitutes goodness? Is the will of God the cause of the law, or does the inherent quality of the law furnish the standard by which God's will is guided. Wesley replies that this question is "more curious than useful." It could not be raised if we did not separate God's will from his nature. According to the Wesleyan conception of creative sovereignty, God is the cause of all things, and none can doubt that God is the cause of his own law. If the will of God be the same thing as God himself, then all difficulty vanishes. Nature and will stand together, and divine creativity is that which defines right and that which gives good its meaning.[132] But once God has defined right and once he has made goodness known to his creatures, then he himself abides by that which he has defined and remains loyal to that which he has given. The insistence on the glory of God which dominates the Calvinistic conception of his nature and which holds that salvation and reprobation alike display his majesty and fulfill his end in the creation of the universe, finds no place in Wesleyan theology. In fact, the Wesleyan emphasis, first and last, is on the righteousness and holiness of God. Thus the moral law is the eternal expression of God's character, divine virtue and wisdom assuming a visible form; [133] and man must learn the lesson that without holiness he cannot see God.[134] Justice and love are aspects of God's character,[135] but apart from holiness they have no meaning.

[128] Sermon XXXIV, part ii, sec. 3.
[129] *Ibid.*, sec. 5.
[130] *Ibid.*, sec. 6.
[131] *Ibid.*, part iii, sec. 1.
[132] *Ibid.*, part iii, sec. 7.
[133] *Ibid.*, part ii, sec. 4.
[134] *Works*, X, 558.
[135] *Ibid.*, pp. 233-34.

Chapter VIII

MAN AND SIN

No ACCOUNT OF JUSTIFICATION IS ADEQUATE WHICH DOES NOT TAKE INTO consideration the creature who is justified. If God is the subject of this all-important transaction, so that his holiness is that which underlies the justifying act and gives meaning to pardon and acceptance, then man is the object of the same transaction; and the condition of his nature is that which necessitates pardon and which calls the religious concept of acceptance into being. In this chapter, therefore, we face the Wesleyan conception of man, his nature and his place in the ultimate scheme of things, and the doctrine of sin, which stands as the negative presupposition of pardon and acceptance.

The Significance of Man in the Order of Creation

The eighteenth century was the heir of the scientific movement of the sixteenth and seventeenth centuries; and the work of Copernicus, Kepler, Galileo, Bacon, Harvey, Gilbert, Descartes, Boyle, and Newton had completely destroyed the old Ptolemaic astronomy and introduced an entirely new conception of the universe. The Copernican theory that the earth revolves about the sun had been verified by the telescopes of both Galileo and Kepler. And what is perhaps more significant than all else, theology and philosophy had been forced to reconsider their basic assumptions concerning man. In the old order of things man had been the physical center of creation. All nature had been construed in such a way as to magnify his pre-eminence and to substantiate his claim to supreme importance in the eyes of his Creator. But the new astronomy had obliterated all "the outer evidence of man's focal and privileged situation in the universe." [1] The earth, of which he was the most important inhabitant, was itself only a small part of the solar system, which in turn was a mere aspect of a universe which possessed no bounds. Thus the old order of thought had been dis-

[1] B. A. G. Fuller, *History of Philosophy*, II, 39.

rupted; a new era in philosophy emerged, of which the eighteenth century was an early instance.

Now as regards the position of man, it would appear that eighteenth-century philosophy was confronted with two alternatives. Either it could accept the negative import of the scientific dictum and acknowledge that, since man has ceased to be the central factor in the physical order of the universe, he no longer can be regarded as the crown of life and the soul of existence; or it could give a more positive interpretation to the findings of science and say that, though it must be recognized that man is of infinitesimal size in the system of creation, it need not be denied that he still possesses inestimable value and remains the most splendid object of nature. The former of these alternatives would lead inevitably to the hesitation and uncertainty of skepticism in philosophy, to the indifference and neglect of agnosticism in religion, and to the confusion and hopelessness of pessimism in life. The second of these alternatives would lead to a more positive appraisal of the power of man and the faculties of human understanding. If it is true that human life, in regard to quantity, amounts to very little in comparison with the vast reaches of space and therefore does not count for much in the universe, it is likewise true that human life, in regard to quality, amounts to a great deal, since man's intellect discovered the vastness of space and brought new planets into view, and therefore counts for everything in the scheme of ultimate reality.

The general temper of the eighteenth century was such that it chose the latter of these two alternatives. The mood of the period was decidedly optimistic, and men were not eager to construe the findings of science in such a way as to discredit human nature and to shatter man's confidence in himself. Religion, considered in its more fundamental meaning of the relationship that exists between man and God and implying a divine concern for and interest in humanity, was in no way tampered with. In fact, the great scientist themselves felt that by their discoveries they had rendered as great a service to religion as they had to science.[2] Nature, though more vast and wonderful, is still adapted to man's needs, because God, the Author of both, has ordained the eternal fitness and relation of all things. Men must discover

2 B. Willey, *Eighteenth Century Background*, p. 4.

the harmony that exists between themselves and nature and act accordingly. Evil lies in setting up one's own self-will in opposition to the rational order of things.[3] The Golden Rule itself is a part of nature's pattern, and to disobey it is actually to commit a contradiction.[4]

Shaftesbury, whom we had occasion to notice in our first chapter in connection with deism, sounds the note of triumphant optimism and expresses his supreme confidence in the harmony that exists between man and nature. The fields and woods are called by him a refuge from the world of business and a sanctuary of retreat and thoughtful solitude. This earth is the "chaste Abode of happiest Mortals," and man is made for contemplation and for meditation on the Cause of things.[5] Indeed, nature's wonders serve to excite and perfect man's idea of their Author. As Addison puts it, in nature "[God] suffers us to see, and even converse with, him in a manner suited to our Frailty."[6] Man should not be afraid of the vastness of creation. Rather, the creation should be "a perpetual Feast" to his mind; everything that he sees should cheer and delight him. Providence is still in control of nature, and it is impossible for a mind, unless it be sunk in gross and sensual delights, to take a survey of nature without secret sensations of pleasure. Virtue itself is built around the love of order and beauty. "In the meanest Subjects of the World, the Appearance of Order gains upon the Mind, and draws the Affection towards it."[7] To behold order in the universe should convince man that he is not a stranger to that order but a part of it, and that regularity and system should be given full reign in his life.[8] Thus in eighteenth-century thought man is considered of supreme significance; he is the "sole judge of truth," and if the "jest," none the less the "glory" and "riddle of the world."[9]

John Wesley, however, does more than accept the cosmic optimism of his century.[10] He employs the findings of science, not to establish the

[3] Samuel Clarke, *Demonstration of the Being and Attributes of God*, pp. 256-57.

[4] Samuel Clarke, *Discourse Concerning the Unchangeable Obligations of Natural Religion*, p. 86.

[5] Shaftesbury, *Works*, II, 344-45.

[6] Addison, *Spectator*, 393.

[7] Shaftesbury, *op. cit.*, II, 75.

[8] *Ibid.*

[9] Pope, *Essay on Man*, epistle ii, ll. 17, 18.

[10] Wesley accepts the general import of the scientific discoveries of his day. A reading of Wesley's five-volume work on natural philosophy is sufficient to indicate his knowledge

thesis of natural religion alone and to secure man's importance by
signifying his essential place in the eternal fitness of things, but rather
to call attention to another fact: namely, that man is the peculiar object
of God's fatherly care and love. In doing this Wesley sets man in
contrast to the gigantic forces of nature and then seeks to measure and
appraise his significance, not in terms of any inherent quality he may
possess or of his state and usefulness in the order of creation, but only
in terms of his relationship to his Creator. If medieval philosophy depicts man's significance in the moral and spiritual order also in terms
of his focal and privileged situation in the physical order, and if the
philosophy of the eighteenth century, recognizing the changes which
science has made in the conception of the universe, depicts man's significance in the physical order only in terms of his central place in the
intellectual order, John Wesley depicts man's significance in terms
of his place neither in the physical order nor in the intellectual order
but solely in the spiritual order. Science, therefore, for Wesley, never
becomes an essential bulwark of religion; rather, it stands as an interesting comment on the observations of God's work in nature and may
be profitably employed to serve religious ends. Man's significance in
the universe cannot be established by what science shows him to be,
but science may be used to amplify and to vivify the real cause of man's
significance and to show more clearly, in the light of the whole created
process, man's peculiar station and his privileged position in the
providence of God.

Wesley begins his discussion of man's place in the order of nature
by asking: What is man with regard to his size, or his magnitude?
One person amounts to very little in comparison with the inhabitants
of Great Britain alone,[11] and he is indeed nothing when the peoples

---

of the discoveries of science and his interest in them. This work is largely made up of
excerpts from the natural philosophers and scientists themselves, and very little of it
represents Wesley's own work. Of course, the observations and deductions are his. Volume IV, on the properties which are common to all bodies, represents Wesley's philo-
sophic and scientific ability at its best; there is some sign of ability and understanding in
a man's being able to pick and choose and arrange in an orderly fashion relevant material. This Wesley does admirably. See *Survey of the Wisdom of God in the Creation,*
Vol. IV. See these additional references for his favorable comments on the scientific de-
velopments of his day: *Works,* X, 483, 492; *Survey of the Wisdom of God in the Creation,* IV, 332-33.
[11] Sermon CIII, part i, sec. 1.

of the whole earth are taken into account. The earth itself is very small when we consider "that vast body, the sun, so immensely larger than the earth," and the whole list of planets, several of the smaller of which—for example, the satellites or moons of Jupiter and Saturn—are a great deal larger than the entire earth.[12] And yet the whole quantity of matter contained in the sun and all the planets which revolve around the sun is of little consequence in comparison with that which goes to compose "those amazing bodies, the comets." Only the Creator himself can tell the number of the comets, describe their composition, and "call them by their names." The comets themselves, however, are not to be compared in magnitude to the fixed stars, "which are so immense a distance from the earth, that they appear when they are viewed through the largest telescope, just as they do to the naked eye." [13] Wesley says that no one can say whether or not the creation extends beyond the region of the fixed stars. All we know is that the creation is finite, for God says he set bounds to it; but we cannot say how vast it is or how far those bounds extend.[14] Even more, we cannot conceive of how small all finite space, all the reaches of all the solar systems, all the vast extent of the universe, is in comparison with the infinite. It cannot be more than a "point, a cipher," compared to that infinite space which is filled by God, who is All in all.[15] Man, seen in the light of his position in such a universe, is not much. We cannot say that he counts for anything in regard to his magnitude in this vast scheme of creation.

What is man in regard to his duration? The size of an object does not count for everything; it is important to know how long it can last. Since the time of Moses, so Wesley tells us, the extent of a man's life, if it reaches the divine standard of fulfillment, is threescore years and ten and, if the man is unusually strong, perhaps fourscore years.[16] And this is a poor pittance of duration in comparison with the length of the lives of those men of old, the first among the sons of God on the face of the earth. Methuselah, who lived the longest of any of the

[12] *Ibid.*, sec. 3.
[13] *Ibid.*, sec. 4.
[14] *Ibid.*, sec. 5.
[15] *Ibid.*, sec. 7.
[16] *Ibid.*, part ii, sec. 1.

human family, lived nine hundred and sixty-nine years. And yet the length of the life of Methuselah is nothing in comparison with that of an angel, whose life began before ever the mountains were brought forth or the foundations of the earth were laid. The length of the life of an angel, however, must be set in a larger frame, for one must consider the time which elapsed before the angels themselves were made. The time which has passed since their creation is in comparison with that which went before no more than a single grain of sand in comparison with all the sands on all the shores of all the seas.[17]

Indeed, it is impossible to consider in any terms of proportion the difference between finite and infinite duration.[18] Time is characterized by bounds or limits; eternity is boundless duration.[19] Though eternity has generally been thought to be divisible into two parts, which have been designated by the terms "eternity *a parte ante*" and "eternity *a parte post*," or eternity which is past and eternity which is future, these terms must not be allowed to confuse our understanding of the true meaning of eternity or cause us to raise the metaphysical question as to how endless duration can have a past. The terms are merely for the sake of convenience; and all we mean by "eternity *a parte ante*" is duration which had no beginning, and by "eternity *a parte post*," duration which will have no end.[20] Past and future, therefore, are applicable to eternity only as we see and conceive it from a particular point in history. Time, since it is co-existent with the beginning of the world, is but a fragment of eternity—that portion of duration broken off at both ends. If it began with the commencement of the world, then it will continue as long as the world continues; and when the world comes to an end, it will expire forever.[21] Thus a period of a thousand years or ten thousand years or ten thousand times ten thousand years can have no meaning whatever in the light of eternity. The inexpressible disproportion between any conceivable part of time and eternity can, in Wesley's mind, be illustrated in no more striking way than the manner in which St. Cyprian expressed it:

[17] *Ibid.*, sec. 2.
[18] *Ibid.*, sec. 3.
[19] Sermon LIV, sec. 1.
[20] *Ibid.*, sec. 2.
[21] *Ibid.*, sec. 4.

Suppose there was a ball of sand as large as the globe of earth, and suppose one grain of this were to be annihilated in a thousand years; yet that whole space of time wherein this ball would be annihilating, at the rate of one grain in a thousand years, would bear less, yea, unspeakably, infinitely less, proportion to eternity, than a single grain of sand would bear to that whole mass." [22]

Having acquainted ourselves with the facts of man's size and his duration, it is no wonder that we men should feel a kind of fear concerning our status in the universe. Why should the Divine Mechanic regard so insignificant and diminutive a creature as man? Such fear rises as the natural consequence of a knowledge of the facts of nature. Though we see in nature the wonders of its Creator's power and wisdom, we find there, also, every reason to doubt our own significance and value. Here Wesley, in contradistinction to the general thought of his age, recognizes the negative import of the scientific dictum and acknowledges the possibility that man may, in comparison with all the other works of nature, be classed among the most miserable.[23] In the recognition of this possibility Wesley anticipates the pessimism of a later age: the world of nature as such may not always be favorable to man's ends; man's aims and ends themselves may count for less than nothing in the total scheme of things. But then Wesley avoids the consequences of that pessimism by recognizing that the cause of man's significance does not rest on any of the proved data of science. All doubt, worry, and fear are eradicated when we consider "what manner of regard the great eternal God bears to little, short-lived man." [24]

The assurance of the reality of that regard, like the knowledge of the existence and the character of God, comes through religious insight alone. Scientific thought, when confronted with the love of God for man, must raise the question: If God so loved the world, did he not love a thousand other worlds as much as he did this; and did he not care for the inhabitants of other planets as much as he did for those who live on the face of the earth? [25] But the love of God for man does not lie within the province of science, and man's significance does

---

[22] Sermon CIII, part ii, sec. 3.
[23] *Ibid.*, sec. 5.
[24] *Ibid.*, sec. 7.
[25] *Ibid.*, sec. 8.

not rest on its data. "Have done, then, with this childish prattle," says Wesley.[26] Suffice it to know this plain, simple, and comfortable truth that the Almighty God has shown such regard for this "poor little creature of a day" that he has given unto him knowledge of his truth and the right to live with him forever.[27] The sole cause of man's significance in the universe is the creative will of God; and the reasons do not appear to us, for they are hidden in the abyss of his infinite wisdom.[28]

The Nature of Man

It is not enough, however, for us to consider man's external status in the universe, his relationship to the other objects of creation. We must go on to consider the composition of man's nature, what he is in himself. It is important to remember that in Wesley's day biology had discovered no discrediting ancestry for the human family, and man had not been subjected to the scathing examinations of anthropology and psychoanalysis.[29] Thus Wesley says that the human machine, curious and strange, is, none the less, "fearfully and wonderfully made." It is a small piece of earth, the individual parts of which cohere and lengthen into innumerable fibers, which cross each other in all directions and which are strangely wrought into what are called membranes, which in turn are wrought into arteries, veins, nerves, and glands. All of these are filled with various fluids, which constantly circulate through the entire human body.[30] The body takes in through its lungs quantities of air, water, and fire. The fire is separated from the air and water and is taken up into the blood, while the air and water are continually being thrown out.[31] Without the fire, which Wesley calls the vital element, there could be no circulation of the blood, consequently no motion of the fluids, and no sensation or muscular action of any kind. The heart, which is generally thought to be cause for the

[26] *Ibid.*, sec. 13.
[27] *Ibid.*, sec. 14.
[28] *Ibid.*, sec. 8.
[29] Willey, *Eighteenth Century Background*, p. 5.
[30] Sermon CIX, sec. 1. It is not possible here to consider in detail the Wesleyan treatment of the four basic elements, which serve as the composition of all things. Earth and water are treated in Vol. III of *Survey of Wisdom of God in Creation*, pp. 3-96; air and fire are treated, pp. 99-186. The detailed treatment of the nature of man is considered in Vol. I of the same work. The parts of the body are treated, pp. 25-104.
[31] Sermon CIX, sec. 2.

circulation of the blood, is, Wesley tells us, altogether inadequate. Why, the force of the heart in a strong man cannot be more than equal to the weight of three thousand pounds, whereas it would take a force equal to the weight of a hundred thousand pounds to cause the blood to circulate from the heart through all the arteries. The real cause of circulation must be the ethereal fire.[32]

Apart, however, from man's physical body Wesley finds something of a quite different nature. He tells us that he finds in himself, for example, something that thinks. Earth, air, water, and fire, which make up the body, cannot think. But this something which he knows he possesses is able to feel, taste, smell, see, and hear. Then, having perceived objects through the senses, it forms inward ideas of them, judges concerning them, sees whether they agree or disagree with one another, and so reasons about them and infers one rational proposition from another. It reflects on its own operations, and may be said to possess imagination and memory.[33] This faculty of thought seems to be situated in some part of the head.[34] It is capable not only of thought but also of love, hatred, joy, sorrow, desire, fear, hope, and the "whole train of other inward emotions, which are commonly called passions or affections." These passions, or affections, are governed by the will, which is itself the only spring of action in that inward principle we call the soul.[35]

What, we ask of Wesley, is the soul? He tells us that he cannot say that the soul is a material substance—that it is water, earth, fire, or air, or a composition of all of these elements put together. He cannot say this for the simple reason that all these, whether separate or compounded in any possible way, are always passive. No one of these elements can move itself; but man's soul has an inward principle of motion, whereby it governs at pleasure every part of the body.[36] Of course, certain vital motions of the body, such as the pulsation of the arteries

[32] *Ibid.*, sec. 4. See also *Survey of Wisdom of God in Creation*, pp. 132-53. Wesley's views on nature and man are taken from such works as Ray's *Wisdom of God in Creation*, Derham's *Physico- and Astro-Theology*, Niewentyt's *Religious Philosopher*, Mather's *Christian Philosopher* and *Nature Delineated*, and Bonnet's *Contemplation de la Nature*. See also F. W. Collier, *John Wesley Among the Scientists*, pp. 75-92.

[33] Sermon CIX, sec. 5.

[34] *Ibid.*, sec. 6.

[35] *Ibid.*, sec. 7.

[36] *Ibid.*, sec. 8.

and the circulation of the blood, are involuntary; and yet we must recognize that a man might kill himself by suspending the motion of his heart or his lungs, or "he might lose his life by mere inattention,—by not remembering, not adverting to" the fulfillment of ordinary bodily functions. But the point is that something besides the body directs the body; and man by a single act of will puts his head, his eyes, his hands, or any part of his body into motion.[37] Thus Wesley reminds us that unquestionably man is something distinct from his body. When the body dies, he does not die; and this self-moving, thinking principle, with all its passions and affections, continues to exist after the body has decayed and "mouldered into dust."[38] Together with thought and will, we are conscious of another distinct property of the soul. That property is freedom, the power of self-determination, which is capable of being exerted with regard to all the faculties of the soul as well as all the movements of the body.[39]

Such, in brief, is the Wesleyan conception of the nature of man.

The Fact of Sin

Now we must ask the question: What is man's moral and spiritual status? Is man by nature wise, good, obedient, and loving; or is he a fallen creature and, therefore, foolish, sinful, and disobedient? Wesley reminds us that it is not enough to offer a theological explanation of original sin. Before attempting to account for any fact, one should make sure of the fact itself.[40] What, for example, was the moral condition of mankind prior to the flood? Not only had moral evil soiled and polluted the works of man's hands, but the contagion had spread itself through man's entire nature and had tainted the very seat of his principles and the foundation of his actions. Indeed, there was no mixture of good anywhere in all this evil. Everything was corrupt and wicked, and the little leaven of piety found perhaps in the single person of Noah was not sufficient to leaven the whole lump. The universality of this wickedness is manifested by the universality of the punishment; God was sorry he had made man, and he sent a flood to

[37] *Ibid.*, sec. 9.
[38] *Ibid.*, sec. 10.
[39] *Ibid.*, sec. 11.
[40] *Works*, IX, 196.

cover the face of the earth.[41] And yet the flood did not destroy wickedness entirely, nor inaugurate a new order of righteousness and good will. We have no record of any universal repentance from the time of the flood to the call of Abraham out of the land of Ur of the Chaldees. And even at the time of this call we find no reason to believe that the majority of mankind was in any way improved in wisdom and virtue; for Lot, Abraham's nephew, because of greed separated himself from his uncle and pitched his tent toward Sodom.[42] The whole history of Israel, from the journey into Egypt, the slavery under Pharaoh, the flight out of bondage and the passage through the Red Sea on dry land, across the forty years of wandering in the wilderness and entrance into the Promised Land, down to the period of exile, is one sad story of human faithlessness in contrast to divine faithfulness, of man's pride and self-will in opposition to God's mercy.[43] Where were knowledge and virtue, even among God's chosen? Why, the men of Israel were like whited sepulchers, outwardly beautiful in their performance of religious rites and in their keeping of solemn assemblies, but inwardly vile, contemptible, unclean—worthy to be compared to dead men's bones. It was they who murdered the Just One and set at nought the work of the very God they pretended to obey.[44]

One can find no relief from the predominant fact of sin by turning to the history of the Gentiles. If the Hebrews destroyed the children of their enemies, the Romans destroyed their own children at pleasure; [45] if Israel bore her thousands of sins, then the heathen world bore its tens of thousands. Cato the Elder did not know the meaning of the word mercy. When any of his servants grew old and decrepit, he turned them out to starve; and his countrymen applauded him for his frugality.[46] Pompey rose to greatness through the villainy of Perpenna and the treachery of Pharnaces. And even the great Caesar, who fought for life rather than for glory, tortured men to death.[47]

The facts of contemporary life but repeat history's story. The heathen

[41] *Ibid.*, p. 197.
[42] *Ibid.*, p. 198.
[43] *Ibid.*, pp. 199-202.
[44] *Ibid.*, p. 202.
[45] *Ibid.*, p. 206.
[46] *Ibid.*, pp. 206-7.
[47] *Ibid.*, p. 208.

world has no real conception of God. If it possesses any notion of him at all, that notion is not worthy of recognition; for it makes God to be no different from men and no better than the creatures whom he has made. And what are the social virtues of the heathen races? These people are not "eminent for justice, for mercy, or truth." Why, when they are angry, they attempt to cut the throat of their adversary; they sell their captives into slavery; they tell lies, always "cozening, cheating, and over-reaching every man that believes a word they say." [48] Wesley's observations on the sin of the heathen are taken largely from the facts of his own experience in Georgia among the American redskins. [49] But he goes on to substantiate these observations by a survey of the wisdom and virtue of all the peoples of the earth. The heathen of Russia are shockingly savage, and those within the borders of Lapland are, if anything, worse. [50] The world of Islam is a state of confusion and animosity. The people observe a sacred book called the *Koran,* which is filled with the most ridiculous absurdities. And yet the adherents of Islam not only condemn all who cannot accept the teachings of the *Koran* to everlasting fire; they even anathematize, "with the utmost bitterness, and adjudge to eternal destruction," all the sect of Hali, an offshoot of Islam, which sect gives a figurative interpretation to the *Koran.* There is no genuine love of God in Islam, for the Mussulmen seek to convert men by the sword and are willing to murder rather than to tolerate any divergence of opinion. [51] But what, we ask, is one to say about the Chinese? These people have been described as men of deep and penetrating wisdom, high learning, and strict integrity. They have honored the scholar, while the soldier they have not even treated with respect. Wesley answers that it is hard to know exactly how virtuous the Chinese really are. They live so many thousand miles away that, if it were affirmed "every Chinese had literally three eyes, it would be difficult for us to disprove it." And yet they appear rather stupid in maintaining an alphabet of thirty thousand letters. It is certainly not consistent with common sense for them to cripple all the women of their empire by "a silly, senseless, affectation of squeezing their feet

[48] *Ibid.,* p. 210.
[49] *Ibid.,* pp. 211-12.
[50] *Ibid.,* p. 215.
[51] *Ibid.,* p. 216.

till they bear no proportion to their bodies." [52] The aristocrat of the land, the mandarin, will not deign to employ his hands in eating but has his food put into his mouth by his servant. The Chinese cannot be very intelligent, for they were astonished at the French Jesuits and honored them far beyond the deserts of any human being merely because the Jesuits could calculate eclipses. But more important than these instances in regard to their general knowledge, in religion they have no more conception of God than the Hottentots, for they worship the souls of their departed ancestors. They do not possess the moral virtues with which they are accredited. They are lazy, full of pride and arrogance; and they rob, defraud, and oppress at will. These people are by nature fawning and artificially polite, which qualities label them among the worst of hypocrites. Such, says Wesley, is the picture of the noblest and best of all the heathen. [53]

Now let us turn to the Christian world and examine the virtues of the people who reside within that city set on a hill, the light of which is supposed to shine forth unto all mankind. Christendom is divided into disputant factions and presents to the outside world a state of disorder and confusion. The gross and barbarous ignorance of the Greek Church is matched by the blind and bitter zeal of Rome. [54] Did not conscience in the past century move good Catholics to murder Protestants? [55] What can we say for Spanish greed in North America? And yet the Protestant world is no haven of justice and truth. Men in these lands fight and kill one another. There is war in the world, yea, among Christians. "Now, who can reconcile war, I will not say to religion, but to any degree of common sense?" [56] Look at our Protestant and Catholic virtues alike; we still have our pickpocket, our gamester, our politician, our traitor, and our murderer. [57] Look at our sailors, so wicked that the ships on which they sail are styled "floating hell." [58] All classes of society within the folds of the Christian world bear the marks

[52] Ibid., p. 213.
[53] Ibid., pp. 214-15.
[54] Ibid., p. 217.
[55] Ibid., p. 218.
[56] Ibid., p. 221.
[57] Ibid., p. 223.
[58] Ibid., p. 226.

of pride, greed, and corruption: the officers in charge of excise and custom,[59] government officials in high places, attorneys employed to thwart rather than to promote justice,[60] the nobility and rich of the land,[61] the housewives, children, and servants,[62] the farmholders and tenants,[63] and even the ministers of the Church, those very men whom the providence of God has called apart to be the guides of others.[64] From the consideration of the empirical data of past and present history, this is "the plain, glaring, apparent condition of human kind:" man is the victim of sin.[65] To deny this fact is impossible. "A man may as modestly deny, that spring and summer, autumn and winter, succeed each other, as deny one article of the ensuing account of the moral world:" namely, that a flood of general wickedness engulfs all mankind; that virtue and truth are not to be found in unregenerate human nature; that fraud and wrong, deceit and violence, the dire thirst for gold, the lust to possess, and the rage to have and to hold and to command are the natural marks or dispositions of the children of men.[66]

Not only do we behold the empirical fact of the universality of wickedness and the absence of moral rectitude and understanding, but we see misery and suffering in the world. Now, says Wesley, universal misery is at once a consequence and a proof of universal corruption. "Men are unhappy because they are unholy," for it is impossible because of the very nature of things that wickedness and happiness can exist in harmony with one another. Thus Wesley calls attention to the fact that an old Roman heathen has observed a truth worthy of the attention of the heathen of the modern world: *Nemo malus felix,* "No vicious man is happy." [67] Men need not be guilty of any gross outward vice in order to be unhappy; as long as vicious tempers have power to reign in their hearts and to make them proud, passionate, angry without reason, desiring always to have their own way in all matters in

[59] *Ibid.,* p. 227.
[60] *Ibid.,* pp. 228-29.
[61] *Ibid.,* p. 229.
[62] *Ibid.,* p. 232.
[63] *Ibid.,* p. 233.
[64] *Ibid.,* p. 230.
[65] *Ibid.,* p. 234.
[66] *Ibid.,* pp. 234-35.
[67] *Ibid.,* p. 235.

which they are concerned, then peace can find no place within them and they are driven like leaves before the angry winds of their own dispositions or like small particles in the midst of a storm. At times they think they could fare very well in life if they were not hindered by some outside factor—if, for example, they were not tormented by the unreasonableness of some wife or husband, upset by the obstinacy or disobedience of a child, or intimidated and harassed by parents with no sympathy and no understanding. If it were not for the wounds of a biting tongue, the provoking manner of a haughty disposition, or the deceit and treachery of a dishonest character, they are sure they could be happy. And they would be right, says Wesley, provided both they themselves and all other men were wise and virtuous. Unhappiness, sorrow, pain, evil of all kinds, are due to sin alone.

Look out of your own doors: "Is there any evil in the city, and" sin "hath not done it?" Is there any misfortune or misery to be named, whereof it is not either the direct or remote occasion? Why is it that the friend or relation for whom you are so tenderly concerned is involved in so many troubles? Have you not done your part toward making them happy? Yes, but they will not do their own: One has no management, no frugality, and no industry; another is too fond of pleasure. If he is not scandalously vicious, he loves wine, women, gaming. And to what does all this amount? He might be happy; but sin will not suffer it.[68]

Perhaps a man suffers when it is not his fault. He falls into the hands of those who mistreat him. This is perfectly true, says Wesley; it is not his own sin which abuses him, but the sin of another. And yet sin itself is the cause of his misfortune.[69] Note this as an axiom: sin, and sin alone, is the "baleful source of all affliction" and the cause of all the miseries which cover the face of the earth, and which not only overwhelm individuals but also engulf and destroy families, cities, and kingdoms, and are "a demonstrative proof of ungodliness in every nation under heaven."[70] Moral evil is always, without exception, the cause of natural evil.[71]

[68] *Ibid.*, p. 236.
[69] *Ibid.*, p. 237.
[70] *Ibid.*, p. 238.
[71] *Ibid.*, p. 332.

The Origin of Sin

The fact of sin is apparent, and the universality of its operation and control is indubitably manifested in the character and behavior of men. But after having recognized the empirical fact of sin, it is necessary to account for it. In November of the year 1756 John Wesley wrote the preface to his treatise on the *Doctrine of Original Sin,* which, not excepting the famous *Plain Account of Christian Perfection,* is the longest single composition included in the fourteen volumes of his *Works.*[72] In the preface Wesley tells us that a few years prior to 1756 he read a treatise by Dr. John Taylor entitled *The Doctrine of Original Sin.*[73] That treatise represents a revival of Pelagianism in eighteenth-century England, and Wesley declares that this old heresy was spreading like poison throughout the universities, the nation, and the Church. One bishop of the land, in recommending Taylor's work, said that he knew of no book more suitable than it to settle the thoughts and principles of young clergymen. Sin is accounted for on the basis of custom; men are by nature inclined to follow custom rather than reason. Now Wesley does not deny this fact, but he says that custom as an explanation of the prevalence of sin does not go far enough. How are we to account for custom itself? How is it, seeing that men are by nature rational creatures and that virtue is more agreeable to rationality than vice, that the custom of all men in all countries and in all ages is on the side of vice rather than virtue? If the answer is given that custom is on the side of vice simply because of a universal process of bad education, this offers no real explanation; for we are then left to account for the origin and perpetuation of bad education itself. When did this bad education first begin to prevail? How was it that wise and good men, for such they must have been before bad education became predominant, failed to train up their children in the same wisdom and goodness in which they themselves were

---

[72] The *Survey of the Wisdom of God in Creation* is Wesley's longest work, though, as we have seen, it is a compilation of material by other authors. His *Notes on the New Testament* and his *Notes on the Old Testament* come next in length among his publications. These three publications are not included in the fourteen volumes of his collected works.

[73] *Works,* IX, 192.

reared? [74] Now it follows as a matter of common sense that the first parents who educated their children in folly and vice either were themselves wise and virtuous or were not. If they were wise and virtuous, then it is impossible to account for the origin of the process of bad education. If they were not wise and virtuous, then their own vice did not proceed from bad education but was itself antecedent to it. In either case bad education offers no satisfying explanation of the cause of wickedness. Why is it that in so long a period of time no single nation on earth has been able by a process of good education to eradicate what bad education is said to have done and so to produce a generation of wise and good men? [75] The cause of evil is more deep-seated and basic. It lies within human nature itself, and we must turn to the scriptural account of the fall of man for its real explanation.

Though man himself was the cause of all the evil in the world, both moral and physical, he was not able to understand what he had caused until it pleased God to reveal it to him. Until God's revelation, man was a "mere enigma to himself." [76] Wesley carries us back to the Garden of Eden and to the sin of our first parents. God had told Adam and Eve that they might eat of the fruit of the garden; but of the fruit of the tree in the midst of the garden God had told them they should not eat lest they die. Eve was tempted by the serpent, who told her that she would not die if she ate of the fruit, that God knew that in the day she ate thereof she would know the difference between good and evil and would be as he. She succumbed to the temptation of the serpent and ate the forbidden fruit. So, says Wesley, sin in its beginning was unbelief and rebellion. Our first parents sinned in their hearts before they were openly disobedient. "They gave more credit to the word of the devil, than to the word of God." They sought their own desire and satisfaction above obedience to the commands of their Maker. Sin, for them, was inward idolatry; they loved the creature more than the Creator.[77]

[74] *Ibid.*, p. 238.
[75] *Ibid.*, p. 239.
[76] Sermon LVII, intro. sec. 2.
[77] *Ibid.*, part i, sec. 1.

192

MAN AND SIN

The Nature of Sin

The nature of sin, therefore, in Wesleyan thought is the same as it is in the thought of Augustine, Luther, and Calvin. It is spiritual pride, that which causes a man to set up idols in his own heart, to bow down to them and worship them, to love himself more than he loves God, and to pay honor unto himself, honor which is due to God alone. "And although pride was not made for man, yet where is the man that is born without it? But hereby we rob God of his unalienable right, and idolatrously usurp his glory." [78] This pride leads man to seek happiness in the creature rather than in the Creator, to turn for satisfaction away from God to the finite. It is in the fixation of man on the finite that sensual appetites of the lowest kind begin to rise to claim dominion over him. These lead him captive "and drag him to and fro, in spite of his boasted reason." [79] The sins of the flesh are the children, not the parents, of pride; and self-love is the root, not the branch, of all evil. Adam was not deceived: he chose to accept the forbidden fruit at Eve's hand and to assert his own will above the will of God. He it was who instigated man's revolt against his Maker. [80]

Why did Adam himself sin? What was there in his nature which prompted him to disobedience and to the open violation of the commands of God? If the nature of sin be conceived as pride, self-love, idolatry, then its source must lie in something other than an act, a deed, or a specific instance of conduct. It must be rooted in character, in that which is fundamental to conduct and which prompts activity and gives action its meaning. Pride as sin is prior to the deed which is its expression. Idolatry is conceived in the heart before open revolt is instigated with the hand. Adam's sin had its origin in the very heart of his being. But, according to Wesley, Adam was created righteous. [81] How, therefore, are we to account for the first sin, or to give any sort of rational explanation of the origin of moral evil? If bad education, according to Wesley, cannot be accounted for apart from the folly and wickedness of its first instigators, how, then, can Adam's disobedience

[78] Sermon XLIV, part ii, sec. 7.
[79] *Ibid.*, sec. 9.
[80] Sermon LVII, part i, sec. 1.
[81] *Works*, IX, 291.

be accounted for apart from an evil nature which both suggested and effected it? Taylor in his work on *Original Sin* has avoided the difficulty of such an explanation by conceiving of sin in terms of specific deeds which, when repeated, develop habits and so influence a man's disposition for better or for worse and in the end give him what character he comes to possess. Holiness likewise must be developed by a man's specific choices and acts. So, according to Taylor, Adam was created neither in a state of original righteousness nor in a state of original evil but in a neutral state, from which he could go on to develop habits of holiness or of wickedness as his free choice directed.[82] Wesley repudiates this view because he holds that practice is merely the expression of something that is more fundamental, and that a man does what is right because of what he himself is. A man must be "righteous before he does what is right: holy in heart before he is holy in life."[83] Righteousness is never the right use and application of a man's powers, as the Pelagians maintain: rather, righteousness is the right "disposition of the soul" and the "right temper" of the mind.[84] Original righteousness, or moral rectitude, was the state in which Adam was created; he loved his Creator supremely;[85] if he had not been made so to love his Creator, but had been created in a state of mere indifference, then his being put in union with flesh and blood and set among a thousand temptations would have itself constituted an overbalance on the side of vice rather than virtue.[86]

But why did Adam sin? Was there not some flaw in his nature which prompted him to pride and pushed him to revolt and idolatry? This Wesley will not admit, for to do so would call into question the power and the goodness of the Creator. All Wesley says is that it pleased God to give Adam absolute freedom of choice, a principle of liberty which separated him from all the other works of creation.[87] Then God put him "upon a trial of his obedience for a season."[88] In this trial Adam failed; he chose the gratification of self-will to divine

[82] Taylor, *Doctrine of Original Sin*, p. 180.
[83] *Works*, IX, 292.
[84] *Ibid.*, p. 293.
[85] *Ibid.*, p. 345.
[86] *Ibid.*, p. 346.
[87] Sermon LVII, intro. sec. 1.
[88] *Works*, IX, 378.

194

obedience. It must be admitted that Wesley gives no adequate explanation of the origin of the first sin: he does not show how a righteous
nature can itself generate unrighteousness, or how that which was
made good and upright can convert itself into evil. But he does affirm
that sin arose as the creative and independent act of man's own nature,
that it emerged as the result of free choice, and that God cannot be
blamed with its existence. If John Calvin, in an effort to guard the
sovereign glory of God, goes so far as to say that God himself planned
and instigated the entrance of sin into the world,[89] then John Wesley,
in an effort to assert human responsibility and freedom, goes to the
other extreme to say that man himself was the sole cause of sin and
the only reason for the emergence of evil in the world. Wesley tells us
that many have written philosophical treatises on the origin of evil;
one man says that it arose from matter, which God himself was not
able to alter. Well, it is very kind of men to "try to make an excuse
for God!" There is really no occasion for it; they had best seek an excuse for themselves. The cause of sin lies at man's own door.[90]

The Result of Sin

The immediate result of the fall of Adam was that pain entered the
world. When the first man lost his innocence, he at the same time lost
his happiness. He had been created to love God, and the source of his
happiness lay in the harmonious unity which existed between his own
righteous will and God's absolute holiness. But now that unity was
broken; by a single act of self-will he chose the finite in preference to
the infinite; he lifted his own humanity out of its natural setting of
humility and obedience and gave it the place of authority and command which belonged by right only unto God. Fear cast its ugly
shadow for the first time across his life.[91] The sense of guilt, like some
horrible sickness, crept over him and took possession of his soul: if his
life at creation had been glorious and wonderful in its innocence, it
now became banal and coarse in its corruption. If he had been made
for Paradise and had been set in the midst of a luxurious garden, he
was now fit only for a habitation upon the uncultivated earth, among

[89] Calvin, *Institutes*, III, xxiii, 5, 8. Cf. *Ibid.*, I, xviii, 4.
[90] Sermon LIX, sec. 15.
[91] Sermon LVII, part i, sec. 2.

the thorns and the thistles, where he would have to earn his bread by the sweat of his face.[92] But not only was the center of his spiritual life altered so that the good things which he had once loved and the noble purposes which he had once cherished ceased to have any attraction for him or to wield any influence over him; the entire physical constitution of his life was also changed, and the hideous stain of moral sin made itself apparent in bodily weakness and deformity. Man by creation, Wesley tells us, was perfectly formed, so that the four elements of earth, water, air, and fire were mingled together in the most exact proportion and no one of them predominated over the others in the least degree.[93] After man sinned, however, the element of earth assumed predominance over the other elements of his body; and he became in literal truth "mortal, corruptible dust." This mortal and weak body began to become a burden to him, to press down upon his soul, and to hinder it in its operations and functions. Mistake as well as ignorance became the common property of the intellect, and the mind felt its dependence on the mortal body in which it was housed.[94] More than all this, however, death was added as the curse of sin. God said unto man: "And unto dust thou shalt return." [95] Yes, and no matter what skill we may have achieved in the art of healing, no matter what success science may have won,[96] it has not been possible to heal the sickness of old age or to halt the march of time in its sure and certain course to the grave.[97] Death stands as the consummate penalty of sin, the uncertain end of man's pilgrimage through this vale of tears.

The Wesleyan conception of the physical consequences of the fall of Adam does not stop with the pain and sorrow which afflict the human race. It goes on to consider the state of the animals and of those orders of life which lie beneath the human level in the scale of existence. We have seen already in our discussion in the last chapter that all nature was, as a result of the creative act of God, good and perfect. Just as Adam in his state of innocence was impassive, incapable of

[92] *Ibid.*, sec. 4.
[93] *Ibid.*, part ii, sec. 1.
[94] *Ibid.*, sec. 2.
[95] *Ibid.*, sec. 3.
[96] *Ibid.*, sec. 4.
[97] *Ibid.*, sec. 5.

suffering, pure in joy, and by nature immortal,[98] so all other living creatures were endowed with the principle of self-motion, a degree of understanding, partial self-direction, absolute happiness, and immortality.[99] In fact, the brute creation differed from man himself in only one instance. Whereas man was created for communion and fellowship with God, the brute creation was not.[100] Man, as the favorite of the Almighty, was given dominion over the brutes, to be the vicegerent of God on earth, through whom the blessings of God flowed to the inferior creatures. "Man," writes Wesley, "was the channel of conveyance between the Creator and the whole brute creation." [101] But as man in the creative chain of being was the great channel of communication between God and the lower orders, it followed, when man sinned and became by his own free act incapable of receiving, much less of transmitting, those divine blessings, that the communication between God and the lower orders of creation was cut off; and the animals were denied those divine blessings which they had been created to receive. Thus every creature was subjected to pain and evil, not by the free choice of its own nature, but by man's sinful act, which God permitted and allowed so to affect his world.[102]

What, we ask, did the lesser creatures suffer when man rebelled against God? Wesley answers that it is probable that they sustained much loss in their physical faculties—in their ability to run, to endure, and to exercise to the fullest their natural vigor and strength. But they unquestionably suffered much more in their understanding, in their will and passion, and in their natural inclination to obey and serve man. Just as man's perfection lay in his loving obedience to God, so the perfection of the brute world lay in its loving obedience to man. After the Fall the brutes were no longer able to trust man. They "studiously avoided his hated presence." [103] Savage fierceness, unrelenting cruelty, took possession of their natures, so that not only did the lion, the tiger, and the wolf among the inhabitants of the land, the shark and the whale among the inhabitants of the water, and the eagle

[98] Sermon LX, part i, sect. 2.
[99] *Ibid.*, secs. 4, 5.
[100] *Ibid.*, sec. 5.
[101] *Ibid.*, sec. 3.
[102] *Ibid.*, part ii, sec. 1.
[103] *Ibid.*, sec. 2.

among the creatures of the air tear "the flesh," suck "the blood," and crush "the bones of their helpless fellow-creatures," but even the seemingly innocent songsters of the grove devoured the fly, the ant, and the beautiful painted butterfly.[104]

"As by one man sin entered into the world, and death by sin; even so death passed upon all men;" and not on man only, but on those creatures also that "did not sin after the similitude of Adam's transgression." And not death alone came upon them, but all its train of preparatory evils: pain, and ten thousand sufferings. Nor these only, but likewise all those irregular passions, all those unlovely tempers, (which in men are sins, and even in brutes are sources of misery,) "passed upon all" the inhabitants of the earth; and remain in all, except the children of God.[105]

The Transmission of Sin

This brings us now to the Wesleyan consideration of the transmission of sin and of the imputation of Adam's guilt to his posterity. Wesley teaches that Adam was a type or representative of mankind, so that the state of all mankind did so far depend on Adam that by his sin all men fell and inherited the pain, sorrow, death, and punishment which his wickedness entailed.[106] Adam, as a public person, the federal head of the whole human race, acted in the stead of all his posterity and represented them in the great transaction which sealed their fate.[107] Thus it may be said, in line with the thought of the divines of the Westminster Assembly, that, since all mankind descended from Adam by ordinary generation, they, therefore, sinned with him and fell with him in that first transgression.[108] Adam's own nature was so corrupted and disabled that it could not produce anything which was free from impurity and sin. Therefore, the descendants of Adam have inherited the corruption of his nature, from which proceeds all the evil and vice which engulf the world. Indeed, the child is like the parent; and the depravity of mankind must be traced to its first representative, who was the parent of the race. This, says Wesley, is the biblical explanation of the fact of original sin, as we see from the read-

104 *Ibid.*, sec. 3.
105 *Ibid.*, sec. 5.
106 *Works*, IX, 332.
107 *Ibid.*, p. 333.
108 *Ibid.*, p. 262.

ing of Romans 5:15-20 and I Corinthians 15:21-22. In those passages we are expressly told that "all men die in Adam" and that "by his offence, judgment is come upon all men to condemnation." [109] It is a hard doctrine, and yet upon the biblical account, without further ado, Wesley rests his case.

What does this do to the justice of God? Is it fair that the fate of the entire human race, of generations then unborn, should have been committed to the keeping of one man and that the state of all posterity should have been made dependent on the behavior of its common parent? John Calvin, who stood in the tradition of Augustine and of Paul and who, like them, explained the origin of sin by the biblical account of the Fall, faced this very same problem. In the thinking of Calvin, to say that Adam had within the power of his own choice as a free individual the fate of the entire human race would be the same as to deify Adam, to make him like unto God, and to ascribe unto him a power which is possessed alone by the Creator. According to Calvin, therefore, Adam, as the representative of the human race, fell because God willed it; and the miserable conditions of pain and depravity which the posterity of Adam inherited because of his fall were themselves planned and determined by the divine will.[110] God's justice lies beyond the scope of man's free inquiry.

I say, with Augustine, that the Lord created those who, he certainly foreknew, would fall into destruction, and that this was actually so because he willed it; but of his will it belongs not to us to demand the reason, which we are incapable of comprehending; nor is it reasonable that the Divine will should be made the subject of controversy with us, which, whenever it is discussed, is only another name for the highest rule of justice.[111]

Wesley's answer to this problem is entirely different. He says that, though it is absolutely true that God so constituted the human race in the original act of creation that man's moral and spiritual nature, as well as his physical nature, should be transmitted from parent to child through all succeeding generations, this fact in itself is in no way inconsistent with either the justice or goodness of God. And that because

---

[109] *Notes on the New Testament*, pp. 375-76, 441-42; *Works,* IX, 262, 264.
[110] Calvin, *Institutes,* III, xiii, 4.
[111] *Ibid.,* 5.

God, after the fall of the first Adam, provided for the recovery of man's nature through the second Adam, Jesus Christ. This "single consideration totally removes all reflections on the divine justice or mercy, in making the state of all mankind so dependent on the behaviour of their common parent: for not one child of man finally loses thereby, unless by his own choice." [112]

Wesley goes all the way with Calvin, with Luther, and with Augustine in his insistence that man is by nature totally destitute of righteousness and subject to the judgment and wrath of God. But to this he adds another principle: By the free grace of God given to all men alike at the very moment of birth, they are able to turn again unto their Heavenly Father and to regain the privilege of which by nature they have been deprived.[113] "Our theological coat," writes W. R. Maltby, in the spirit if not in the language of Wesley, "was cut for the figure of Total Depravity, but when it was tried on, it was found not to fit any kind of human nature. Accordingly we let out a seam in the back, as far as it would go, and the margin thus gained, with the stitches still showing, we called prevenient grace." [114]

[112] *Works*, IX, 332.

[113] *Ibid.*, p. 326. Wesley's insistence on human freedom characterized every aspect of his thought. This God never destroys. See his "Thought on Necessity," in which he discusses freedom in regard to scientific determinism and the determinism of Jonathan Edwards.—*Works*, X, 457-80. The Wesleyan view of the transmission of sin is the semipelagianism of the Roman Catholic Church, save only that Wesley does not go to the extreme of insisting that infants must of necessity be baptized. God will on the basis of the universality of Christ's atonement save them if they die in infancy, for though their nature is corrupt they have not actually merited the condemnation of guilt since they have not had the chance to accept or to reject the free grace of God. Cf. Moxon, *Doctrine of Sin*, "Semipelagianism," pp. 110-40; *Canons and Decrees of the Council of Trent*, Session V. See Pope, *A Compendium of Christian Theology*, II, 72-81.

[114] From an article published in the *Methodist Recorder*, Dec., 1916. Preventing grace given to all men alike enables them to turn unto God and be saved. All men possess the urge after God, which if they yield to it will increase more and more. There is, therefore, a light wherewith the Son of God enlighteneth every one that cometh into the world and shows every man to do justly, to love mercy, and to walk humbly with God.—Sermon XLIII, part i, sec. ii. God himself, says Wesley, if he be truly love, will not behold the noblest of his creatures under heaven necessitated to evil and incapable of any relief without affording that relief. God can cure evil, and he will if we *choose he should.*—*Works*, X, 473-74. Free will, though powerless to rectify man's nature, is none the less that which enables him to respond to the Holy Spirit. We can do all things through Christ strengthening us.—*Ibid.*, p. 478. If perhaps it is true that by nature man is free only to do evil, it is likewise true that every man has free will returned to him by grace so that he can return to God.—*Ibid.*, X, 392. No man can be lost except by his own choice.—Sermon LIX, sec. 14.

Chapter IX

REDEMPTION AND ASSURANCE

Justification in Relation to Its Cause

HUMAN WICKEDNESS CANNOT BE VIEWED ALONE IN THE LIGHT OF THE absolute demands of divine righteousness without producing in mankind a sense of utter frustration and despair. If man is by nature helpless as well as sinful and, therefore, powerless to rectify his character and alter the fundamental disposition of his life, and if God is by nature perfect holiness and, therefore, incapable of receiving into harmonious relationship with himself anything that is vile and corruptible, then it follows that either mankind must be denied forever the privilege of communion and fellowship with God or else God himself must provide some way for the rectification of man's character and the transformation of his life. Justification, as an act of divine pardon of sin and acceptance of the sinner, must, in the last analysis, be viewed in relationship to its fundamental cause, to the provision which God has made for the bestowal of his mercy in a manner consistent with his justice, and to the instrument of its effective actualization in human life. In this chapter, therefore, it is necessary for us to consider the work of God in redemption and to give attention to the doctrines both of the person and work of Christ and of the Holy Spirit. In the doctrine of Christ we deal with the formal cause of man's forgiveness, with the ultimate reason for pardon and acceptance; in the doctrine of the Holy Spirit we deal with the efficient cause of man's rectification, with the instrument whereby the work of Christ is applied to the needs and conditions of particular men. The one has reference to a completed act in history; the other, to a present, ongoing, continuing process.

Since Adam, as the parent of the human family, chose for himself and his posterity the way of pride and rebellious self-assertiveness, it is not strange that men through all succeeding ages have blamed him for their trouble and have laid all their misfortunes, both physical and moral, at his door. By his disobedience the future destiny of the race was altered; and as many as were then in his loins were constituted sinners and deprived not only of the favor of God but also of his image —of all virtue, righteousness, and true holiness—left to sink into the image of the devil—in pride, malice, and those other diabolical tempers which stir the passions and break the heart.[1] For the irregularities of nature, for pain and sickness, for death itself, we may thank Adam, they say, and look to him as the instigator of all our woe.[2] Thus men shift the responsibility for sin from their own shoulders back upon those of their first parent and bewail the condition in which they were born.

But, says Wesley, they are not content to let their charge rest here. From miserable Adam they lift their accusing eyes to the Creator, who made him; and from the fact of Adam's sin they turn to question the justice of God that the penalty of that sin should be continued on them.[3] Indeed, Taylor, in his consideration of sin, writes that the doctrine of natural depravity cannot be maintained if one holds to the justice, righteousness, and love of God. It is dishonorable to God to suppose that he is displeased with us for what he himself has infused into our nature.[4] Does not God create the nature of every man that is born into the world? Yes, and if God produces men in the womb with certain qualities, then it must be said that those qualities, even if sinful, are none the less according to his will.

Wesley replies that the circumstances of the formation of man's nature in the womb are beyond his understanding and that he does not know how the body is fashioned or how the soul is united to it.[5] Therefore, he is not able to say how sin is propagated from father to son; but of the fact that it is propagated he is as certain as of life itself.[6] Yet it does not follow that God creates sinful men and that he directly continues the corruption which Adam started. Here Wesley falls back on the basic principle which underlies his doctrine of creation: God is loyal to the nature of the things he has made. Man's essential nature

[1] Sermon LIX, intro. sec. 1.
[2] *Ibid.*, sec. 2.
[3] *Ibid.*, sec. 3.
[4] Taylor, *Doctrine of Original Sin*, p. 142.
[5] *Works*, IX, 334.
[6] *Ibid.*, p. 335.

was planned and made before Adam's fall; and it follows, as a part of the divine order of things, that like produces like and that the child is similar to the parent who bears him. To say, writes Wesley, that, since it is the power of God whereby a sinful father begets a sinful son, God is himself the author of sin, is just as foolish as to say that, since it is the power of God which enables a murderer to lift his club, God himself perpetrates his wickedness and performs the crime which he commits. Even so, the power of God which men call "nature" acts from age to age under its fixed laws. God set those laws at the time of creation. It is the power of God, therefore, which continues the human species from age to age, yet he "who this moment supplies the power whereby a sinful nature is propagated (according to the fixed rules established in the lower world) is not chargeable with the sinfulness of that nature."[7] God does not, in the last analysis, create each newborn child. He merely produces its body in the same sense in which he produces the oak; he merely supplies the power whereby one creature begets another of its kind.[8]

God does produce the action which is sinful; and yet (whether I can account for it or no) the sinfulness of it is not his will or work. He does also produce the nature which is sinful (he supplies the power by which it is produced) and yet (whether I can account for this or no) the sinfulness of it is not his will or his work. I am as sure of this as I am there is a God; and yet impenetrable darkness rests on the subject. Yet I am conscious my understanding can no more fathom this deep than reconcile man's free will with the foreknowledge of God.[9]

Set over against the fact of evil and its attendant woes, which, in Wesley's thought, is entirely due to man and to his freedom, is the fact of redemption, of what God does in behalf of man in order to restore him to his original state of righteousness. Indeed, the doctrine of sin, according to Wesley, must always be considered in the light of the doctrine of redemption; for, if it portrays man's character at its worst and shows what he can do in deeds of violence and of hatred, then redemption portrays God's character in the fullness of its holiness and shows what he is both able and willing to do in deeds of mercy and of

[7] *Ibid.*
[8] *Ibid.*, p. 336.
[9] *Ibid.*, p. 337.

203

love. In the preface to his work on *The Doctrine of Original Sin,* Wesley reminds us that the Pelagian view of man's nature as represented by the work of Taylor is dangerous solely because of what it does to the work of God in redemption. It sets at nought the very foundation of the Christian faith and saps all the vitality out of revealed religion. It is nothing more than "old Deism in a new dress." If man is by nature upright and capable of knowing the good and performing the good in the power of his own might, then what need is there for Jesus Christ? Men that are whole have no need for a physician. Christ came into the world for no other purpose than to save sinners from their sin.[10] If it is true that God in his infinite wisdom made a creature who was capable of freedom, even to the extent of open rebellion, and that he permitted Adam to fall into sin and to bring evil and suffering upon all his children, it is likewise true that his infinite love conceived a plan for man's recovery and made provision for his restoration more complete and more wonderful than anything yet devised. The fact of redemption looms so large and is so powerful in its import that sin itself, interpreted in its light, becomes an advantage; and the fall of Adam, a defeat in itself, prepares the way for the ultimate victory in Christ.[11] Wesley descends unafraid into the blackness and night of inherited human depravity because of his unfaltering trust in the sunrise of God's redeeming love.

The Person of Christ

The person of Christ, therefore, is set forth in Wesleyan thought always in terms of his work, and the historical Jesus is never limited to his date in time but is interpreted solely as a manifestation of eternity. He both symbolizes and embodies the redemptive work of God; and, though he stands in history as a particular person occupying a particular place and performing a particular task at a particular time, the effects of his mission are eternal; for in the purposes of divinity the Lamb of God was slain from the beginning of the world.[12] The

[10] *Ibid.,* pp. 193-94.
[11] Wesley teaches that the effects of redemption, which come only as a result of the fall of Adam, are more glorious than man's original state at creation. See Sermon LIX, intro. sec. 3; part i, secs. 1-11.
[12] Sermon LXI, sec. 3.

work of redemption was made available for our first parents in the Garden centuries before the Redeemer took human form,[13] and the efficacy of that work will abide until the end of time. Though it was necessary for the Redeemer to be born into the world and to assume our humanity in order to save us, he none the less recapitulated in his person all generations of mankind and made himself the center of salvation for all ages as well as races of men.[14]

Wesley begins in accordance with the teachings of historic Christianity by affirming the deity of Christ. If, he says, the inspired writers give Jesus of Nazareth all the titles of the most high God and ascribe unto him all the attributes and all the works of the Almighty, then we need not scruple to pronounce him "God of God, Light of Light, very God of very God: in glory equal with the Father; in majesty coeternal." He was with God the Father in the creation of the universe; and, since the Scripture teaches that all things were made by him,[15] we may say that he is Creator and Cause of all things in the same sense and in the same degree as the Father.[16] Likewise, he is at one with the Father in that he is the Supporter,[17] Preserver,[18] Governor,[19] and End[20] of all

[13] Sermon LXII, part ii, sec. 2.

[14] Sermon CXLI, part ii.

[15] *Notes on the New Testament*, p. 212.

[16] Sermon LXXVII, part i, sec. 2. In Wesleyan thought there is the emphasis on the absolute unity between Father and Son, the mutual pervasion of each by the other, the oneness of nature, will, and action. There is a strange parallel in this between the thought of Wesley and the doctrine of Hilary of Poitiers in the controversy which followed the Council of Nicaea. See Seeberg, *History of Doctrine*, I, 255-56. Such an emphasis in Wesleyan thought never goes to the extreme of Sabellianism, or the flat denial of the distinct personality of the Son. The latter part of the seventeenth century saw the beginning of the Trinitarian Controversy in English theology, and both Burnet and Tillotson tend to make the three persons in the Godhead only three manifestations of One God. Suffice it to say that Wesley took no part whatever in this controversy, and his purpose always is merely to reaffirm the Catholic position of Nicaea and of Chalcedon. For a full discussion of the Trinitarian Controversy in England, see Abbey and Overton, *The English Church in the Eighteenth Century*, pp. 197-226.

[17] Sermon LXXVII, part i, sec. 3.

[18] *Ibid.*, sec. 4. Wesley's statements are not broad and general affirmations but rather specific indications of his meaning. Thus in calling Christ Preserver of the universe he indicates that by him and in him are all things compacted into one system, that he is the Author of motion, and that he generates the movement of the planets. All this is shared with God the Father and God the Spirit. Wesley is trying to leave no room for uncertainty concerning Christ's absolute equality with the Father in power as well as goodness.—*Ibid.*, secs. 5, 6.

[19] *Ibid.*, sec. 8-9.

[20] *Ibid.*, sec. 10.

the objects of creation, "the cement of the whole universe." [21] He is the Author of eternal life [22] as well as the Fountain from whose stream flows the present life of man and of animals. [23] More than this, Jesus Christ is the person by whom God will judge the world in the last day, and in the light of whose goodness he will appraise the deeds of both the living and the dead. [24] But Jesus Christ is precious to the sons of men in that he is Redeemer and Saviour, the manifestation of God in his nearest and dearest relation, [25] the incarnate Word, who assumed flesh and became a real man and was in all things like as we are yet without sin. For our iniquities he was bruised, and for our transgressions he poured out his soul and washed us in his own blood. [26]

Though it is true that Jesus possessed the spirit of divinity in all of its fullness so that the Godhead dwelt in him bodily, it is likewise true that he possessed the spirit of humanity in all its fullness so that he had all the attributes of the children of men. [27] By the Holy Ghost's coming upon the Virgin Mary and the power of God the Father overshadowing her, his incarnation was wrought, and he entered into our world to learn our language and to adopt our ways in order that we might learn God's language and adopt God's ways. The purpose of his becoming man was that we, by receiving his adoption, might become the sons of God once again and at last "be carried into immortality." [28] The divine wisdom, therefore, presented itself in the Saviour

---

[21] *Ibid.*, sec. 4.

[22] *Ibid.*, part ii, sec. 1.

[23] *Ibid.*, sec. 3.

[24] Sermon XV, part i, secs. 1, 2.

[25] Sermon LIX, part i, sec. 3.

[26] *Ibid.*, sec. 4.

[27] Sermon CXLI, part ii. Wesley, in line with the thought of the Council of Chalcedon, is content merely to affirm the two natures in Christ and to say our Lord Jesus Christ, "the same perfect in Godhead and also perfect in manhood; truly God and truly man, . . . consubstantial with the Father according to his Godhead and consubstantial with us according to his Manhood, . . . one and the same Christ, Son, Lord, Only-begotten, to be acknowledged in two natures, inconfusedly, unchangeably, indivisibly, inseparably, the distinction of the two natures being by no means taken away by the union," and to offer no explanation of the metaphysical manner in which they are joined. See Schaff, *Creeds of Christendom,* II, 62-63.

[28] Sermon CXLI, part ii. Wesley was a careful student of the Fathers, and many of his teachings reflect ideas in the theology of the early Church. His statement that Christ assumes our nature in order that he may confer his nature upon us and restore us to the blessings of immortality is in line with the temper of Eastern thought prior to A.D.

of the world as a union between God and man.[29] In his humanity Christ submitted himself to all the necessary stages in the progress of our life, and his heavenly nature was hidden for the most part in the "secret of his soul" until death. He was crucified at the hands of sinful men. The third day he rose again from the dead, clothed his body with the attributes of immortality, and ascended into heaven and seated himself at the right hand of the Father.[30]

The Nature of the Work of Christ

This concludes the Wesleyan statement of Christ's person and brings us now to the consideration of his work. The work of Christ stands, in the first instance, as the supreme manifestation of human righteousness and holiness, the highest moral and spiritual example ever to be viewed by the children of men. Christ's righteousness in this world belonged to his human nature; it was a copy of divine righteousness, to be sure, but it was imparted to the human spirit and so was not alien to the ethical and spiritual ideals of ordinary men. He showed men what it was to live out in this world of flesh and blood the perfect life, and his few years on this earth furnish us with a transcript of divine purity, justice, mercy, and truth.[31] It was the least part of Christ's external righteousness that he did nothing amiss, that he knew no outward sin of any kind, and that not a single improper word ever crossed his lips. He went on to achieve positive righteousness, to do all things well, and to obey the will of God as perfectly on earth as the angels obey it in heaven.[32] Not only so, but his absolute loyalty to God led him to the passive obedience of suffering, to the endurance of humility which receives without retaliation both ridicule and oppression,

---

300. The Eastern theologians tend to stress the incarnation, while the Western theologians tend to stress the atonement. See Seeberg, *op. cit.,* I, 185-91.

[29] Sermon CXLI, part ii.

[30] *Ibid.* Irenaeus taught that Christ fulfilled all the stages in human life. See Seeberg, *op. cit.,* I, 118-38. Starting with Andrewes, there developed a tendency among English theologians to draw heavily upon the thought of the early Fathers and in a measure to substitute their thought for the later expressions of the Reformation. Wesley stands in this tradition, and even a hurried reading of his works would be sufficient to make one aware of Wesley's debt to early Christian thought.

[31] Sermon XX, part i, sec. 2.

[32] *Ibid.,* sec. 3.

and to the courageous acceptance of death on the cross.[33] The manner of Christ's life and death as a human being; his love, reverence, and resignation to his heavenly Father; his humility, meekness, and gentleness in contrast to the hatred and violence of his enemies; and his love for saints and sinners alike, stand as a faultless picture of human goodness, a representation of perfect righteousness to all ages.[34]

The work of Christ stands, in the second instance, as the perfect sacrifice for sin and the ground of redemption and reconciliation. If Adam, as the representative of the human race, chose sin and damnation for himself and his posterity, then Christ, as the second Adam, representing all mankind, made himself an offering for sin, bore the iniquities of the human race, and became a sufficient satisfaction for the evils of the whole world.[35] Thus in consideration of the fact that the Son of God tasted death for everyone, God the Father now vouchsafes to every sinner, on the condition of his acceptance of the merits of Christ's death, both to remit the punishment due to sin and to reinstate him into favor, to restore his soul in all holiness, and to set him on the way of eternal life.[36]

There is in all of Wesley's writings no single work on the atonement, and there is no reason whatever for us to believe that he had any clear, well-thought-out theory of the meaning of Christ's death. He seems only to have repeated the fact that the work of Christ, taken as a whole and including both his life and death, stands as the objective ground for the forgiveness of sins. Christ is the Author of faith and grace, and, therefore, the sole cause of man's redemption. And yet in presenting this fact Wesley uses the language of Anselm and of Calvin. He writes that the words of St. Paul representing Christ as a propitiation for sin must be understood to mean that Christ actually made appeasement to an angry and offended God. If God were not offended, then there would be no occasion for the use of the word "propitiation." But the point is that propitiation is the word used, and Christ is said to declare God's righteousness, which means that he demonstrates not

[33] *Ibid.,* sec. 4.
[34] *Ibid.,* sec. 2.
[35] Sermon V, part i, sec. 7.
[36] *Ibid.,* sec. 8.

only God's clemency but his justice, "even that vindictive justice, whose essential character and principal office is to punish sins." In the punishment of Christ he evidences himself to be strictly and inviolably righteous. Every attribute of God's character must be preserved, and his justice must be manifested as well as his mercy.[37]

It might appear from the writings of subsequent Methodist theologians that Wesley accepted the Grotian theory of the atonement, that Christ's death was a satisfaction due, not to any internal principle of the divine nature, but to the necessities of the government of the universe. God's government cannot be maintained or divine authority upheld apart from law, and the violation of law must be punished. God, therefore, accepts Christ's death as a substitute for the penalty which man deserves for violating the law.[38] And indeed, Wesley writes, God must "evidence himself as righteous in the administration of his government." But this phrase is used merely as an expression of his character, which is always to be just, and the administration of the universe is one of the areas in which it is exemplified. Indeed, as we have seen in Chapter VII of this work, one of the supreme manifestations of God's character is in his government of the universe, and nothing is more alien to Wesley's thought than to separate the principle of the government of nature from the character of God. The necessities of the government of the universe are what they are simply because of the character of God, and the satisfaction of sin is related to the internal principle of the divine nature, which, as we have seen in Chapter VII, is holiness itself. Wesley's position is Anselmic—that sin, as a violation of God's honor, deserves infinite punishment—and he goes all the way with Calvin in his insistence that God's wrath must be expressed against sin and his vindictive justice satisfied.[39]

In commenting on forgiveness Wesley writes that it should appear that every sin would automatically call forth its punishment, and yet such is not the case if the sinner comes to God with a believing and penitent heart. Why? Simply because, on the basis of the evangelical principle of the atonement, the debt of sin is paid by Christ, and it is

---

[37] *Notes on the New Testament*, p. 370.

[38] See A. H. Strong, *Systematic Theology*, p. 740.

[39] See *ibid.*, pp. 747-48; cf. Hodge, *Systematic Theology*, II, 470-540. For Calvinistic theory of the atonement, see *Institutes*, II, xvi, 1-6.

"the part of equity to cancel the bond and to consign over the pur-chased possession." Christ's satisfaction has taken away all guilt.[40]

In calling attention to the similarity in language between Wesley and Calvin, we dare not overlook two very important factors which attach themselves to Wesley's view of the work of the Redeemer and which separate his thought on that subject from the thought of the Reformer of Geneva. In the first place, Wesley teaches that the work of Christ is universal in its extent, that the Son of God died for every-one and that no single creature is excluded from the merits of his atonement.[41] Christ, writes Wesley, obtained for all the possibility of salvation; [42] his death was in behalf of all men; otherwise, those for whom he did not die have every reason to complain.[43] Particular re-demption is ruled out of Wesleyan thought,[44] and this is one of the reasons why he and Whitefield could never unite. Indeed, in April of the year 1741 Wesley wrote a letter to George Whitefield in which he said, "You rank all the maintainers of universal redemption with the Socinians themselves. Alas! my brother, do you not know even this, that the Socinians allow no redemption at all?" [45] And he wrote to John Fletcher on March 20, 1768, that it was a matter of common knowledge that all the lay preachers who were connected with him were maintainers of general redemption.[46] James Hervey stands as a Calvinistic representative of the doctrine of particular redemption, that Christ died for the elect alone; and Wesley, in commenting on this doctrine as it is set forth in Hervey's *Theron* and *Aspasio,* writes that on the basis of this he cannot understand what becomes of those people who are not among the elect. Is it true that they must perish forever, that the die was cast in regard to their destiny before ever they were born? If so, writes Wesley, "I could sooner be a Turk, a Deist, yea an Atheist, than I could believe this. It is less absurd to deny the very being of God than to make him out an almighty tyrant." [47]

[40] *Notes on the New Testament,* p. 631.
[41] Sermon LXXX, sec. 8.
[42] *Works,* X, 332.
[43] *Ibid.,* p. 319.
[44] *Ibid.,* VIII, 184.
[45] *Ibid.,* XII, 158.
[46] *Ibid.,* p. 162.
[47] *Letters,* III, 387.

In the second place, Wesley teaches that the work of Christ, though universal in the sense that it is offered to all men alike, is none the less conditional in the sense that it is made dependent on man's willingness to accept it in order for it to become effective in his life. Wesley repudiates the teaching that God the Father made a covenant with God the Son before the world began in which covenant the Son agreed to suffer and die and the Father to give him certain particular souls for a recompense.[48] The covenant of God, on the contrary, is with men.[49] If men are to receive its benefits, they must fulfill its conditions. Christ's atonement is offered freely unto all who believe. Salvation is bought by the blood of Christ for every child of man, and yet its benefits are bestowed only on those who willingly receive them.[50]

The Results of the Work of Christ

But if Christ came into the world to destroy sin and to rectify the evil which has emerged as a by-product of man's depraved nature,[51] what, we ask, are the objective results of his mission, and what is the lasting effect of his work in the world? To begin with, Christ's work makes possible the redemption and restoration of all created things in a manner consistent with their nature and with the justice and the mercy of Almighty God. If it is true that we cannot go beyond the creative act itself and ask why God made things the way they are, we none the less have a right to expect of God that he will preserve them in their own integrity and will remain eternally loyal to the nature he has given them. Wesley goes so far as to say that God is "pleased to appeal to man himself touching the justice of His proceedings." [52] But is it not true that because of the sin of the first man evil entered the world and not only captured the souls of the human race but upset the original harmony of nature and threw the animal kingdom into a state of disorder, violence, and pain? The animals did not choose to disobey God; neither were they constituted in Adam's loins, so that he represented them in that awful transaction. They suffer because of

[48] *Works*, X, 238.
[49] *Ibid.*, pp. 39-41.
[50] *Ibid.*, p. 254.
[51] Sermon LXII, intro. sec. 4.
[52] *Works*, X, 216.

man's sin, and that alone. And yet, says Wesley, we dare not so much as entertain the thought that the animals will remain forever in such a state; for, whereas they did not choose to sin but had evil, which is the consequence of sin, thrust upon them, even so they will automatically be restored and given the blessings of redemption.[53] Likewise inanimate nature will reflect the glory of God's redemptive power,[54] and no single object of creation will be isolated from the effects of Christ's work. And yet the effects of Christ's work must always be applied in a manner consistent with the nature of created things. Therefore, redemption cannot be applied automatically to man, for by nature he is free—free to accept or to reject God's offer. Though it is true that the life and death of our Lord have made possible not only the restoration of the original privileges which man lost in the garden but the addition of blessings which he did not there possess,[55] God still respects his

[53] The notion of the redemption of animals and of all lower forms of life was a conviction which Wesley consistently held and constantly refused to surrender. It did not arise from any sentimental attachments, such as his fondness for his horse, which he said he expected to find in heaven. Rather, it emerged as a necessary consequence of God's eternal loyalty to the things which he made and his absolute justice and righteousness and mercy which do not limit themselves to the level of human life. It was likewise an integral factor in his solution of the problem of evil. He maintained that physical evil emerged as a consequence of moral evil; and, if physical evil caused the innocent to suffer, it at the same time worked for their benefit in the long run and added blessings to the state of their final redemption.—Sermon LIX, part i, secs. 15-16. If animals suffer, as indeed they do because of Adam's fall, then their suffering will be recompensed by even greater rewards in the world to come.—Sermon LX, part iii, sec. 1.

[54] Inanimate nature, as we have seen in Chapter VII, is passive in the hands of God, and he employs the forces of nature to display his wrath against sin. Wesley devotes an entire sermon to the "Cause and Cure of Earthquakes," which are interpreted as the judgments which a righteous God inflicts on sinners.—Sermon CXXIX. But the redemptive work of God will finally be applied to nature, and it will display once again its original harmony and beauty in manner far surpassing its state in creation.—Sermon LXIV.

[55] Sermon LIX, part i, secs. 1-12. Wesley does not consider that in saying man's state in redemption is better and more glorious than his state in creation he implies that his state in creation was not absolutely good. Of course, he is trying to drive home the practical lesson of a preacher and to make people believe that if they accept the benefits of the atonement, they really gain by Adam's fall; for if Adam had not fallen, Christ would not have come. This is an accepted fact in historic Christianity; and, though it is always possible for us to raise the unanswerable question and to ask why God did not confer the privileges of redemption at creation and make it impossible for sin ever to exist, it must, nevertheless, be admitted that, accepting the world as it is and the facts of life as they present themselves, John Wesley offers a solution to the problem of evil on the basis of his doctrine of redemption and goes a long distance in justifying the ways of God to man.

212

essential nature and gives him, alone of all the objects of creation, the right to decide whether or not he will receive the merits of our Lord. The work of Christ is redemption, but the effects of his atonement must be received by man, and the purification "through his blood" must be applied to the human soul.[56]

The Work of the Holy Spirit

It is, therefore, as the instrument whereby the work of Christ is applied to the souls of individuals throughout all time that we understand the function of the Holy Spirit. Wesley is not content to stop with a consideration of what God does *for* us through the life and death of his Son but moves on to a positive statement of what God does *in* us through his Spirit. We must learn that Christ is not only God above us. If he were, he might keep us in awe, but he could not save. It is necessary for us to learn also that he is "Immanuel, God with us and in us," and that by the power of the Holy Spirit he makes his tabernacle with us and dwells by faith in our hearts.[57] If it is true that the work of Christ establishes the foundation of justification and is the cause of our pardon and our acceptance with God, and if it is legitimate to say that faith is imputed to us for righteousness[58] and that the righteousness of Christ is the sole ground of all our hope,[59] it is likewise true, as soon as we are justified and delivered from guilt and punishment, that the Holy Spirit operates constructively in our lives, that *Christ is formed in our heart,*[60] that we put on the robes of his righteousness, casting aside the filthy rags of our own trespasses and sin, and that we come to possess inherent righteousness ourselves,[61] which is the result of faith in his name. Wesley dreaded the implications of the phrase *"the imputed righteousness of Christ,"* for it signified to so many of his hearers that Christ's righteousness was a substitute for their own,[62] and that what he did at Calvary was sufficient to relieve them of all obligation and to set them free from

[56] *Works,* VIII, 342.
[57] Sermon CXLI, part ii.
[58] Sermon XX, part ii, sec. 10.
[59] *Ibid.,* sec. 13.
[60] Sermon I, part ii, sec. 7.
[61] Sermon XX, part ii, sec. 12.
[62] *Works,* X, 315.

the law of holiness and obedience.[63] Such an interpretation of the work of Christ, Wesley likens to a "blow at the root" and says that it is the means whereby "Christ is stabbed in the house of his friends." [64] There is indeed no substitute for personal righteousness; without holiness no man can see God.[65] "I testify to you," writes Wesley, "that if you still continue in sin, Christ shall profit you nothing; that Christ is no Saviour to you, unless he saves you from your sins; and that unless it purify your heart, faith shall profit you nothing. O when will you understand, that to oppose either inward or outward holiness, under colour of exalting Christ, is directly to act the part of Judas, to 'betray the Son of man with a kiss'?" [66]

The Holy Spirit, as the agency of the actual bestowal of Christ's holiness and the power of inherent goodness manifesting itself in man's soul, keeps alive the work of Christ in the world and, in the practical thought of Wesley, is inseparable from Christ's mission itself. Indeed, so intimately does he associate the Holy Spirit with the character of Jesus as it is portrayed in the Gospels that at times it seems that all Wesley means by the Holy Spirit is merely the continuing inspiration of Christ. But the important thing is that the Holy Spirit represents God's immanence, and that he is always present to serve the needs of men. It is useless to search Wesley's thought for any systematic presentation of the doctrine of the Third Person of the Trinity, but it is only necessary to read a few of his sermons in order to realize the tremendous emphasis that he gave to the work of the Holy Spirit in the lives of men. "But I think," he writes as a young man, "that the true notion of the Spirit is, that it is some portion of, as well as preparation for, a life in God." [67] Without the Spirit of power descending upon men, Christ remains a pattern, the ideal of which is ever beyond reach. But know, says Wesley, that the power of God is forever about us. It hovers over our beds; it stands beside our path; it besets us behind and before, and offers us the strength to become like our Lord.[68]

[63] Sermon XXXV, part ii, secs. 1-7.
[64] *Works*, X, 364, 366.
[65] *Ibid.*, p. 364.
[66] *Ibid.*, pp. 367-68.
[67] Sermon CXLI, part iii.
[68] Sermon LXXVII, part iii, sec. 9.

The Doctrine of Assurance

Not only does the Holy Spirit communicate the blessings of Christ's work in the act of man's justification by giving him power over sin and by infusing righteousness into his life, but also the Holy Spirit becomes the voice of divine assurance within him and generates that confidence whereby he knows that he is a child of God. The *witness of the Spirit* assumes, therefore, a role of cardinal significance in Wesley's theology; for it is the means whereby a man's justification is made manifest, the internal sign that the power of God has touched his life, that his sins have been forgiven, and that he has been set on the road to holiness and final salvation. It holds the same place in the spiritual life that visual perception holds in the world of sense and things. For, as a man is most readily convinced of the reality of those things which he has seen with his own eyes, even so he is most certain of those truths which he has experienced in his heart.[69] In referring to his own experience at Aldersgate, Wesley writes: "The Spirit itself bore witness to my spirit that I was a child of God, gave me an evidence hereof, and I immediately cried, Abba, Father!"[70] On the basis of his own experience Wesley laid down as a principle of the religious life that the direct witness of the Spirit, providing the believer with a sense of assurance, is the natural accompaniment of justification itself and is granted unto every child of God.[71]

Such a doctrine as the direct testimony of the Holy Spirit to the individual believer did not commend itself to the theologians of eighteenth-century England. Though it is true that the Caroline divines of the seventeenth century had treated the doctrine of assurance with approval [72] and that Thomas Sherlock continued to acknowledge its validity, albeit he found its evidence in good works alone,[73] the majority of ministers of the Church of England felt that it was a form of enthusiasm [74] and reacted to the Wesleyan statement of it

[69] *Journal*, Wed., May 24, 1738, sec. 15.
[70] Sermon XI, part iii, sec. 6.
[71] Sermon X, intro. sec. 2.
[72] H. Watkin-Jones, *The Holy Spirit from Arminius to Wesley*, pp. 306-9.
[73] *Ibid.*, pp. 311-13.
[74] See U. Lee's short but thorough monograph *The Historical Backgrounds of Early Methodist Enthusiasm*, pp. 58-119.

with open antagonism.[75] Indeed, William Warburton, in the year 1750, published a work entitled *The Doctrine of Grace; or the Office and Operations of the Holy Spirit Vindicated from the Insults of Infidelity and the Abuses of Fanaticism: with Some Thoughts Regarding the Right Method of Defending Religion Against the Attacks of Either Party*.[76] "The abuses of fanaticism," he applies to the work of Mr. Wesley; and he says that his doctrine of the direct witness of the Spirit, though it is in the language of Scripture, is neither scriptural doctrine nor history. Wesley teaches that the work of God begins in the heart, while it is plain that the beginning of all religion is in the understanding. Rational conviction must win the allegiance of the heart, for the seat of such conviction is within the mind, not the emotions.[77] Where prudence governs, there is no God wanting to keep everything in order; where imprudence governs, there is no devil needed to throw all things into confusion.[78] Wesley's doctrine, Warburton held, represents zeal run mad; and if anyone will read the accounts of spiritual fanatics in the past and then compare them with the Wesleyan expressions upon such subjects as faith, grace, redemption, regeneration, justification, and so forth, he will see that Wesley is of the same stock and that his work will produce the same results.[79]

Bishop Butler shared the opinions of his colleague Bishop Warburton in this regard; "probability," for him, was "the very guide of life." [80] In a conversation with John Wesley, Butler himself is reported to have said: "Sir, the pretending to extraordinary revelations and gifts of the Holy Ghost is a horrid thing, a very horrid thing." [81] At least, whether this interview occurred or not, we do know that Butler went so far as to write in the *Analogy* that enthusiasm weakens the testimony to facts and that the powers of enthusiasm and disease operate in a like manner.[82] So foreign was the doctrine of the witness

---

[75] See Wesley's letter to Bishop Warburton in reply to Warburton's attack. This gives some indication of the opposition in the Church of England.—*Works*, IX, 117-73.
[76] W. Warburton, *Works*, VIII, 237-455.
[77] *Ibid.*, p. 349.
[78] *Ibid.*, p. 361.
[79] *Ibid.*, pp. 363-64.
[80] Butler, *Works*, I, 3-9.
[81] Watkin-Jones, *op. cit.*, p. 313.
[82] Butler, *op. cit.*, I, 313.

of the Spirit to the religious thinking of the time that Susannah Wesley herself frankly confessed that she had scarce heard of such a thing mentioned as God's Spirit bearing witness with our spirit; much less did she imagine this was the common privilege of all true believers.[83]

But such was the conviction of her son. In the conversation with Bishop Butler he is reported to have replied: "I pretend to no extraordinary revelations or gifts of the Holy Ghost: none but what every Christian may receive, and ought to expect and pray for." [84] To be sure, many fanatics have laid claim to a knowledge of God which they did not possess. It is true that many have mistaken the voice of their own imagination, the whisperings of their own diseased brain, for the witness of God's Spirit, and so have deluded themselves into thinking that they were the children of God while they were doing the works of the devil.[85] Their mistakes present no valid reason, however, for repudiating the Christian teaching of direct assurance. There is a way to steer a middle course—to keep a sufficient distance from the errors of fanaticism and uncontrolled enthusiasm and at the same time to hold fast to the conviction of the witness of God's Spirit as the great privilege of the justified.[86] Accordingly, Wesley describes what he calls the testimony of the Holy Ghost as "an inward impression on the soul, whereby the Spirit of God directly witnesses to my spirit, that I am a child of God; that Jesus Christ hath loved me, and given himself for me; and that all my sins are blotted out, and I, even I, am reconciled to God." [87] Not only does the Spirit of God work in us every manner of thing that is good, but he also "shines upon his own work, and clearly shows what he has wrought." [88]

Immediately the question arises, however, as to whether or not such testimony really is the work of God's Spirit. Is it not true that man is endowed with a conscience? Perhaps what appears to be the witness of the Holy Ghost is nothing more than the rational testimony of man's own spirit. Fortunately, Wesley gives his own definition of

[83] *Journal*, Mon., Sept. 3, 1739.
[84] Watkin-Jones, *op. cit.*, p. 316. The entire interview between Wesley and Bishop Butler is reported in J. Crowther, *History of Wesleyan Methodists*, p. 38.
[85] Sermon X, intro. sec. 1.
[86] *Ibid.*, sec. 2.
[87] *Ibid.*, part i, sec. 7.
[88] *Ibid.*, sec. 10.

conscience, in which he says it is "that faculty whereby we are at once conscious of our own thoughts, words, and actions; and of their merit or demerit, of their being good or bad; and, consequently, deserving either praise or censure." [89] Thus everyone has it at the very dawn of understanding, and even the barbarian is aware that there is a distinction between good and evil.[90] It is hardly just to speak of conscience as natural; for, though it is found in the breast of every human creature born into the world,[91] it is conferred on man as a supernatural gift and is a part of the preventing grace of God.[92] It fulfills three necessary duties of the moral life. First of all, it supplies us with a clear knowledge of what we have done in thought, in word, and in deed. Secondly, it passes sentence on what we have done and indicates to us whether it is good or evil. Thirdly, it executes its own sentence by occasioning complacency in us when we have done well, giving us a sense of satisfaction, and by occasioning uneasiness in us when we have done evil, giving us a sense of fear and sorrow.[93] Such a testimony of our conscience applies to spiritual matters, also; and when we love our neighbor sincerely, engage in charitable acts toward him, are pure in life and thought, we are immediately conscious of it; our own spirit bears testimony to what we do and to what we are.[94]

But, says Wesley, this faculty of conscience applies only to the knowledge of those states and conditions, those affections and tempers, which actually possess us; it furnishes us solely with a judgment of the merit and demerit of what we are and what we do. The witness of God's Spirit, on the other hand, is superadded. It furnishes us with a knowledge of what God has done for us in Christ and what we shall become through the power of Christ's Spirit. Indeed, we must be actually holy of heart and life before we can be conscious that we are so. But the Spirit of God comes to us while we are sinners, assures us of his pardoning grace, and claims us through the inspiration of his love.[95] The manner in which the divine testimony is manifested to

[89] Sermon CV, sec. 3.
[90] Ibid., sec. 4.
[91] Ibid., sec. 5.
[92] Ibid., sec. 9.
[93] Ibid., sec. 7.
[94] Sermon X, part i, secs. 1-6.
[95] Ibid., secs. 8-9.

the human heart is a mystery, but the fact itself can never be denied. A man cannot help but know the moment that he comes to delight and rejoice in God, the moment he comes to love him as the Object of his life.[96] When the Spirit of God is present in the soul, "a man can no more doubt the reality of his sonship, than he can doubt the shining of the sun while he stands in the full blaze of its beams." [97]

But how, we ask, is one to distinguish the witness of the Spirit from the presumptions of the natural mind and the frenzy of enthusiasm? We need not suppose, Wesley tells us, that because certain mad French prophets imagined that they had experienced the Holy Ghost in their hearts, others have not really experienced it. The fact that a madman imagines himself a king does not prove that there are no real kings.[98] Therefore, if a man is genuinely repentant, believes in Christ, and earnestly desires salvation, then, when peace and assurance come to him, he has no reason to think that he is "grasping a mere shadow." [99] He may know that he is a child of God and that the Spirit does not deceive if he is possessed with humble joy, abhors his old self in dust and ashes, and is filled with meekness, patience, gentleness, long-suffering, and love,[100] consumed with the desire to do good.[101]

Finally, Wesley tells us, two inferences can be drawn from his teaching. The first is this: Let no one rest in any supposed testimony of the Spirit which is separate from its fruits—from love, joy, peace, long-suffering, gentleness, goodness, meekness, fidelity, and temperance.[102] The second is this: Let no one rest in any supposed fruit of the Spirit without the witness. A man may display certain moral virtues, but he must hear the divine voice within his soul and know by experience that he is a child of God.[103] The doctrine of the direct

96 *Ibid.*, sec. 11.
97 *Ibid.*, sec. 12.
98 Sermon XI, part iv, sec. 2.
99 Sermon X, part ii, sec. 4.
100 *Ibid.*, sec. 6.
101 *Ibid.*, sec. 7.
102 Sermon XI, part v, sec. 3.
103 *Ibid.*, sec. 4. It has not seemed necessary to indicate that Wesley believed that the witness of the Spirit is destroyed by sin, since the point was sufficiently labored in Chapter VI that faith itself must die before a man can commit an actual sin. Of course sin kills the Spirit in a man's life; there is no Calvinistic bent here; there is no guarantee of final perseverance. See Sermons LXXXII, LXXXIV, LXXXVI. Temptation

witness of the Holy Spirit was an emphasis in Wesley's preaching all the days of his life; and it is a fact worth remembering that the last words John Wesley attempted to write in this world were—GOD IS WITH US.[104]

often causes a man to doubt momentarily and to worry. Wesley himself was led to doubt his own conversion more than once in his life. This in itself does not kill the Spirit of God. "It is true," writes Wesley, "that the Holy Ghost may be withdrawn in the hour of trial. Yea, the soul may be exceedingly sorrowful while the hour and power of darkness continue; but even this is generally restored with increase, till we rejoice with joy unspeakable and full of glory."—Sermon XI, part v, sec. 3. See *Journal*, Wed., May 24, 1738, secs. 15-18; Fri., May 26, 1738; Sat., May 27, 1738; Sun., May 28, 1738.

[104] Tyerman, *Life and Times of John Wesley*, III, 652-53.

Chapter X

THE MORAL LIFE AND CHRISTIAN PERFECTION

Justification in Relation to Moral Goodness

IN OUR STUDY OF THE WESLEYAN THEOLOGY WE COME NOW TO CONSIDER the moral and religious life which emerges as a consequence of pardon and acceptance and which exhibits a symmetry between the holiness of God and the righteousness of his children. A sinner cannot think of the Author of his being without abasing himself before him; for he is conscious of the distance which separates him, a worm of corruption, from God, who is perfection itself. "In His presence he sinks into the dust, knowing himself to be less than nothing in His eye; and being conscious, in a manner words cannot express, of his own littleness, ignorance, foolishness." [1] But the Christian man is no longer a sinner. Though he continually feels a sense of dependence on the Parent of good for his being and for all the blessings which attend it, he possesses at the same time the strongest affection for God and has the firmest confidence in him. This confidence does not lead him to self-abnegation; it is far from creating moral sloth or spiritual indolence. Rather, it pushes a man on

to the most vigorous industry. It causes him to put forth all his strength in obeying Him in whom he confides. So that he is never faint in his mind, never weary of doing what he believes to be His will. And as he knows the most acceptable worship of God is to imitate Him he worships, so he is continually labouring to transcribe into himself all His imitable perfections; in particular, His justice, mercy, and truth, so eminently displayed in all His creatures. [2]

Too long, Wesley reminds us, has the word "Christian" been abused by those who separate it from moral obligation. If it is not synonymous with the highest ethical attainments, then it means nothing at all. It

[1] *Works*, X, 67.
[2] *Ibid.*, p. 68.

is high time to rescue it out of the hands of "wretches that are a reproach to human nature," and to show that a genuine Christian does not use his religion as a "cloak for the vilest hypocrisy," [3] but lives out in life and character, in body and spirit, the will of God, whom he claims to obey.[4]

The Wesleyan system of Christian ethics rests securely on the foundation of Wesleyan theology. If justification implies the concomitant act of regeneration, and if the deed of God in pardon and acceptance is accompanied by the work of the Holy Spirit in rectification, and if both occur instantaneously as well as simultaneously so that a man is rectified in the very moment that he is justified, then it follows that, immediately after the experience of justification and regeneration, a man is introduced into the privileges and responsibilities of the Christian life and is given the power to fulfill its duties and to demonstrate its ideals. This is a point of no small consequence in Wesleyan thought; for, though it is true that the process of sanctification is just begun at the moment of conversion, this process has to do, as we shall see, solely with man's internal dispositions which still trouble him and which provide the occasion of falling into outward sin, but in no sense does it signify a gradual conquest over sinful acts themselves or a steady improvement in a man's external moral relationships. Man, in the very moment that he is justified, is given power over sin and actually does not commit sin in any of his dealings with his fellow creatures.[5] Thus any moral failure or any act of willful violation of the divine law on the part of a believer presupposes, first of all, the loss of faith;[6] for faith, working by love, excludes all deeds of outward sin.[7]

Wesleyan Ethics in Contrast to Ethics of the Reformation

Justification and regeneration, for Wesley, though they stand at the very beginning of the Christian life, signify none the less a completed

[3] *Ibid.*, p. 67.

[4] *Ibid.*, p. 71.

[5] Wesley writes: "A Christian is so far perfect, as not to commit sin. This is the glorious privilege of every Christian, yea, though he be but a babe in Christ."—*Works*, XI, 376.

[6] Sermon XIX, part ii, sec. 9.

[7] *Ibid.*, part iii, sec. 1.

act, not an ongoing process—something actually wrought out and accomplished, not a gradual transformation. Wesley abandons the Reformation conception of regeneration as continuing throughout life and as never actually reaching completion until flesh and blood are no more and death is swallowed up in victory.[8] He does not acknowledge the sixteenth-century Protestant idea that the Christian man is on the way toward righteousness but does not really attain the goal until his earthly pilgrimage is ended and he is ushered into the presence of his Lord.[9] In place of this, he substitutes the conception of a growth in holiness, of a genuine righteousness, not in the process of being attained and therefore marked by the vestiges of corruption, but actually having been reached and hence, once reached, subject to further development.[10] The real distinction between the two points of view lies—more than anywhere else, it seems to me—in the religious motive which prompts the use of the word "righteousness" and which assigns all Christian development either to a process *prior* to its attainment, as in the case of the Reformers, or to a process *subsequent* to its attainment, as in the case of Wesley.

Luther, for example, never denies the reality of Christian virtue; what he says is that man is in the process of being healed but, since sin is not altogether banished or dead, we cannot call him righteous in himself but only in Christ. He is forgiven for Christ's sake, and his sins will not be imputed to him.[11] And we might say to Wesley: If

[8] Luther, *Werke* (Weimar ed.) II, 495, 497.

[9] Calvin, *Institutes,* III, vi, 5. "Therefore, let us not cease to strive, that we may be incessantly advancing in the way of the Lord; nor let us despair on the smallness of our success; for however our success may not correspond to our wishes, yet our labor is not lost when the day surpasses the preceding one; provided that, with sincere simplicity, we keep our end in view, and press forward to the goal, not practicing self-adulation, nor indulging our own evil propensities, but perpetually exerting our endeavours after increasing degrees of amelioration, till we shall have arrived at perfection of goodness, which indeed, we seek and pursue as long as we live, and shall then attain, when, divested of all corporeal infirmity, we shall be admitted by God into complete communion with him."

[10] "The Plain Account of Christian Perfection" repeats this idea on every page.— *Works,* XI, 366-449.

[11] The matter is expressed in the Smaldcald Articles of 1537: "That we, through faith, secure another and new heart, and God, for Christ, our mediator's sake, will and does consider us as entirely righteous and holy. Though sin in the flesh is not entirely banished or dead, yet he will not impute nor recognize it. And upon such faith, re-

223

the righteousness which a man possesses is subject to improvement, then he cannot be said to be really righteous. If man is regenerate and yet must go on to perfection, then the state of regeneration itself is not synonymous with all that it implies. But the point is that Wesley is constrained to assign the term "righteousness" to the very first stages of the Christian life in order to express his conviction that a real moral similarity exists between Christians and their heavenly Father and that the weakest Christian man is capable of imitating the character of his Lord. The religious motive of the Reformers, which leads them to assign everything to the operation of God's grace and which causes them to interpret the merits of the moral life in terms of the imputation of the righteousness of Christ whereby a believer is accounted righteous by faith,[12] is drastically modified in the thought of John Wesley. Though he recognizes faith in Christ as essential to the continuance as well as the beginning of the moral life,[13] he at the same time uncompromisingly affirms that a man is not accounted righteous unless he is righteous and that the holiness of Christ is of no avail apart from a genuine personal holiness exemplifying itself in the life of the Christian man.[14] Thus the religious conviction which prompts Calvin, for example, to say that "man cannot without sacrilege arrogate to himself the least particle of righteousness, because it is so much detracted and diminished from the glory and the righteousness of

newal, and forgiveness of sin then follow good works. And what in these are yet sinful and defective, just for Christ's sake shall not be reckoned sinful or defective, but the man shall both in person and in his works be called and be entirely righteous and holy, out of pure grace and mercy shed abroad and poured out upon us in Christ."—Seeberg, *History of Doctrines,* II, 261. Cf. Luther, *op. cit.,* II, 13-14, 424; VIII, 106, 111.

[12] "We rest, I say, in the righteousness of Christ, by which he is righteous, because we cling to this, through which he is acceptable to God and intercedes as our advocate for us and makes himself entirely ours. . . . As impossible as it is therefore that Christ in his righteousness should not be acceptable, so impossible is it that we by our faith, by which we cling to his righteousness, should not be acceptable."—Luther, *op. cit.,* VI, 133; Seeberg, *op. cit.,* II, 261, n. 2. "Man is not righteous in himself but because the righteousness of Christ is communicated to him by imputation. . . . For he must be destitute of all righteousness of his own, who is taught to seek a righteousness out of himself. . . . Our righteousness is not of ourselves but in Christ; and . . . our title to it rests in our being partakers of Christ; for in possessing him, we possess all his riches with him."—Calvin, *op. cit.,* III, xi, 23.

[13] The moment faith is lost, unbelief will poison the whole soul.—*Works,* VIII, 399. Cf. "The Scripture Way of Salvation," Sermon XLIII. Faith in Christ is essential to all the stages of the Christian life.

[14] *Works,* X, 364-69.

God,"[15] prompts Wesley, on the other hand, to say that man can do all things through Christ strengthening him[16] and that Christians are so far righteous as to be "lively portraitures of Him" whom they are appointed to serve.[17] Therefore, the religious idea of Luther and of Calvin that in the ethics of salvation God is everything and man is nothing is not maintained by Wesley; and the difference between them is a difference not merely of degree but also of kind. What might appear as a superficial distinction, manifesting itself in the Reformers' refusal to say that man is inherently righteous in this world, as against Wesley's insistence that he *is* righteous, is really of ultimate significance. That man is not righteous and cannot be righteous means that his final salvation depends on something totally different from moral attainment and personal purity. On the other hand, that man can be righteous and indeed must be righteous if he is to be Christian means that his final salvation includes moral attainment and personal purity as essential elements. Without inherent personal holiness, Wesley says, no man can see God.[18]

Ethics of Christian Self-Realization

The Wesleyan system of ethics, therefore, stands in contrast to the systems of Luther and of Calvin in that it is an ethics of realization, not of aspiration. If everyone who believes in Christ is, as Luther maintains, righteous, not in reality, but only in hope, then the Christian life is a quest and a striving, a continuous struggle in pursuit of a goal which lies forever beyond the reach of actual attainment.[19] And yet that goal is not an idle dream; its reality for man consists in the faith that is given him, in his unfaltering trust that, though what he does as a finite creature is tarnished by sin, it is none the less acceptable in the eyes of God for Christ's sake and that both he and his actions are in the process of being rectified and healed. Though, as Calvin says, not even the holiest servant of God (so accounted in the eyes of men) can select from all the deeds of his life that which he conceives to have been the best and not find there some taint of the corruption of the

[15] Calvin, *op. cit.*, III, xiii, 2.
[16] *Works*, X, 369.
[17] Sermon IV, part iv, sec. 5.
[18] *Works*, X, 364.
[19] Luther, *op. cit.*, II, 495, 497.

THE THEOLOGY OF JOHN WESLEY

flesh or some mixture of an impure motive,[20] he still remains constant in his moral endeavor;[21] for he knows "that the kingdom of heaven is not the stipend of servants, but the inheritance of children, which will be enjoyed only by those whom the Lord adopts for his children, and for no other cause than on account of this adoption."[22] The moral law displays a perfection of righteousness, for it is the revelation of the holiness of God; and yet, if we view it alone, we shall be filled only with despair, since it condemns and curses us all by setting before us a demand which we can never fulfill.[23] Thus it cannot serve as the pattern of Christian duty, for righteousness is taught in vain by its precepts until Christ bestows it by his own gratuitous imputation.[24] With Calvin the starting point of ethics is the sovereign glory of God, and yet Christian duty is the earnest but imperfect striving toward that absolute ideal.[25]

With Wesley, on the other hand, the law is not only the disclosure of God's holiness but the pattern which we observe and the duty which we fulfill. He reminds us again and again that under the color of preaching Christ and magnifying the gospel we dare not neglect the law and, therefore, make void its precepts.[26] It is not enough "to coax sinners to Christ," to preach justification by faith alone. This is only half the gospel; and if it is substituted for the whole of it, it ceases to be the gospel at all. The true gospel minister insists on sanctification and universal holiness, on the great salvation, which is the deliverance from all sin, both inward and outward, and the absolute conformity unto the pattern of Christ. This is offered to every child of man, to whom it is said God willeth you to be perfect even as your Father in heaven is perfect.[27]

---

[20] Calvin, *op. cit.*, III, xiv, 9.

[21] *Ibid.*, vi, 5.

[22] *Ibid.*, xviii, 4.

[23] *Ibid.*, II, vii, 3-4.

[24] *Ibid.*, 2.

[25] This is not to imply any degree of antinomianism in the ethics of Calvin himself; man's imperfect striving is none the less characterized by Calvin in rules of rigid discipline. Note the rigid rules for the Christian life in the *Institutes*, III, vii-x. Yet he does insist that no man can be found who is not still a great distance from gospel perfection, and that the law is the goal toward which we must earnestly tend.—*Ibid.*, vi, 5.

[26] Sermon XXXVI, intro. sec. 1.

[27] *Works*, X, 455-56.

THE MORAL LIFE AND CHRISTIAN PERFECTION

The Wesleyan system of Christian ethics is embraced in thirteen discourses which are expositions by Wesley of our Lord's Sermon on the Mount. The Sermon on the Mount is Christ's own description of the way to heaven. The ethical standards embodied in its teachings are not for a small group of men who are withdrawn from the world; neither are they descriptive of some ideal state free from the turmoil and corruption of wicked men. They are given to all mankind alike; [28] and they are descriptive of the whole of religion—a full prospect of the Christian life as it ought to be.[29] Wesley, free from the findings of critical biblical scholarship, believes that the Sermon on the Mount was delivered by Jesus as a unified and systematic public address and that it is, therefore, perfect in method, each part harmonizing with the others and setting forth exactly what our Lord intended for us to know. It divides itself consequently into three distinct branches, the first of which covers chapter five of St. Matthew's Gospel; the second, chapter six; and the third, chapter seven.[30]

In the first branch of his discourse our Lord lays down the sum of all true ethical religion in eight particulars. Some people have imagined that these particulars are instances of the several stages in Christian development, the successive steps which a Christian takes in his journey toward perfection. Others have felt that all these particulars belong at one and the same time to every Christian. Wesley tells us that we must accept both points of view. Undoubtedly poverty of spirit, which is the first beatitude, is found in a greater or less degree in every Christian, and so likewise are all the other states described in the beatitudes. But it is equally true that real Christianity begins in poverty of spirit, and then goes on successively in the manner here presented until the babe in Christ develops into a full-grown man. If we begin at the lowest of these gifts and move on up the scale to the highest, it does not mean that we relinquish the lower as we progress but that we add to and build on the foundation which is laid.[31]

Poverty of spirit, which is the foundation of the religious life, must

[28] Sermon XXI, intro. secs. 5-6.
[29] Ibid., sec. 7.
[30] Ibid., sec. 10.
[31] Ibid., part i, sec. 1.

227

not be taken to mean a love for poverty;[32] rather, it refers to the disposition of those who are in a state of penitence, who have received that first repentance which is prior to faith, and who are, therefore, convinced that they have no spiritual good abiding in them and that they are still covered with "the loathsome leprosy sin," which they have brought with them from their mother's womb.[33] Some have called this the "virtue of humility," and have taught us to be proud of knowing we deserve damnation and yet are saved for Christ's sake. Nothing is further from the truth of our Lord, when he teaches that we must be of a sorrowful spirit and repent in dust and ashes for our transgressions.[34] It is only when our sorrow is genuine and our penitence is sincere that we may expect the promise that the Kingdom of Heaven is ours. And in what sense is it ours? It is ours because God actually washes us and purifies us and stamps the righteousness of his own nature upon our souls.[35] To be sure, this poverty of spirit continues on through the course of our Christian life, but then it is not a sense of hopeless sorrow because of unforgiven sins but rather a continual sense of our utter dependence on God for every good thought, word, and work, of our inability to remain righteous unless he "water us every moment."[36]

But after our sins are forgiven and righteousness manifests itself in our lives, we begin to imagine that the Christian way is easy and that we shall be "borne aloft in chariots of joy and love" to our heavenly home.[37] Such is not the case; our old dispositions are not dead; they still trouble us, and we are subjected to all manner of temptations. So our Lord calls those of us blessed who mourn in temptation and trouble, not on account of some worldly matter such as the loss of reputation, friends, or fortune, but solely on account of our desire for the blessed assurances of our God.[38] And when our mourning is brought to an end by the return of the Comforter and we are released from our stage of depression by a greater abundance of heavenly joy,

[32] Ibid., sec. 3.
[33] Ibid., sec. 4.
[34] Ibid., secs. 7-8.
[35] Ibid., secs. 11-12.
[36] Ibid., sec. 13.
[37] Ibid., part ii, sec. 1.
[38] Ibid., secs. 3, 4, 5.

there is another form of Christian mourning which abides with us forever, a mourning which is akin to the suffering of the Son of God —we mourn for the sins and miseries of mankind, for those creatures who remain in moral corruption and who persistently refuse the regenerative power of God's Spirit.[39]

Next in the scale of the Christian virtues comes meekness, that property of the soul which demonstrates itself in our relationships both to God and to our fellow men. It is a composure of mind which, with reference to God, we term resignation, a calm acquiescence to his will in all matters concerning our lives; and which, with reference to our neighbors, we term mildness and kindness to the good and gentleness and understanding to the evil.[40] Meekness enables us to bear up under the strain of evil and to regulate even our zeal for God by a genuine love for our fellow men.[41] It is interesting to note in what sense Wesley interprets our Lord's promise that the meek shall inherit the earth. The wise of all ages have counseled us that if we are too meek, we shall be abused and there will be no living left for us. But Wesley says that God takes peculiar care to provide for the meek and to supply them with all things needful for life and godliness. They inherit the earth in the sense that by their very meekness they are content with what God gives them, and they richly enjoy what little they have in spite of the force, fraud, and malice of men.

It is sweet to them, be it little or much. As in patience they possess their souls, so they truly possess whatever God hath given them. They are always content, always pleased with what they have: it pleases them because it pleases God; so that while their heart, their desire, their joy is in heaven, they may truly be said "to inherit the earth."[42]

The first three Christian virtues, which are characteristic states of the soul, serve to remove the hindrances to true religion, such as pride, which is taken away by poverty of spirit; levity and thoughtlessness, which are removed by holy mourning; and anger, impatience, and discontent, which are banished by genuine meekness. But then there

39 *Ibid.*, sec. 6.
40 Sermon XXII, part i, sec. 4.
41 *Ibid.*, sec. 5.
42 *Ibid.*, sec. 12.

is a more positive disposition which asserts itself in the soul of the Christian, and that is a spiritual hunger and thirst after righteousness.[43] Wesley defines righteousness as "every holy and heavenly temper in one; springing from, as well as terminating in, the love of God, as our Father and Redeemer, and the love of all men for his sake." [44] All the rest of our spiritual appetites are swallowed up in this one great desire—to be renewed after the likeness of him who created us. Just as the bodily appetites of hunger and thirst cannot be satisfied apart from meat and drink,[45] even so it is impossible to satisfy the soul who is athirst for the living God with what the world calls religion: the doing no harm, the abstaining from outward sin, and the using of the means of grace.

This is only the outside of that religion which he insatiably hungers after. The knowledge of God in Christ Jesus: "the life which is hid with Christ in God;" the being "joined unto the Lord in one spirit;" the "having fellowship with the Father and the Son;" the "walking in the light as God is in the light;" the being "purified even as he is pure;"—this is the religion, the righteousness he thirsts after; nor can he rest, till he thus rests in God.[46]

The more a Christian is filled with positive righteousness, the more tenderly will he be concerned for those who are without God in the world. He will be compassionate and tender-hearted and will display genuine mercy.[47] Mercy, for Wesley, always means love, for love alone is the instigator of compassion.[48] Love envieth not,[49] is completely unselfish,[50] does not willingly think evil,[51] weeps over sin and rejoices in goodness,[52] is glad to find a reason to excuse whatever is amiss, and is easily convinced of the sincerity of a penitent.[53]

Does this mean that love conceals evil and winks at sin? No, certainly not to the extent that a righteous man makes himself an ac-

[43] *Ibid.*, part ii, sec. 1.
[44] *Ibid.*, sec. 2.
[45] *Ibid.*, sec. 3.
[46] *Ibid.*, sec. 4.
[47] *Ibid.*, part iii, sec. 1.
[48] *Ibid.*, sec. 3.
[49] *Ibid.*, sec. 5.
[50] *Ibid.*, sec. 9.
[51] *Ibid.*, sec. 11.
[52] *Ibid.*, secs. 12-13.
[53] *Ibid.*, sec. 15.

complice to a crime or encourages wrongdoing by remaining indifferent to it. But it does mean that a righteous man dare not, for the glory of God, seek to destroy evil by injuring the evildoer; and Wesley goes so far as to say: "Wheresoever and with whomsoever he is, if he sees anything which he approves not, it goes not out of his lips, unless to the person concerned, if haply he may gain his brother." Only for the benefit of the innocent is a righteous and merciful man ever constrained to declare the guilty, and Wesley lays down five standards which must be met before such a declaration of another's guilt may be made:

1. He [a righteous and merciful man] will not speak at all, till love, superior love, constrains him.

2. He cannot do it from a general confused view of doing good, or promoting the glory of God, but from a clear sight of some particular end, some determinate good, which he pursues.

3. Still he cannot speak, unless he be fully convinced that this very means is necessary to that end; that the end cannot be answered, at least not so effectually, by any other way.

4. He then doeth it with the utmost sorrow and reluctance: using it as the last and worst medicine, a desperate remedy in a desperate case, a kind of poison never to be used but to expel poison. Consequently,

5. He uses it as sparingly as possible. And this he does with fear and trembling, lest he should transgress the law of love by speaking too much, more than he would have done by not speaking at all.[54]

Finally, love cannot be motivated by an interest in self; it must be outgoing and universal, the expression of one's willingness to lay down his life for the sake of others.[55] Motivated by the power of such love, mercy exercises itself, and the mercy of the Christian man shall obtain the mercy of God, which not only repays him a thousandfold in his heart but likewise bestows an exceeding and eternal weight of glory.[56]

On what foundation, Wesley asks, is true love built? He then answers that it rests upon the love of God alone. Blessed are the pure in heart, for they shall see God.[57] Genuine purity of heart has received

---

[54] Ibid., sec. 14.
[55] Ibid., sec. 18.
[56] Ibid., sec. 17.
[57] Sermon XXIII, part i, sec. 1.

scant emphasis from the ethical teachers of the past; they have spent their time guarding men against outward impurities alone.[58] But the pure in heart are those whose souls are pure after the fashion of the purity of God; having been washed clean of every unholy affection, they now love the Lord their God with all their heart and with all their soul, mind, and strength.[59] They will not retain anything which is the occasion for the return of impurity. If a person as dear to them as their right eye be an occasion to them for doing wrong and for offending God by exciting any unholy desire in their soul, they will forcibly separate from that person at once. "Any loss whether of pleasure, or substance, or friends, is preferable to the loss of thy soul." [60] People who are pure in heart not only shall see God but do actually see him: in all his providences relating to themselves, in pleasure, in sorrow, in health, in pain, in honor, in abuse; [61] for they live by the conviction that

God is in all things, and that we are to see the Creator in the glass of every creature; that we should use and look upon nothing as separate from God, which indeed is a kind of practical Atheism; but, with true magnificence of thought, survey heaven and earth, and all that is therein, as contained by God in the hollow of his hand, who by his intimate presence holds them all in being, who pervades and actuates the whole created frame, and is, in a true sense, the soul of the universe.[62]

True religion, however, is not alone a state of being; it is a state of doing also.[63] Blessed are the peacemakers, those lovers of God and man who detest all strife and contention and who labor "with all their might, either to prevent this fire of hell from being kindled, or, when it is kindled, from breaking out; or, when it is broke out, from spreading any further." It would appear, says Wesley, that a righteous man and a promoter of peace would be "the darling of all mankind." But our Lord knew the true character of human nature and the vast ex-

[58] *Ibid.*, sec. 3.
[59] *Ibid.*, sec. 2.
[60] Before any final separation, however, from friends, try to drive the unclean spirit of temptation out by fasting and prayer and consult with someone else who has experience in the ways of God.—*Ibid.*, sec. 4.
[61] *Ibid.*, secs. 6-10.
[62] *Ibid.*, sec. 11.
[63] *Ibid.*, part ii, sec. 1.

tent of sinfulness, and he went on to say: "Blessed are they which are persecuted for righteousness' sake; for theirs is the kingdom of heaven." [64] The fact that a man is righteous is not the reason why he is persecuted. If he would keep his religion to himself, he would be tolerated; but it is when he seeks to spread his goodness to others that he runs into danger and persecution.[65] But such persecution is the badge of discipleship: "if we have it not, we are bastards, and not sons: straight through evil report as well as good report lies the only way to the kingdom." [66] But how, we ask, is a Christian to act in the face of persecution? He should not actively seek it or designedly do things to bring it upon him.[67] Neither should he try to avoid it or escape from it when it comes, and one can be sure that it will come. He should let no persecution turn him from the Christian way, but he should love his persecutors, bless them in their bitterness, and reprove them by repeating a better lesson before them, by rendering them good in deed and in prayer.[68]

Such, in brief, are the marks which characterize the true Christian and which, in Wesley's own words, present "a picture of God so far as he is imitable by man." [69] To those who have been thus transformed into the likeness of God, who created them,[70] comes the charge to let their goodness shine before men,[71] for religion is ordained not for the individual alone but for society also. True godliness cannot exist in isolation.[72] Such virtues as gentleness, mildness, endurance in the midst of evil, and the desire for peace in strife and the striving to achieve it cannot subsist alone in a desert or in the total solitude of a hermit's cell.[73] But though religion is social in the sense that it is ordained for all mankind, still the individual is the agency of its promulgation and the means whereby it spreads. It is the very nature

[64] *Ibid.*, part iii, sec. 1.
[65] *Ibid.*, sec. 3.
[66] *Ibid.*, sec. 7.
[67] *Ibid.*, sec. 9.
[68] *Ibid.*, sec. 13.
[69] *Ibid.*, part iv.
[70] Sermon XXIV, intro. sec. 1.
[71] *Ibid.*, sec. 5.
[72] *Ibid.*, part i, sec. 1.
[73] *Ibid.*, sec. 2.

of the divine savour which is in you, to spread to whatsoever you touch; to diffuse itself, on every side, to all those among whom you are. This is the great reason why the providence of God has so mingled you together with other men, that whatever grace you have received of God may through you be communicated to others; that every holy temper and word and work of yours may have an influence on them also. By this means a check will, in some measure, be given to the corruption which is in the world; and a small part, at least, saved from the general infection, and rendered holy and pure before God.[74]

In Wesleyan thought man is not saved from sin and converted to goodness by a general renovation of society or perfection of the social system. The reverse of the matter is true: society is changed into a better place in which to live by the conversion and ethical purification of individual men. Therefore, Wesley charges his followers not to conceal their religion; indeed, if they have it, it will not be concealed, for holiness makes one as "conspicuous as the sun in the midst of heaven." [75]

In the second branch of his discourse on the Sermon on the Mount our Lord gives practical application to what he has already set forth as the ethical principles of true religion, those inward tempers contained in spiritual holiness which pervades the soul. He proceeds to show, Wesley tells us, how all human actions, even those that are indifferent in their own nature, may be made good and acceptable to God by a pure and holy intention.[76] Pure intention keeps all outward actions free from corruption and delivers us from worldly desires and the anxious cares of daily life.[77] Thus in regard to works of mercy, we are not to seek the attraction of men, but rather we are to do good merely for the sake of the body and soul of the person in whose behalf that good is performed.[78] Works of piety likewise, such as attendance at church and public prayers, are to be executed with no view to any temporal reward but solely for the design of promoting the glory of God.[79] Fasting is to be considered not as some meaningless ceremony

[74] *Ibid.,* sec. 7.
[75] *Ibid.,* part ii, sec. 2.
[76] Sermon XXVI, intro. sec. 1.
[77] Sermon XXI, intro. sec. 10.
[78] Sermon XXVI, part i, secs. 1-4.
[79] *Ibid.,* part ii, sec. 2.

to be fulfilled because it is commanded but rather as the outward expression of genuine sorrow for sin, either our own sin or that of others,[80] and as a help to prayer.[81] But purity of intention does not characterize our religious actions alone; it follows us to our houses of business, and vain and worldly desires are no more allowable in our employment than in our religious devotions.[82] It is a truth which can never be denied that we cannot receive the things of God unless our eyes be singly fixed on God.[83] In our business, therefore, we are to attempt to succeed only to the extent that we are enabled to meet our financial obligations, to provide adequately for ourselves and for our family; but beyond this we dare not go.[84] If it is true that we are to be industrious and to gain all we can,[85] and if it is likewise true that we are to be thrifty and save all we can,[86] it is solely for the purpose of love, so that we may give all we can.[87] No man can serve two masters; we cannot be devoted to ourselves and at the same time be loyal to God.[88]

In the third branch of his discourse on the Sermon on the Mount our Lord cautions us against the most fatal hindrances to true holiness and then finally exhorts us to rise above them and to secure the prize for which we were in the first instance justified.[89] He tells us not to judge other people for what they do or to assign evil motives for their evil deeds.[90] Passing judgment on another, says Wesley, is thinking of him in a manner contrary to love.[91] But neither are we to cast holy thing to dogs nor the pearls of the faith to swine: that is, we are not to defile the precious things of our religion by repeating them to those who openly ridicule them and make fun of what they stand for.[92]

[80] Sermon XXVII, part ii, secs. 2-5.
[81] *Ibid.*, sec. 6.
[82] Sermon XXVIII, sec. 1.
[83] *Ibid.*, sec. 7.
[84] *Ibid.*, secs. 11-12.
[85] Sermon L, part i, sec. 1.
[86] *Ibid.*, part ii, sec. 1.
[87] *Ibid.*, part iii, sec. 1.
[88] Sermon XXIX, secs. 3-4, 13.
[89] Sermon XXX, sec. 3.
[90] *Ibid.*, sec. 4.
[91] *Ibid.*, sec. 9.
[92] This does not have reference to preaching, but to continued argument and personal conversation.—*Ibid.*, secs. 16-17.

Rather, we are to seek the good of such evildoers through prayer,[93] and make sure our prayer reaches the heavenly throne by presenting it with a clean heart and with charity for all men.[94] In all cases relating to our neighbor we must abide by the Golden Rule and make his cause our very own.[95] We must carefully guard ourselves against all sin, and know that to violate the least commandment of God constitutes sin.[96] To stop to enumerate the sins that are common to most people is impossible. "Rather," writes Wesley, "go and count the drops of rain, or the sands on the sea-shore." [97] And yet sin is an abomination unto the Lord, and all who are its victims are on that broad road that leadeth to destruction. How greatly will they swell the number of the children of hell! [98] We are to know the worth of any doctrine and of any life by the fruit that it produces, by the effects it has for moral power and goodness in the character and disposition of men.[99] Thus it behooves every man to examine the foundation on which he builds. If he builds on what men call orthodoxy or right opinion, his foundation possesses no more stability than sand or "the froth of the sea." [100] He must build on personal trust in the cross of Christ alone; [101] he must labor in the spirit of holiness and unselfish love.[102]

The Wesleyan ethics is, in the last analysis, an ethics of Christian self-realization; and as such it takes its place among those systems of moral discipline in which the Christian society is conceived in terms of its indivdual members, the quality of whose lives and the earnestness of whose work constitute its power and its success.

Ernst Troeltsch, in his work on the social teachings of the Christian groups throughout history, distinguishes between two major types of Christian society, or rather two major ideas as to what Christian society really is. The one, which he calls the church type, considers Christian society in a relative sense as embracing the whole of social life as it is

[93] *Ibid.*, sec. 18.
[94] *Ibid.*, sec. 21.
[95] *Ibid.*, sec. 24.
[96] Sermon XXXI, part i, sec. 2.
[97] *Ibid.*, sec. 4.
[98] *Ibid.*, sec. 5.
[99] Sermon XXXII, part iii, secs. 1-4.
[100] Sermon XXXIII, part iii, sec. 1.
[101] *Ibid.*, sec. 4.
[102] Sermon XXXI, part iii, sec. 5.

lived under the aegis of the Church. The Church, therefore, is a universal institution, endowed with absolute authoritative truth and the sacramental power of grace and redemption. It takes up into its life the secular institutions, groups, and values which have arisen out of man's fallen state. The Christian fellowship is not dependent on individualism, or the individual's fulfilling the duties of the Christian life. It depends alone on the sacraments and on the Church as a supernatural institution. It is able to discard the ideal of moral perfection for its members and so to adapt itself to the relativities of the social order, which it frankly accepts and tolerates. The other, which he calls the sect type, regards the religious community as that group of people who live according to the ideals of the gospel. It does not recognize the evils which exist in society at large as essential parts of man's life on this earth, and it either withdraws completely from society or else seeks to remake society after the pattern of the Christian ideal.[103]

Wesleyan ethics, viewed in the light of Wesley's social teachings (which can be put in a sentence—that society is rectified by the rectification of its individual members through genuine conversion and the pursuit of the moral life), is a clear and unquestionable example of the sect ethics. Any attempt to interpret it otherwise or to attempt to construe it in terms of the recognized moral relativities of the church type as Troeltsch defines it is impossible. The demand for absolute holiness is not reconcilable with compromise freely admitted and accepted as such. It is possible to effect a compromise without being conscious that it is a compromise; and yet for the one who so effects it, it is not a compromise. Wesley is not conscious of making any compromise in his moral demands on Christians, although he conceives of those demands always in individualistic terms. Individuals are the measure of all things spiritual, the very blocks of the Christian social order. Troeltsch is perfectly correct, therefore, in characterizing Wesleyanism as an example of the sect type.[104]

For Wesley, the Christian whole is made up of the sum of its parts, and any defect in any individual leaves its mark on the structure as a whole. Thus the ethical standards set forth by Wesley in his thirteen

[103] See E. Troeltsch, *The Social Teaching of the Christian Churches*, II, 461-65.
[104] *Ibid.*, pp. 721-24.

discourses on our Lord's Sermon on the Mount are binding on all the
members of the Christian fellowship alike and are the marks whereby
the true children of God are distinguished from the children of wrath
and the servants of this present world. The Christian, in a very real
sense, is set apart and separated from the world, and he must keep
himself free from the contamination of wicked men. But immediately
the question arises: Is not this the pharisaical self-righteousness which
characterized Wesley's life prior to Aldersgate? In form there is perhaps no distinction. In motive the two are worlds apart. Before Aldersgate, Wesley was righteous from a sense of fear and a feverish desire
to fulfill all the commandments of the law. His attitude toward those
whose sins were fleshly and, therefore, pronounced was one of contempt
and pharisaical condemnation. If he performed works of charity in
their behalf, it was merely for the sake of fulfilling the external commandment, "Love thy neighbor," and of thus increasing his own
chances of salvation. But after Aldersgate his motive was changed,
and he viewed the sinful with pity and genuine love. Thus, if the
Christian is separate from the world, it is not in the sense that he takes
no interest in the needs of the world and refuses to converse with evil
men. Rather, he goes to all men—fornicators, idolaters, railers, drunkards, extortioners—and yet he goes, not as one familiar with their
habits or desiring to keep intimate company with their faults, but as
the servant of Christ seeking to win them to the standards of his
Lord.[105] Thus Wesley never repudiates, or even so much as modifies,
the extreme outward righteousness of pharisaism: he accepts its form
and adheres to its expression, but he rejects its motive and substitutes
for its love of self the love of God and of the neighbor.[106]

It is not surprising, therefore, that Wesleyan ethics assumes an
extreme form of outward discipline in the performance of duty and
in the conduct of personal life. Wesley is pedantic in his enumeration
of the faults that his followers are to abstain from; and he lists as a
requirement for remaining a member of the United Societies that a
man evidence his desire for salvation by

[105] Sermon XXIV, part i, sec. 5.
[106] Sermon XXV, part iv, secs. 1-13.

doing no harm, by avoiding evil in every kind; especially that which is most generally practiced: Such is, the taking the name of God in vain; the profaning the day of the Lord, either by doing ordinary work thereon, or by buying or selling; drunkenness, buying or selling spirituous liquors, or drinking them, unless in cases of extreme necessity; fighting, quarreling, brawling; brother going to law with brother; returning evil for evil, or railing for railing; the using many words in buying or selling; the buying or selling uncustomed goods; the giving or taking things on usury, that is, unlawful interest; uncharitable or unprofitable conversation, particularly speaking evil of Magistrates or of Ministers; doing to others as we would not they should do unto us; doing what we know is not for the glory of God, as the "putting on of gold and costly apparel!" the taking such diversions as can not be used in the name of the Lord Jesus; the singing those songs, or reading those books, which do not tend to the knowledge or love of God; softness, and needless self-indulgence; laying up treasure upon earth; borrowing without a probability of paying; or taking up goods without a probability of paying for them.[107]

Wesley is careful likewise to list the specific good works that his followers are to perform and the noble lives that they are to exemplify; and then he closes by saying of anyone who proves unfaithful: "We will admonish him of the error of his ways; we will bear with him for a season: But then if he repent not, he hath no place among us. We have delivered our own souls."[108]

Christian Perfection: the Goal of Justification and the Moral Life

If Wesleyan ethics is extreme in its form of outward discipline to the extent that it will not countenance the open violation of the moral law, it is even more extreme in its conception of inward holiness and in its insistence on absolute, not relative, Christian perfection. We have seen already that, if man is rectified by an act of God in justification and regeneration and is so far perfect as to have absolute power over

[107] "The Nature, Design, and General Rules of the United Societies, in London, Bristol, Kingswood, Newcastle-Upon-Tyne, Etc.," *Works,* VIII, 270. See Sermons XLVIII, XLIX, LII, LXXIX, LXXX, LXXXI, LXXXII, LXXXVII, LXXXVIII, XCVII, XCVIII, XCIX, CI, CIV, CVIII, CXVIII, CXIX, CXXVI, CXXX. Sermon CXL, on public diversions, though it was never published by Mr. Wesley himself, is no more extreme in its sectarian strictness than the others and is in line with his temper of moral discipline and purity.

[108] *Works,* VIII, 271.

outward sin, it is none the less true that he is not completely sanctified and that there are latent within him his old dispositions which still trouble him and which furnish the occasion for his falling back again into sin. And in our exposition of Wesleyan ethics we noted the fact that the various dispositions of the Christian soul which are the heritage of the justified are at the same time capable of development and that they exist in varying degrees of perfection in the various Christians who embody them. Christian perfection, or entire sanctification, is the end of Wesleyan moral development, the goal of justification itself, and indeed the final condition for salvation and the entrance into the eternal presence of God.

Now it is interesting to note that the doctrine of Christian perfection was embraced by Mr. Wesley as a consequence of the moral and spiritual insights gained from his training in the home and from his study of Taylor, Thomas à Kempis, and William Law and that he held absolute holiness as the goal of the Christian life before his religious experience at Aldersgate.[109] To be sure, the Aldersgate experience modified his theology; for it shifted the emphasis from self to God and opened Wesley's eyes to the inherent sinfulness of human nature, to the impotence of man to fulfill the divine law unaided, and to the true meaning of justification by grace through faith. It did not abrogate the requirements of the moral law, however, as regards either external or internal holiness, but rather it established the law more firmly by generating the power to fulfill it and by actually producing holiness in the heart. Thus Wesley set forth in his sermon entitled "The Circumcision of the Heart," preached on January 1, 1733, what he believed on Christian perfection; and he wrote as late as the year 1777 in regard to this, the first of all his writings to be published, that it expressed "without any material addition or diminution" all he believed in regard to perfection.[110]

Perfection, in Wesley's own words, is nothing more nor less than

that habitual disposition of the soul which, in sacred writings, is termed holiness; and which directly implies, the being cleansed from sin, "from all filthiness both of flesh and spirit;" and, by consequence, the being endued

[109] Ibid., XI, 266-67.
[110] Ibid., p. 369.

THE MORAL LIFE AND CHRISTIAN PERFECTION

with those virtues which were also in Christ Jesus; the being so "renewed in the spirit of our mind," as to be "perfect as our Father in heaven is perfect." [111]

Or, put in another way:

Here, then, is the sum of the perfect law; this is the true circumcision of the heart. Let the spirit return to God that gave it, with the whole train of its affections. "Unto the place from whence all the rivers came," thither let them flow again. Other sacrifices from us he would not; but the living sacrifice of the heart he hath chosen. Let it be continually offered up to God through Christ, in flames of holy love. . . . Let your soul be filled with an entire love of him, that you may love nothing but for his sake.[112]

Perfection is the completion of the development of sanctification begun at regeneration. There man is given power over outward sin, and love becomes the dominating motive of his life. But, though love dominates in all his dealings with other men and is the guide of all his actions, it is not the only motive of his life; and he is tormented by the urges, cravings, and dispositions of his old nature, by evil thoughts and suggestions which furnish the occasion for returning to open sin. However, when the Christian reaches the state of entire sanctification, when he attains the goal of perfection, these wrong tempers are taken away, the dispositions which trouble him are made to vanish, and the craving and urge after wrong which by grace he has kept in subjection no longer remain in his soul. Love has entire possession of him.[113]

Christian perfection, for Wesley, means, therefore, only one thing, and that is purity of motive: the love of God, freed entirely from all the corruptions of natural desire and emancipated completely from any interest in self or in any other person or thing apart from God, guides unhindered every thought and every action of a man's life. In body and mind the perfect Christian is still finite; he makes mistakes in judgment as long as he lives; these mistakes in judgment occasion mistakes in practice, and mistakes in practice often have bad moral consequences. Thus perfection in the sense of infallibility does not exist on the face of the earth.[114]

[111] Sermon XVII, part i, sec. 1.
[112] Ibid., part ii, sec. 10.
[113] Works, XI, 394.
[114] Ibid., p. 395; Sermon XL, part i, secs. 1-9.

241

But how, we ask, is Christian perfection to be achieved? How long do we have to continue in the moral struggle, fighting temptation and by grace keeping our natural passions in subjection? What can we do to win this priceless gift? To this Wesley answers by saying that perfection is not achieved by effort; there is not a single moral act that a man can perform to win it. Like justification, it comes by faith and is the free gift of God. All we can do is continue patiently in the faith that is given us, remain loyal morally and spiritually, and steadfastly believe that what God has promised he will perform. In fact, in his sermon on "The Scripture Way of Salvation," Wesley indicates that if we sincerely believe that God will do it, then it is reasonable for us to expect him to do it at any moment. "Look for it then every day, every hour, every moment! Why not this hour, this moment? Certainly you may look for it now, if you believe it is by faith." [115] Does this mean that perfection, entire sanctification, is instantaneous, comes in a moment? Wesley replies that the act of faith wherein perfection is finally wrought in the soul does come in a moment, just as in the case of justification; but a gradual work precedes that moment, so that sanctification, considered as a whole, is a process of development which begins at the very moment a person is justified. [116] Often the act of perfection seems itself to be gradual, and not instantaneous, in that the person in whom it is wrought does not know the particular moment in which all his sinful urges ceased to be; [117] but "it is often difficult to perceive the instant in which a man dies; yet there is an instant in which life ceases. And if ever sin ceases, there must be a last moment of its existence, and a first moment of our deliverance from it." [118]

[115] Sermon XLIII, part iii, sec. 18.

[116] *Works*, XI, 446. Dr. Umphrey Lee very wisely points out the reason why Wesley is forced to hold that entire sanctification must come in a moment. Wesley, as we have seen, believes that a man must be absolutely holy in order to see God. In the case of a death-bed confession in which a man is justified just prior to his death, then God must at the same time sanctify him and make him entirely holy: there is no time for a gradual development in such an instance, so Wesley must hold that sanctification in the sense even of perfection can come in a moment by faith. See U. Lee, *John Wesley and Modern Religion*, p. 189. This is not the usual procedure, however, for Wesley tells us that entire sanctification generally comes many, many years after justification, in most cases just before the hour of death itself.—*Works*, XI, 446.

[117] Sermon XLIII, part iii, sec. 18.

[118] *Works*, XI, 442.

242

It must be remarked at this point that perfection, or the rule of per- fect love supreme, is not in Wesley's thought a static state with no further progress and development. Though it is true that he does not succeed in explaining the nature of spiritual development beyond per- fection, he does himself raise the question: "Is it improvable?" And he answers: "It is so far from lying in an indivisible point, from being incapable of increase, that one perfected in love may grow in grace far swifter than he did before." [119] Thus there is no further develop- ment in which the dispositions which trouble us and furnish the oc- casion for the return to open sin are gradually being overcome. Perfect love is in complete control. And yet there are new occasions always for the demonstration of love and thus for the enrichment of life. These are the means of growth in grace. It is a pity that Wesley did not have access to A. E. Taylor's notion of "a possibility which com- bines attainment and aspiration and which leaves room in a society of just men made perfect for a very real and intense moral life." This is exactly the idea that Wesley is trying to get across in his emphasis on growth in grace subsequent even to entire sanctification.[120] It must be noted here, also, that Wesley believed that a man can fall from the state of entire sanctification and be lost. Everything depends on his own freedom in willing to remain in any spiritual state in which God by his faith has placed him.[121] "I do not," Wesley writes, "include an impossibility of falling from it, either in part or in whole." [122]

Christian perfection, or full sanctification, is "the grand depositum which God has lodged with the people called Methodist; and for the sake of propagating this chiefly he appeared to have raised us up." [123] It is the end of which justification is the beginning—the final goal toward which all ethical development moves.

[119] *Ibid.*
[120] *Ibid.*, p. 446. See Taylor, *The Faith of a Moralist,* I, 386-434.
[121] *Ibid.*, X, 296-97.
[122] *Ibid.*, XI, 446.
[123] *Ibid.*, XIII, 9. This was certainly not the position of the Anglican Church. Richard Hooker held: "There is a glorifying righteousness of men in the world to come; and there is a justifying and sanctifying righteousness here. The righteousness, wherewith we shall be clothed in the world to come, is both perfect and inherent. That whereby here we are justified is perfect, but not inherent. That whereby we are sanctified, in- herent, but not perfect."—*Works,* III, 485.

CONCLUSION

IT HAS BEEN THE THESIS OF THIS BOOK THAT WESLEY'S DOCTRINE OF JUSTI-fication was the source and determinant of all the rest of his theology. It remains now to gather together the separate strands of this presentation into a coherent whole.

It is possible to consider the nature of the Christian conception of justification in one of two ways. Either it may be viewed as the means whereby a sinner, who stands in condemnation before the righteous law of God, is actually converted into a righteous person and is thereby enabled to meet the standards of divine holiness and in a manner consistent with absolute justice to merit the right of eternal fellowship with God;[1] or it may be interpreted solely as divine mercy which even in spite of sin claims the sinner and pardons him for Christ's sake and accepts him into the everlasting fellowship of the redeemed. The former of these alternatives leads to a limitation of the extent of justification in the process of salvation as a whole and makes it, not the sum total or even the final goal of religion, but merely the start. The second of these alternatives, on the other hand, extends the bounds of justification until it comes to include almost the whole of the Christian life and makes it synonymous with final salvation itself. In the one instance, what God does in pardon and acceptance is relative to its consequences, and the act of forgiveness is not in itself ultimate but is a means to a more glorious end. In the other instance, the exact opposite is the case: what God does and continues always to do in pardon and acceptance is final, and all moral and spiritual effects in life and character are manifestations of the one fundamental act of forgiveness, which is the end as well as the beginning of man's religious

[1] This statement must be taken in a cautious and guarded sense. What is meant by the standard of holiness is simply the highest moral possibility for human life to attain under given conditions, and what is meant by absolute justice is that God will not account a man as just unless he really is just—that is, unless he has met the highest possible standard of holiness. Thus to merit the right of eternal fellowship comes to mean that a person is what he ought to be in order to have communion and keep company with God. Note carefully that these characteristics follow the act of justification, and justification is that which enables them to come into existence.

life. Reformation theology is a classic expression of this latter, all-inclusive concept of justification,[2] while Wesleyan thought stands as a representation within the stream of Protestantism of the former, less inclusive concept of justification.[3]

Thus the Reformers always refer to a religious act, to what God does for man in Christ; and justification is the abiding, lifelong expression of the mediatorial and perfectly righteous work of Christ apportioned to the believer by divine grace through the instrument of faith. Wesley always refers to a religious and moral condition, to a living expression of the result of divine grace in the form of human holiness; and justification, for him, is the prior act which makes possible that condition and produces that result. Therefore, though degrees of similarity are apparent in the two conceptions of justification, especially in the nature and statement of the justifying act itself, the religious emphasis of the two doctrines is entirely different, and the starting point of the one is as far removed from that of the other as the east is from the west. The Reformers always begin with God, and the cause of man's justification has no meaning apart from the electing

[2] For a most excellent discussion and critical analysis of the Reformation principle of justification by faith in Christ, see A. Ritschl, *Die Christliche Lehre von der Rechtfertigung und Versohnung*, B. I, K. 4.

[3] It has not seemed necessary to compare and to contrast Wesleyan thought with the Roman Catholic conception of justification, which likewise is interpreted as a means of making man actually acceptable to God. The Roman notion does not bear a direct relationship to Wesleyan thought at this point because of the fact that Wesleyanism, in line with Protestant thought in general, views the effects of justification as a subjective experience of the individual, not as an objective process of infused grace bestowed on the individual through the sacraments. The Catholic concept is not a simple notion but is bound up with the use of the sacraments on the part of the individual and with his active fulfillment of the laws of God and of the Church. To be sure, the Roman conception is not limited to a single act either at the start or at the finish of man's life but is continuous and is increased and decreased as man exercises his faith in good works or fails to do so. It more nearly corresponds to Wesley's conception of sanctification than to that of justification—at least, in its stress on holiness and the increase of grace through good works. These works are said actually to merit reward. "If any one saith, that the good works of one that is justified are in such manner the gifts of God, as that they are not also the good merits of him that is justified; or that the said justified, by the good works which he performs through the grace of God and the merit of Jesus Christ, whose living member he is, does not truly merit increase of grace, eternal life, and the attainment of that eternal life,—if so be, however, that he depart in grace,—and also an increase of glory; let him be anathema."—*Canons and Decrees of the Council of Trent*, Session VI, Canon XXXII. See the entire account of Session VI for the Roman Catholic doctrine of justification. See A. Ritschl, *op. cit.*, B. I, K. 3; also, S. 141, S. 142.

power of divine grace. Justification is the sign of God's mercy and the seal of his promise delivered unto the elect through the offices of his Son and the effectual calling of the Holy Spirit. Wesley always begins with man; and the cause of man's holiness has no meaning apart from his free and willing acceptance of divine grace. Justification is the sign of God's mercy, and as such it rests on the merits of Christ's work; but it is delivered to all those who earnestly desire and gratefully receive it, and the deciding factor in its attainment does not lie with God but remains solely within the bounds of man's own decision. While the religious emphasis of the Reformation is always on the forgiveness of sins and the habitual renewal of the justified, the Wesleyan emphasis, though forgiveness is included as the primary fact in the beginning of religion, is on perfection, and holiness is the final label of the Christian. The one starts and ends with God's act, for which man must remain continually and forever thankful; the other starts with man's condition, asks how it may be made conformable to God's righteousness and preserved in a state of purity and love. Thus Wesley writes:

Suppose then you stood with the "great multitude which no man can number, out of every nation, and tongue, and kindred, and people," who "give praise unto Him that sitteth upon the throne, and unto the Lamb for ever and ever;" you would not find one among them all that were entered into glory, who was not a witness to the great truth, "Without holiness no man shall see the Lord;" not one of that innumerable company who was not sanctified before he was glorified. By holiness he was prepared for glory; according to the invariable will of the Lord, that the crown purchased by the blood of his Son, should be given to none but those who are renewed by his Spirit. He is become "the author of eternal salvation" only "to them that obey him;" that obey him inwardly and outwardly; that are holy in heart, and holy in all manner of conversation.[4]

And yet justification, according to Wesley, is the indispensable means to holiness; and it stands, apart from human effort and achievement, solely as an act of divine mercy and a demonstration of divine grace. The first fact, therefore, which stands out in a review of the material which we have covered is that man cannot in himself merit the right

[4] Sermon LVIII, sec. 11.

246

to be justified. Neither the quality of his works nor the nature of his character is of sufficient goodness to warrant acceptance of God or approval at the tribunal of divine holiness. Indeed, he is altogether sinful, a creature of pride, passion, and self-will. The notion that he can save himself through the performance of good deeds, acts of charity, attendance at church, intellectual assent to the teachings of Christendom, or any other means which are centered in himself and are motivated by the desires and aspirations of his own nature is entirely surrendered. Wesley repudiates the Anglican doctrine of justification by faith in the form of rational belief and by works in the form of moral and ecclesiastical obedience and labels all human striving, the hope of attaining heaven as a result of moral endeavor, as "beating the air" or attempting to build on "the froth of the sea." Man's sole hope is with God, who finds him in his sinfulness and who provides the means as well as sets the conditions for his recovery and restoration into the fellowship of the redeemed. Wesley stands at this point with Paul, Augustine, and the Reformers and adds his testimony to that of the saints in all the ages that justification comes not of him that willeth, nor of him that runneth, but of God who showeth mercy.

Moreover, the mercy of God is described by Wesley as universal and his love as extending over all his works. The second fact which leaps to view, then, is that the privilege of justification is denied by God to no one and that all men everywhere are the objects of his saving grace. The Calvinistic doctrine of predestination by which some are elected to eternal life from the foundation of the world and others are set apart as the peculiar objects of divine wrath, vessels of dishonor fitted for destruction, is described by Wesley as "full of blasphemy," as having "a direct and manifest tendency to overthrow the whole Christian Revelation," and as picturing God in a form "more false, more cruel, more unjust" than even the devil. In place of special or particular grace, Wesley affirms his doctrine of grace as *free for all* and *free in all*. It is as broad as life, and it extends to the farthest reaches of created existence. This grace which is the beginning of justification is planted by God in the soul of every man born into the world, and it expresses itself as a man's first wish to please God, as his "first slight transient conviction of having sinned," as his first desire for forgiveness and deliverance "from a blind unfeeling heart, quite insensible to God and the things of God." It is through the means of this divine spark within him that he is led to a knowledge of his helplessness, is enabled to confess his sins, and is empowered to make his way to the foot of the cross and ask for divine mercy.

The third fact which compels our attention, therefore, is that active human responsiveness in the form of man's willingness to receive, yea, earnest desire to possess, the gift of faith, is the sole condition of his justification. If grace be free for all and to a certain extent already present in all, then it follows that, unless all men are said to be justified without exception, the justifying act must itself be conditioned by some other factor which lies outside the bounds of divine grace. Wesley tells us that faith is the means of man's justification just as grace is its source, but faith, like grace, is the free gift of God. But then he goes on to say that faith is only conferred on those who sincerely desire it, who actively manifest that desire in repentance, and who, if there is time, bring forth works meet for repentance. It is important to note that repentance is man's own act effected in conjunction with prevenient grace, which is the possession of every creature. Whether a man is justified or not, whether he is pardoned of his sins or left in the bonds of their captivity and subject to guilt and punishment, is, in the thought of Wesley, dependent on his own free choice alone. God desireth not the loss of a sinner but rather that he turn unto him in true repentance and be saved. To be sure, man cannot generate his own faith and, therefore, claim and lay hold of justifying grace. But likewise God does not violate man's nature, destroy his freedom, and confer justifying grace upon him by the irresistible power of his will. No, faith is planted in the human soul through the agency of God operating in co-operation with and not in violation of free human response, so that there is neither merely an apportionment of justifying grace to man by God nor simply an appropriation of that same grace by man from God but both divine apportionment and human appropriation standing together in a single process.

Justification, in the fourth place, having been defined as the act in which a sinner is pardoned by God solely on the condition of his possessing faith, is accompanied by regeneration, or conversion, in which act a man's life is changed, his character is rectified, and he is made into a new creature and is set on the way toward entire sanctification. After conversion he is so far perfect as not to commit acts of sin, and love is the dominating motive of his life. But his old passions are still present, and they furnish the occasion for his yielding to temptation and falling back into open sin. God's grace, however, is always present to sustain him, and God will not permit him to fall as long as he himself remains faithful to the heavenly vision. Thus he who finds the love of God shed abroad in his heart at conversion and is delivered from the bondage of sin in the act of justification is henceforth enabled to walk in the commandments of God blameless and is carried on to that state of perfection without which no man can see God.

The emphasis on justification as a means to holiness, and on free human responsiveness as the condition both of pardon and acceptance and of perseverance in the way of entire sanctification, is borne out in all the major doctrines of Wesley's theology and is at last substantiated in his treatment of Christian ethics and of the religious life. Thus the character of God is set forth in terms of the moral law, which is the eternal expression of his holiness; his nature is such that he cannot condone sin, that he cannot account a person as righteous unless he is in fact righteous. And yet, though God hates sin and loves the sinner, he cannot save a man apart from that man's willingness to be saved. God in the act of creation defined the nature of all the objects which he made; he endowed man with freedom; and, because God is eternally loyal to the nature of the things which he has created, he cannot violate man's freedom or take away that gift which in very truth makes man what he is. In his *Thoughts upon Necessity* Wesley writes that there is no subject of greater importance than human freedom,[5] and he proves his own belief in it by acknowledging it as the one principle which limits the power and redemptive activity of Almighty God.

Likewise, the Wesleyan doctrine of man and sin teaches that evil, both physical and moral, entered the world through the free choice of the first man, that it was passed on to all subsequent generations, and that no person born into the world is free from corruption or without

[5] *Works*, X, 457.

the taint of original sin. And yet Wesley shies away from the Augustinian conception of total depravity in which man's freedom is denied also and he is left helpless in his own misery and is dependent solely on the divine ordinance concerning his fate. With Wesley man is always free to return unto God by gratefully accepting the gift of faith.

Consequently, the work of Christ, which is the sole cause of redemption, is interpreted in a universal sense, so that Christ is said to have lived and died for every man whether a man accepts the gift of his atonement or not. The effects of Christ's work for the individual are conditional, however, being dependent on man's willingness to receive them. The Holy Spirit is the power of actualizing goodness in human life and is the divine witness within man of his own justification and of his progress in love. And yet the Spirit will not abide in an unwilling or recalcitrant heart, and man always possesses the power to quench the spark of holiness within him and to kill the life of God in his own soul.

Finally, what God does for man in justification and conversion makes its marks on man's moral and spiritual life and expresses itself in a holy character and disposition, free from the hindrances of outward sin, progressively overcoming all inward desires that are evil, and being led on toward perfect love, which is the highest gift of sonship and the final goal to be reached on this earth before admission is granted into the Kingdom of God beyond the years. The Wesleyan ethics, therefore, is an ethics of realization and development; for a man is finally judged at the last day on the basis of what he is, not of what he might hope to become. Justification alone is partial and incomplete; it must be followed by entire sanctification of heart and life so that the forgiven sinner is transformed into the likeness of his Lord.

It has been frequently observed, that very few were clear in their judgement both with regard to justification and sanctification. Who has wrote more ably than Martin Luther on justification by faith alone? And who was more ignorant of the doctrine of sanctification, or more confused in his conceptions of it? . . . On the other hand, how many writers of the Romish Church (as Francis Sales and Juan Castaniza, in particular) have wrote strongly and scripturally on sanctification, who, nevertheless, were entirely unacquainted with the nature of justification! insomuch that the whole body of their Divines at the Council of Trent, in their *Catechismus ad Parochos*, (Catechism which every parish Priest is to teach his people,) totally confound sanctification and justification together. But it has pleased God to give the Methodists a full and clear knowledge of each, and the wide difference between them.

They know, indeed, that at the same time a man is justified, sanctification properly begins. For when he is justified, he is "born again," "born of the Spirit;" which, although it is not (as some suppose) the whole process of sanctification, is doubtless the gate of it. Of this, likewise, God has given them a full view. They know the new birth implies as great a change in the soul, in him that is "born of the Spirit," as was wrought in the body when he was born of a woman: Not an outward change only, . . . but an inward change. . . .

And, as in the natural birth a man is born at once, and then grows stronger and stronger by degrees; so, in the spiritual birth, a man is born at once, and then gradually increases in spiritual stature and strength. . . .

Therefore, they [the Methodists] maintain, with equal zeal and diligence, the doctrine of free, full, present justification, on the one hand, and of entire sanctification both of heart and life, on the other; being as tenacious of inward holiness as any Mystic, and of outward, as any Pharisee.[6]

What, finally, can we say by way of evaluating the Wesleyan doctrine of justification? To be sure, it is impressive in its moral earnestness, in the manner in which it conjoins the religious conception of pardon and acceptance with the ethical demand of conversion and the rectification of character and of life. The religious man, for Wesley, is always the good man; and, if the Author of true religion provides the only power which can generate goodness in human life, then it is likewise true that goodness itself is that quality which defines religion, which provides it with content and with meaning, and which is the highest insignia of its worth and its claim to the allegiance of all the races of mankind. And yet the Wesleyan emphasis on goodness, on the realization of moral perfection here on earth, is, viewed in one way, a source of weakness and of danger. By making justification merely the gate of religion, the means to a higher end, and by laying stress not on the religious act of forgiveness but on the quality or state of life which that act is said to produce, Wesley throws himself open to

[6] Sermon CVII, part i, secs. 5-8.

the peril of reducing religion to an appendage of morality and of raising virtue to that throne which rightfully belongs only to its Source.
It is not enough simply to say that the state could not be reached apart
from its Source or that perfection could not exist if it were not for the
prior act of forgiveness. It must be shown also that the state is sub-
sidiary to its Source; otherwise, there is always the danger of making
a realizable quality of human life the ultimate end of religion and of
subordinating the worship of Almighty God to those benefits which
it is supposed to confer. Such a danger manifests itself in an undue
emphasis on the subjective evidence, whether in the form of internal
feelings or of external behavior, that man is in a condition worthy of
final salvation; in a narrow conception of postregenerate sin as the
willful violation of some known law; [7] and in a strict separatism which,
though it does not forbid contact and fellowship with the unregenerate,
limits such contact and such fellowship to the one purpose of saving
souls and absolutely forbids it if and when it proves dangerous to the
moral and spiritual life of the redeemed. Goodness ceases to be itself
when it becomes self-conscious, and the highest aspirations of human
life arise oftentimes from a sense of unworthiness and yet of being
continuously forgiven and perpetually healed.

But the Wesleyan emphasis on goodness, viewed in another way,
is a source of power and strength. For it must be remembered that,
though Wesley teaches that justification, which is the act of God, is
but the beginning of religion, he also teaches that sanctification, or
perfect holiness, which is the end of religion, is as much God's act as
justification; and that it comes to man as a free gift. Thus the quality
of holiness, though it takes expression in the form and substance of
humanity, is not of man's making; and whatever good there is in
personal life is not an occasion for human pride and self-satisfaction

[7] Wesley employs the word "sin" in a double sense. He uses it to characterize man's
underlying state of nature prior to conversion and, as such, all man's deeds are evil, for
they spring from a corrupt nature. After conversion, however, man's nature has been
sufficiently purified so that he has power over outward sin. Here sin bears the narrow
meaning of willful violation of divine law. Thus it is a mark of man's conversion that
he is so far perfect as not to commit sin; and, if he does commit sin, he is not a child
of God but of the devil. Here the standard is external and atomistic, and the Pelagian
concept that a man has within himself the power to do right or wrong in the performance of a given act is thoroughly adhered to by Wesley in regard to the redeemed. Of
course, Wesley is always careful to add that this power is of God.

252

but for humble gratitude and praise. If there is a distinction between regenerate and unregenerate humanity, it is a distinction which God himself has made; for the power of his holiness is sufficient to overcome sin in the lives of those who have chosen him; and the effects of the operation of his Spirit are of such strength as to make themselves apparent in the character and disposition of all who have been born again. Human holiness, therefore, does not usurp the throne of God; for man's perfection, hedged within these walls of flesh and bone, is not a rival of God's glory but a reflection of God's image, and "any sinlessness of ours is the adoration of his."[8] Viewed in this light, the Wesleyan teaching takes on new meaning; and human goodness can never become self-conscious, for it does not look to the body in which it is cast but to the Source from whence it comes and to which it hopes always to return.

It is important to note that Wesley never equated human perfection with the absolute perfection of God. He claimed that in motive a man can be like God. In everything he thinks or says he is guided entirely by love. But of course man is subject to mistakes and the wrongs that follow from them. Wesley always felt the need of Christ's atonement, even in cases where men reached the state of Christian perfection. He was never able to explain why he felt this need, at least in a satisfactory way. He says, for example, to heal the mistakes which arise from unintentional error; and yet error, for him, is not a sin. Or he says to make up for the defect which still remains between our perfection and the absolute perfection of God.[9]

On Sunday, Feb. 27, 1791, just three days before his death, he repeated the words:

I the chief of sinners am,
But Jesus died for me!

Then Miss Ritchie asked, "Is this your language now?"
"Yes," Wesley replied, "Christ is all! He is all!"[10]
Perfection, therefore, is the realization of the best moral and spiritual

[8] A line from Principal Forsyth's *Christian Perfection*, quoted in R. N. Flew, *The Idea of Perfection in Christian Theology*, p. 394.
[9] Sermon LXXVI, sec. 3; *Works*, XI, 443.
[10] Tyerman, *Life and Times of John Wesley*, III, 651.

possibilities in a life dominated completely by God and motivated entirely by love. Justification, in the last analysis, is not superseded; it is transfigured and transformed, for the same Lord who is rich in mercy and plenteous in redemption is able also to do exceeding abundantly above all that we ask or think and, according to the power that worketh in us, to deliver us from the bondage of sin and to make us conformable to the blessed image of his Son.

APPENDIX

BIBLIOGRAPHY

The Writings of John Wesley

The Sermons of John Wesley constitute the most significant of his theological writings. The first series, consisting of fifty-three discourses, was published by Mr. Wesley in four volumes in the year 1771. The second series, consisting of fifty-five discourses, most of which were first inserted in the *Arminian Magazine,* was afterward revised by Mr. Wesley and published in four volumes in the year 1788. The third series, consisting of eighteen discourses, was published by Mr. Wesley in the *Arminian Magazine* but never revised by him for further publication. The fourth series consists of only seven discourses, each one of which was published by Mr. Wesley in a separate form and yet none of which was embodied in any collection of his sermons. The fifth series consists of eight discourses which were published from Mr. Wesley's manuscripts after his death but which were never designed by him for publication. Seven of these were written prior to his Aldersgate experience. It is necessary to call attention to the fact that most editions of Wesley's sermons print only the first series of fifty-three discourses and that the numbering of the sermons varies with the different editions. All five series, however, containing without abridgment the whole of Wesley's one hundred forty-one sermons, are printed in Volumes V, VI, and VII of the Thomas Jackson edition of *Wesley's Works,* which edition has been employed in all references to the sermons in this book.

The Works of the Reverend John Wesley, A.M., Sometime Fellow of Lincoln College, Oxford, with the Last Corrections of the Author. Ed. Thomas Jackson, 3rd ed., 14 vols.; London: Wesleyan-Methodist Book-Room, 1831.

Explanatory Notes upon the New Testament. New York: Lane & Tippett, 1847.

The Journal of the Reverend John Wesley, A.M., Sometime Fellow of Lincoln College, Oxford, Enlarged from Original Mss., with Notes from Unpublished Diaries, Annotations, Maps, and Illustrations. Ed. Nehemiah Curnock, 8 vols.; London: The Epworth Press, 1938.

The Letters of the Reverend John Wesley, A.M., Sometime Fellow of Lin-

coln College. Ed. John Telford, 8 vols.; London: The Epworth Press, 1931.

A Survey of the Wisdom of God in the Creation: or a Compendium of Natural Philosophy. 3rd ed. enlarged, 5 vols.; London: printed for J. Fry & Co., 1777.

The Poetical Works of John and Charles Wesley. Collected and arranged by G. Osborn, 13 vols.; London: Wesleyan Methodist Conference Office, 1868-72.

A Christian Library: Consisting of Extracts from and Abridgements of the Choicest Pieces of Practical Divinity Which Have Been Published in the English Tongue, 30 vols.; London: printed by T. Cordeaux for T. Blanshard, 1819.

SUPPLEMENTARY BIBLIOGRAPHY

ABBEY, C. J. *The English Church and Its Bishops.* 2 vols.; London: Longmans, Green, & Co., 1887.

ADDISON, JOSEPH. *Works.* Ed. Thomas Tickell, 4 vols.; London: printed for J. Tonson, 1721.

ANDREWES, LANCELOT. *Works.* 11 vols.; Oxford: Library of Anglo-Catholic Theology, John Henry Parker, 1841-54.

ANNET, PETER. *The History and Character of St. Paul Examined.* London: F. Page.

———. *The History of the Man after God's Own Heart.* London: 1766.

———. *The Resurrection of Jesus Considered; In Answer to the Trial of the Witnesses.* London: printed for the Author, 1744.

The Ante-Nicene Fathers. Ed. Alexander Roberts and James Donaldson, 10 vols.; New York: Charles Scribner's Sons, 1885-87.

ARMINIUS, JAMES. *Works.* 3 vols.; London: Longman, Hunt, Rees, Orme, Brown, & Green, 1825.

Athenian Oracle (magazine), *Being an Entire Collection of all the Valuable Questions and Answers in the Athenian Mercuries.* 2nd ed., 4 vols.; London: printed for J. and J. Knapten, 1728.

BACON, FRANCIS. *Works.* Ed. Spedding, Ellis, and Heath; Boston: Brown & Taggart, 1861.

BAINES-GRIFFITHS, D. *Wesley the Anglican.* London: Macmillan & Co., 1919.

BIBLIOGRAPHY

BARING-GOULD, S. *The Evangelical Revival*. London: Methuen & Co., Ltd., 1920.

BARROW, ISAAC. *Theological Works*. Ed. A. Napier, 9 vols.; Cambridge: University Press, 1859.

BAXTER, RICHARD. *Aphorisms of Justification, with Their Explication Annexed*. London: printed for F. Tyton, 1649.

———. *The Practical Works*. 4 vols.; London: George Virtue, 1888.

———. *Richard Baxter's Account of His Present Thoughts Concerning the Controversies About the Perseverance of the Saints*. London: printed for T. Underhill, 1657.

———. *The Saints' Everlasting Rest, or A Treatise of the Blessed State of the Saints in Their Enjoyment of God in Heaven*. London: printed by W. Clover for T. Kelly, 1822.

BENGEL, JOHANN ALBRECHT. *Abriss der so genanten Brudergemeine, in welchem die Lehre und die ganze sache geprufet, das gute und lose dabey unterschieden und insonderheit die Spangenhergische Declaration erlauteste wird Johann Albrecht Bengel*. Stuttgart: J. B. Metzler, 1751.

BERKELEY, GEORGE. *The Works of George Berkeley*. 4 vols.; Oxford: Clarendon Press, 1801.

BEVERIDGE, WILLIAM. *Theological Works*. 12 vols.; Oxford: Library of Anglo-Catholic Theology, John Henry Parker, 1845.

BICKNELL, E. J. *The Christian Idea of Sin and Original Sin*. New York: Longmans, Green & Co., 1923.

BLOUNT, CHARLES. *Miscellaneous Works of Charles Blount, Esq.*, 1695.

BOEHMER, H. *Luther and the Reformation in the Light of Modern Research*. London: G. Bell & Sons, Ltd., 1930.

BOLINGBROKE, HENRY ST. JOHN, VISCOUNT. *Works*. 4 vols.; Philadelphia: Casey & Hart, 1841.

BONNET, CHARLES. *Oeuvres d'Histoire Naturelle et de Philosophie de Charles Bonnet*. Neuchatel: Chez S. Franche, 1779-83.

———, *Philosophical and Critical Inquiries Concerning Christianity*. Trans. John L. Boissier; London: J. Stockdale, 1791.

BRAMHALL, JOHN. *Works*. 5 vols.; Oxford: Library of Anglo-Catholic Theology, John Henry Parker, 1845.

BROWNE, ROBERT. *A Treatise of Reformation without Tarying for anie, and of the Wickedness of those Preachers which will not reforme till the Magistrate Commands or Compells them*. Middleborough, 1582.

259

BROWNE, SIR THOMAS. *Works.* 6 vols.; London: Faber and Grover, Ltd., 1928.

BULL, GEORGE. *Examen Censurae: or an Answer to Certain Strictures before unpublished, on a book entitled Harmonia Apostolica to which is added an Apology for the Harmony and its Author in Answer to the Declamations of T. Tully, D.D., in a book lately published by him, and entitled Justification Paulina.* Oxford: John Henry Parker, 1844.

———. *Harmonia Apostolica: Or Two Dissertations; in the Forms of which the Doctrine of St. James on Justification by Works is Explained and Defended: in the latter the Agreement of St. Paul with St. James is clearly shown.* Oxford: Library of Anglo-Catholic Theology, John Henry Parker, 1844.

BURNET, GILBERT. *Exposition of the Thirty-Nine Articles.* Oxford: Clarendon Press, 1796.

———. *History of His Own Time.* Oxford: Clarendon Press, 1823.

———. *History of the Reformation of the Church of England.* Ed. N. Peacock, 7 vols.; Oxford: Clarendon Press, 1845.

BURNET, THOMAS. *The Sacred Theory of the Earth, Containing an Account of the Original of the Earth, and of All the General Changes Which It Hath Undergone or Is to Undergo till the Consummation of All Things.* London: printed by R. Norton for W. Kettilby, 1684.

BURY, ARTHUR. *The Danger of Delaying Repentance.* London, 1692.

———. *The Doctrine of the Holy Trinity Placed in Its Due Light.* London, 1694.

———. *The Naked Gospel.* London, 1690.

BURY, J. B. *History of the Freedom of Thought.* New York: Henry Holt & Co., 1913.

BUTLER, JOSEPH. *The Works.* 2 vols.; New York: The Macmillan Co., 1896.

CALAMY, EDMUND. *An Abridgement of Mr. Baxter's History of His Life and Times, With an Account of Many Others of those Worthy Ministers who were ejected after the Restauration of King Charles II and their History to the Year 1691.* London: S. Bridge, 1702.

CALVIN, JOHN. *Institutes of the Christian Religion.* 7th Amer. ed., trans. John Allen, 2 vols.; Philadelphia: Presbyterian Board of Christian Education, 1936.

The Canons and Decrees of the Sacred and Oecumenical Council of Trent. Trans. J. Waterworth; London: C. Dolman, 1848.

The Catechism of the Council of Trent. Trans. J. Donovan; New York: Catholic Publication Society.

CELL, G. C. *The Rediscovery of John Wesley.* New York: Henry Holt & Co., 1935.

Certain Sermons or Homilies Appointed to be Read in Churches in the Times of Queen Elizabeth of Famous Memory. London: printed for J. Fuller, 1766.

CHERBURY, LORD EDWARD HERBERT, BARON OF. *The Antient Religion of the Gentiles and Causes of their Errors Consider'd: the Mistakes and Failures of the Heathen Priests and Wisemen, and Matters of Divine Worship are examin'd; with regard to their being Altogether Destitute of Divine Revelation.* London: printed for John Nutt, 1705.

——. *De Veritate.* Bristol: J. W. Arrowsmith, 1937.

CHILLINGWORTH, WILLIAM. *Works.* 12th ed.; London: printed for B. Blake, 1836.

CHUBB, THOMAS. *The Posthumous Works of Mr. Thomas Chubb.* 2 vols.; London: R. Baldwin, 1748.

CLARKE, ADAM. *Memoirs of the Wesley Family, Collected from Original Documents.* 2 vols.; London: J. Haddon, 1834.

CLARKE, ELIZABETH. *Susanna Wesley.* Boston: Robert Bros., 1886.

CLARKE, SAMUEL. *A Demonstration of the Being and Attributes of God.* Boyle Lectures of 1704; London: printed for J. Knapton, 1705.

——. *Dicourse Concerning the Unchangeable Obligations of Natural Religion, and the Truth and Certainty of the Christian Revelation.* London: printed by W. Botham for J. Knapton, 1716.

COKE, THOMAS, AND HENRY MOORE. *Life of the Reverend John Wesley Including an Account of the Great Revival of Religion in Europe and America of Which He Was the First and Chief Instrument.* London: G. Paramore, 1792.

COLLIER, F. W. *John Wesley Among the Scientists.* New York: Abingdon Press, 1928.

COLLINS, ANTHONY. *A Discourse of Free-Thinking, Occasioned by the Growth of a Sect Call'd Freethinkers.* London: 1713.

——. *A Discourse on the Ground and Reason of the Christian Religion.* 1724.

CONYBEARE, JOHN. *A Defense of Reveal'd Religion Against the Exceptions of a Late Writer in His Book entitled Christianity as Old as Creation.* London: printed for S. Wilmont, 1732.

COSIN, JOHN. *Works.* 5 vols.; Oxford: Library of Anglo-Catholic Theology, J. H. Parker, 1843-55.

CROOK, WILLIAM. *The Ancestry of the Wesleys.* London: Epworth Press, 1938.

CROWTHER, J. *A True and Complete Portraiture of Methodism; or, The History of the Wesleyan Methodists.* New York: Daniel Hitt & Thomas Ware, 1813.

The Daily Words of the Brethren's Congregation for the Year 1781. London: 1781.

The Daily Words of the Brethren's Congregation for the Year 1784. London: 1784.

DERHAM, WILLIAM. *Astro-Theology, or a Demonstration of the Being and Attributes of God, from a Survey of the Heavens.* London: W. Innys, 1714.

————. *Physico-Theology, or a Demonstration of Beings and Attributes of God from His Works of Creation.* London: Boyle Lecture Sermon, 1712.

DESCARTES, RENÉ. *Philosophical Works.* 2 vols.; London: Cambridge University Press, 1931.

DIMOND, S. G. *The Psychology of the Methodist Revival.* Oxford: University Press, 1926.

DODDRIDGE, PHILIP. *Works.* 10 vols.; Leeds: E. Baines, 1802-5.

DODSLEY, R. *The Art of Preaching: in Imitation of Horace's Art of Poetry.* London: printed for R. Dodsley, 1735.

DORNER, J. A. *History of Protestant Theology.* 2 vols.; Edinburgh: T. & T. Clark, 1871.

EARLE, JOHN. *Microcosmography, The World Display'd.* London: C. Ward & R. Chandler, 1740.

EICKEN, ERICH VON. *Rechtfertigung und Heiligung bei Wesley dargestellt unter Vergleichung mit den Anschauungen Luther und des Luthertums.* Heidelberg: 1934.

English Puritanism. Documents Relating to the Settlement of The Church of England by the Act of Uniformity of 1662. London: W. Kent & Co., 1862.

FABER, GEORGE STANLEY. *The Primitive Doctrine of Justification.* 2nd ed.; London: R. B. Seeley & W. Burnside, 1889.

FLETCHER, JOHN. *Works.* 9 vols.; London: printed by T. Cordeux, 1815.

FLEW, R. NEWTON. *The Idea of Perfection in Christian Theology.* London: Oxford University Press, 1934.

FLYNN, JOHN STEPHEN. *The Influence of Puritanism on the Political and Religious Thought of the English.* London: John Murray, 1920.

BIBLIOGRAPHY

FROST, STANLEY B. *Die Autoritätslehre in den Werken John Wesleys.* Munchen: Ernest Reinhardt.

FULLER, B. A. G. *History of Philosophy.* New York: Henry Holt & Co., 1938.

GREEN, J. R. *History of the English People.* 4 vols.; New York: Harper & Bros, 1878.

GREEN, RICHARD. *The Works of John and Charles Wesley.* A Bibliography: Containing an exact account of all the publications issued by the brothers Wesley arranged in chronological order, with a list of the early editions, and descriptive and illustrative notes. London: C. H. Kelly, 1896.

HACKET, JOHN. *A Century of Sermons upon Several Remarkable Subjects.* London: Thomas Plume, 1675.

HAGEN, F. F. *Old Landmarks: or Faith and Practice of the Moravian Church, at the Time of Its Revival and Restoration in 1727, and Twenty Years After.* Bethlehem, Pennsylvania, 1886.

HALL, EDWIN. *The Puritans and Their Principles.* New York: Baker & Scribner, 1846.

HALL, JOSEPH. *Works.* 12 vols.; Oxford: D. A. Talboys, 1837.

HALL, ROBERT. *Works.* 8th ed., 6 vols.; London: Henry Bohn, 1843.

HAMILTON, JOHN TAYLOR. *A History of the Church Known as the Moravian Church, or the Unitas Fratrum, or the Unity of the Brethren During the Eighteenth and Nineteenth Centuries.* Bethlehem, Pennsylvania: Times Publishing Co., 1900.

HAMMOND, HENRY. *Miscellaneous Theological Works.* 3 vols.; Oxford: Library of Anglo-Catholic Theology, John Henry Parker, 1849.

HARDWICK, CHARLES. *History of the Articles of Religion,* to which is added a series of documents from A.D. 1536 to A.D. 1615. Philadelphia: Herman Hooker, 1852.

HARNACK, ADOLPH. *History of Dogma.* Trans. Neil Buchanan, 7 vols.; Boston: Robert Bros., 1897.

HARRISON, A. W. *Arminianism.* London: Duckworth, 1937.

———. *The Beginnings of Arminianism to the Synod of Dort.* London: University of London Press, 1926.

———. *John Wesley, the Last Phase.* London: Epworth Press, 1934.

HENRY, JAMES. *Sketches of Moravian Life and Character.* J. B. Lippincott Co., 1859.

HERBERT, GEORGE. *The Complete Works in Verse and Prose of George Herbert.* Ed. A. B. Grosart; London: Robson & Son, 1874.

263

HICKES, GEORGE. *How the Members of the Church of England Ought to Behave themselves Under a Roman Catholic King with Reference to the Test and Penal Laws.* London: Randel Taylor, 1687.

———. *A Plain Defence of the Protestant Religion Fitted to the Meanest Capacity: Being a Full Confutation of the Net for the Fishes of Men.* Published by two Gentlemen lately gone over to the Church of Rome. London: printed by S. L. and sold by R. Taylor, 1687.

HOBBES, THOMAS. *The English Works of Thomas Hobbes of Malmesbury.* London: John Bohn, 1839.

HODGE, CHARLES. *Systematic Theology.* 3 vols.; New York: Scribner, Armstrong, & Co., 1873.

HOOKER, RICHARD. *Works.* 3 vols.; Oxford: Clarendon Press, 1874.

HORNECK, ANTHONY. *The Crucified Jesus: or, A Full Account of the Nature, End, Design, and Benefits of the Sacrament of the Lord's Supper.* 5th ed.; London: 1705.

———. *God's Providence in the Midst of Confusions.* London: 1682.

———. *The Happy Ascetick: or, the Best Exercise, To Which Is Added a Letter to a Person of Quality Concerning the Holy Lives of the Primitive Christians.* 3rd ed.; London: 1693.

HUME, DAVID. *Essays, Literary, Moral, and Political.* London: Ward, Lock, & Co.

HUNT, JOHN. *Religious Thought in England.* 3 vols.; London: Strahan & Co., 1870-73.

HUTTON, WILLIAM H. *A History of the English Church from the Accession of Charles I to the Death of Queen Anne.* New York: The Macmillan Co., 1903.

———. *A Short History of the Church in Great Britain.* London: Rivingtons, 1904.

JACKSON, THOMAS. *The Life of the Reverend Charles Wesley.* 2 vols.; London: John Mason, 1841.

———. *Works.* 12 vols.; Oxford: University Press, 1844.

JAMES I. *The Works of the Most High and Mightie Prince James, by the Grace of God, King of Great Britaine, France, and Ireland, Defender of the Faith, etc.* Ed. James Montague; London: printed by Robert Barker & John Bill, 1616.

JENNINGS, A. C. *Ecclesia Anglicana.* London: Rivingtons, 1889.

JENYNS, S. *Free Enquiry into Nature and Origin of Evil, In Six Letters.* London: printed for R. & J. Dodsley, 1790.

KANT, IMMANUEL. *Critique of Practical Reason and Other Works on the*

BIBLIOGRAPHY

Theory of Ethics. T. K. Abbott trans.; London: Longmans, Green, & Co., 1883.

KIRK, JOHN. *The Mother of the Wesleys.* London: Henry James Tresidder, 1864.

LAUD, WILLIAM. *A Relation of the Conference between William Laud, then Lord Bishop of St. Davide, now Lord Archbishop of Canterbury and Mr. Fisher, the Jesuit with an Answer to such Exception as A. C. takes against it.* London: Richard Badger, 1639.

————. *Works.* 7 vols.; Oxford: Library of Anglo-Catholic Theology, J. H. Parker, 1847-60.

LAW, WILLIAM. *Works.* 9 vols.; London: printed for J. Richardson, 1762.

LECKY, W. E. H. *A History of England in the Eighteenth Century.* 8 vols.; New York: D. Appleton & Co., 1878-90.

LEE, UMPHREY. *The Historical Backgrounds of Early Methodist Enthusiasm.* New York: Columbia University Press, 1931.

————. *John Wesley and Modern Religion.* New York and Nashville: Abingdon-Cokesbury Press, 1936.

LEGER, AUGUSTIN. *La Jeunesse de Wesley, L'Angleterre Religieuse et Les Origines du Methodisme au XVIIIe Siècle.* Paris: Libraire Hachette et Cie., 1910.

LELAND, JOHN. *A View of the Principal Deistical Writers that have appeared in England in the last and present Century, With Observations upon them and some account of the Answers that have been published against them.* 5th ed., 2 vols.; printed for T. C. Cadill, Jr., & W. Davis, 1798.

LOCKE, JOHN. *Works of John Locke.* 11th ed., 10 vols.; London: printed for W. Olridge & Son, 1812.

LUCCOCK, HALFORD E., and PAUL HUTCHINSON. *The Story of Methodism.* New York: Methodist Book Concern, 1926.

LUNN, A. *John Wesley.* New York: Dial Press, 1929.

LUTHER, MARTIN. *Werke, Erlangen ed.* German Works, 67 vols.; Latin Works, 38 vols.; 1826.

————. *Werke, Weimar ed.,* 1884.

————. *Works.* 6 vols.; Philadelphia: A. J. Holman Co., 1915.

MACDONALD, JAMES ALEXANDER. *Wesley's Revision of Shorter Catechism.* London: George A. Morton, 1906.

MACKINNON, JAMES. *Calvin and the Reformation.* London: Longmans, Green, & Co., 1936.

————. *Luther and the Reformation.* 4 vols.; New York: Longmans, Green, & Co., 1925.

McConnell, F. J. *John Wesley.* New York and Nashville: Abingdon-Cokesbury Press, 1939.

McGiffert, A. C. *A History of Christian Thought.* 2 vols.; New York: Charles Scribner's Sons, 1931-32.

————. *Protestant Thought Before Kant.* New York: Charles Scribner's Sons, 1936.

McTyeire, H. N. *A History of Methodism.* Nashville: Southern Methodist Publishing House, 1885.

Meyer, Henry Herman. *Child Nature and Nurture According to Nicolaus Ludwig von Zinzendorf.* New York: The Abingdon Press, 1928.

Middleton, Conyers. *Free Inquiry into the Miraculous Powers Which Are Supposed to Have Subsided in the Christian Church.* London: R. Manby & H. S. Cox, 1749.

————. *An Introductory Discourse to a Larger Work.* London: R. Manby & H. S. Cox, 1747.

Moore, Henry. *The Life of the Reverend John Wesley, A.M., in which are included the Life of the Reverend Charles Wesley and Memories of this family.* 2 vols.; New York: N. Bangs & J. Emory, 1826.

More, Hannah. *The Complete Works of Hannah More.* 7 vols.; New York: Harper & Bros., 1835.

More, Paul Elmer, and Frank Leslie Cross. *Anglicanism.* Milwaukee: Morehouse-Gorham Co., 1935.

Mossner, E. C. *Bishop Butler and the Age of Reason.* New York: The Macmillan Co., 1936.

Moxon, R. S. *The Doctrine of Sin.* New York: Geo. H. Doran Co., 1922.

Müller, Julius. *The Christian Doctrine of Sin.* Trans. William Urwick, 2 vols.; Edinburgh: T. & T. Clark, 1868.

Nelson, Robert. *The Life of Dr. George Bull, later Lord Bishop of St. David's, with the history of those controversies in which he was engaged; and an abstract of those fundamental doctrines which he maintained and defended in the Latin tongue.* London: R. Smith, 1713.

Newton, John. *The Works of the Reverend John Newton.* 4 vols.; New Haven: Nathan Whitney, 1826.

The Nicene and Post-Nicene Fathers. 1st series, ed. Philip Schaff, 14 vols.; New York: Christian Library, 1886-90.

The Nicene and Post-Nicene Fathers. 2nd series, ed. Philip Schaff and Henry Wace, 14 vols.; New York: Christian Library, 1890-1900.

BIBLIOGRAPHY

Norton, William, J., Jr. *Bishop Butler, Moralist and Divine*. New Brunswick, Rutgers University Press, 1940.

Original Records of Early Non-Conformity Under Persecution and Indulgence. Ed. G. Lyon Turner, 2 vols.; London: T. Fisher Unwin, 1911.

Orr, John. *English Deism; Its Roots and Its Fruits*. Grand Rapids: William B. Eerdmans Publishing Co., 1934.

Overall, John. *The Convocation Book of 1606, Concerning the Government of God's Catholick Church and the Kingdom of the Whole World*. Oxford: Library of Anglo-Catholic Theology, H. Parker, 1844.

————. *Reflections on Bishop Overall's Convocation Book 1606, Concerning the Government of God's Catholick Church; and of the Kingdoms of the Whole World*. London: 1615.

Overton, John H. *The Evangelical Revival in the Eighteenth Century*. Epochs of Church History; London: Longmans, Green, & Co., 1900.

————. *John Wesley*. London: Methuen & Co., 1891.

————. *Life in the English Church, 1660-1714*. London: Longmans, Green, & Co., 1885.

————. *The Nonjurors, Their Lives, Principles, and Writings*. London: Smith, Elder, & Co., 1902.

————. *William Law, Nonjuror and Mystic*. London: Longmans, Green & Co., 1881.

————, and Frederick Relton. *The English Church from the Accession of George I to the End of the Eighteenth Century, 1714-1800*. New York: The Macmillan Co., 1906.

Paley, William. *The Works of William Paley*. 5 vols.; London: G. & J. Robinson, 1825.

Pearson, J. *An Exposition of the Creed*. London: William Tegg, 1878.

Philip, Robert. *The Life and Times of the Reverend George Whitefield*. D. Appleton & Co., 1838.

Piette, Maximin. *John Wesley in the Evolution of Protestantism*. New York: Sheed & Ward, 1937.

Plummer, Alfred. *The Church of England in the Eighteenth Century*. London: Methuen & Co., 1910.

————. *Continental Reformation in Germany, France, and Switzerland from Birth of Luther to the Death of Calvin*. London: R. Scott, 1912.

Pope, W. B. *A Compendium of Christian Theology*. 3 vols.; New York: Phillips & Hunt, 1881.

Portus, Garnet V. *Caritas Anglicana, or An Historical Inquiry into Those Religious and Philanthropical Societies That Flourished in England*

Between the Years 1678 and 1740. London: A. R. Mowbray & Co., 1912.

POTTER, JOHN. *Theological Works.* 3 vols.; Oxford: printed at the Theatre, 1753-54.

Proceedings of the Wesley Historical Society. 3 vols.; London: Gazette Printing Works, 1898.

RATTENBURY, J. ERNEST. *The Conversion of the Wesleys, A Critical Study.* London: Epworth Press, 1938.

RAY, JOHN. *The Wisdom of the God Manifested in the Works of Creation.* 5th ed.; printed by J. B. for B. Walford, 1709.

REICHELT, G. T. *The Literary Works of the Foreign Missionaries of the Moravian Church.* Trans. Bishop Edmund de Schweinitz; Nazareth, Pennsylvania: Moravian Historical Society, 1886.

RIMIUS, HENRY. *A Candid Narrative of the Rise and Progress of the Herrnhuters, Commonly Call'd Moravians or Unitas Fratrum, with a Short Account of their Doctrine, drawn from their own writings.* London: printed for A. Linds, 1753.

RITSCHL, ALBRECHT. *Die christliche Lehre von der Rechtfertigung und Versöhnung.* Band I; *Die Geschichte der Lehre;* Bonn: Marcus und Webers, 1903.

———. *Die Geschite des Pietismus.* 3B.; Bonn: A. Marcus, 1880-86.

———. *The Christian Doctrine of Justification and Reconciliation, The Positive Development of the Doctrine.* Eng. trans., ed. H. R. Mackintosh and A. B. Macaulay; Edinburgh: T. & T. Clark, 1902.

ROUSSEAU, JEAN JACQUES. *Émile, or Treatise on Education.* New York: D. Appleton & Co., 1901.

———. *The Social Contract, or the Principles of Political Rights.* London: G. P. Putnam's Sons, 1893.

ROWDEN, A. W. *The Primates of the Four Georges.* London: John Murray, 1916.

SCHAFF, PHILIP. *The Creeds of Christendom.* 3 vols.; New York: Harper & Bros., 1877.

SCHMID, HEINRICH. *Die Geschichte des Pietismus.* Nordlingen: C. H. Beck, 1863.

SCHWEINITZ, EDMUND DE. *The Moravian Manual: Containing an Account of the Moravian Church, or Unitas Fratrum.* 2nd ed.; Bethlehem, Pennsylvania: Moravian Publication Office, A. C. & H. T. Clauder, 1869.

SECKER, THOMAS. *Works.* 6 vols.; London: 1825.

BIBLIOGRAPHY

SEEBERG, REINHOLD. *Text-Book of the History of Doctrines.* Trans. C. E. Hay, 2 vols.; Philadelphia: United Lutheran Publication House, 1905.

SELBIN, W. B. *English Sects, A History of Non-Conformity.* New York: Henry Holt & Co.

SELDEN, JOHN. *Table Talk.* Ed. S. H. Reynolds; Oxford: Clarendon Press, 1892.

SHAFTESBURY, ANTHONY, EARL OF. *Characteristics of Men, Manners, Opinions, Times, etc.* London: Grant Richards, 1900.

———. *The Life, Unpublished Letters, and Philosophical Regimen of Anthony, Earl of Shaftesbury.* London: Swan Sonnenschein & Co., Ltd., 1900.

SHEDD, WILLIAM G. T. *Dogmatic Theology.* 3 vols.; New York: Charles Scribner's Sons, 1888.

SHERLOCK, THOMAS. *The Case of Abraham and Melchizedeck, the History of Esau and Jacob, and the Story of Balaam, Considered and Explained, and the Mistakes of Mr. Chubb, and others, corrected; With a Postscript Relating to the Expulsions of the Canaanites by Joshua.* London: printed for J. Roberts, 1746.

———. *The Tryal of the Witnesses of the Resurrection of Jesus.* 5th ed.; London: printed for J. Roberts, 1729.

SIMON, JOHN S. *John Wesley and the Advance of Methodism.* London: Epworth Press, 1925.

———. *John Wesley and the Methodist Societies.* London: Epworth Press, 1923.

———. *John Wesley and the Religious Societies.* London: Epworth Press, 1921.

———. *John Wesley the Master-Builder.* London: Epworth Press, 1927.

SIMPKINSON, C. H. *Life and Times of William Laud, Archbishop of Canterbury.* London: John Murray, 1894.

SMITH, GEORGE. *History of Wesleyan Methodism.* 5th ed., 3 vols.; London: C. H. Kelly.

SMITH, HAROLD. *The Thirty-Nine Articles of Religion: Their History in Relation to Other Formularies, English and Foreign.* London: Society for Promoting Christian Knowledge, 1930.

SOMMER, J. W. ERNST. *John Wesley und die soziale Frage.* Bremen: Verlagshaus der Methodistenkirche, 1930.

SOUTHEY, ROBERT. *The Life of John Wesley; and the Rise and Progress of Methodism.* 3rd ed.; London: Longman, Brown, Green, & Longmans. 1846.

269

Spangenberg, A. G. *An Exposition of Christian Doctrine as Taught in the Protestant Church of the United Brethren.* London: W. & A. Strahan, 1784.

Spangenburg, A. G. *The Life of Nicholas Lewis Count Zinzendorf.* Trans. Samuel Jackson; London: Samuel Holdsworth, 1838.

Spooner, W. A. *Bishop Butler.* New York: Houghton Mifflin Co., 1901.

Stephen, Leslie. *English Literature and Society in the Eighteenth Century.* London: Duckworth & Co., 1904.

———. *History of English Thought in the Eighteenth Century.* London: Smith, Elder, & Co., 1881.

Stevens, Abel. *The History of the Religious Movement in the Eighteenth Century, called Methodism, Considered in Its Different Denominational Forms and Its Relations to British and American Protestantism.* New York: Carleton & Porter, 1858-61.

Strong, A. H. *Systematic Theology.* Philadelphia: Judson Press, 1907.

Sykes, Norman. *Church and State in England in the Eighteenth Century.* Cambridge: University Press, 1934.

Taine, H. A. *History of English Literature.* Trans. H. Van Laun, 2 vols.; New York: Grosset & Dunlap.

Taylor, A. E. *The Faith of a Moralist.* 2 vols.; New York: The Macmillan Co., 1930.

Taylor, Isaac. *Wesley and Methodism.* New York: Harper & Bros., 1855.

Taylor, Jeremy. *Works.* Ed. Reginal Heber, 3rd ed., 15 vols.; London: Longman, 1839.

Taylor, John. *The Scripture Doctrine of Original Sin Proposed to a Free and Candid Examination.* 4th ed.; London: 1767.

Taylor, Vincent. *Forgiveness and Reconciliation.* London: Macmillan & Company, Ltd., 1941.

Telford, John. *The Life of John Wesley.* New York: Eaton & Mains.

Thomas à Kempis. *The Christian's Pattern: or a Treatise of the Imitation of Jesus Christ.* Trans. George Stanhope; London: ninth edition printed by W. Bonyer, 1714.

———. *Soliloquy of the Soul.* Trans. George Stanhope; Hartford: John Babcock, 1800.

Thorndike, Herbert. *Theological Works.* 6 vols.; Oxford: Library of Anglo-Catholic Theology, 1844-56.

Tillotson, John. *Works.* Ed. Thomas Birch; printed by J. F. Dove for K. Priestly, 1820.

TINDAL, MATTHEW. *Christianity as Old as the Creation, or the Gospel a Republication of the Religion of Nature.* London: 1730.

TOLAND, JOHN. *Christianity not Mysterious or a Treatise showing that there is nothing in the Gospel contrary to Reason nor above it and that no Christian Doctrine may be properly called a Mystery.* London: 1696.

TOPLADY, AUGUSTUS MONTAGUE. *The Church of England Vindicated from the Charge of Arminianism; and the Case of Arminian Subscription Particularly Considered.* London: 1769.

————. *The Doctrine of Absolute Predestination Stated and Asserted, with a Preliminary Discourse on the Divine Attributes, Translated, in Great Measure, from the Latin of Jerome Zanchius.* Wilmington: printed at Adam's Press, 1793.

————. *A Letter to the Reverend Mr. John Wesley: Relative to His Pretended Abridgement of Zanchius on Predestination.* Printed for J. Gurney, 1770.

————. *More Work for Mr. John Wesley: or, A Vindication of the Decrees and Providence of God from the Defamations of a Late Printed Paper, entitled, "The Consequence Proved."* London: printed for J. Matthews, 1772.

————. *The Scheme of Christian and Philosophical Necessity Asserted in Opposition to Mr. John Wesley's Tract on that Subject.* London: 1775.

TOWNSEND, W. J., W. B. WORKMAN, and GEORGE EARYS. *A New History of Methodism.* 2 vols.; London: Hodder & Stoughton, 1909.

TROELTSCH, ERNST. *The Social Teaching of the Christian Churches.* Trans. Olive Wyon, 2 vols.; London: George Allen & Unwin, Ltd., 1931.

TULLOCK, JOHN. *Rational Theology and Christian Philosophy in England in the Seventeenth Century.* 2 vols.; Edinburgh: William Blackwood & Sons, 1872.

TYERMAN, LUKE. *The Life and Times of the Reverend John Wesley, M.A.* 3 vols.; New York: Harper & Bros., 1872.

————. *The Life and Times of the Reverend Samuel Wesley, M.A.* London: Simpkin, Marshall & Co., 1866.

————. *The Life of the Reverend George Whitefield.* 2 vols.; New York: Anson D. F. Randolph & Co., 1877.

————. *The Oxford Methodists.* New York: Harper & Bros., 1873.

————. *Wesley's Designated Successor.* London: Hodder & Stoughton, 1882.

Ussher, James. *Whole Works.* 17 vols.; Dublin: Hodge, Smith & Co., 1864.

Wakeman, H. O. *The Church and the Puritans.* Epochs of Church History; London: Longmans, Green & Co., 1912.

Warburton, William. *Works.* Ed. Richard Hurd, 12 vols.; London: printed for T. Cadell & W. Davies, 1811.

Ward, R. *Life of the Learned and Pious Dr. Henry More.* London: Joseph Downing, 1710.

Waterland, Daniel. *Works.* 6 vols.; Oxford: University Press, 1856.

Watkin-Jones, Howard. *The Holy Spirit from Arminius to Wesley.* London: Epworth Press, 1928.

Watson, John Selby. *Life of William Warburton.* London: Longmans, Green, Longmans, Roberts, & Green, 1863.

Watson, Richard. *Life of Reverend John Wesley.* New York: Carlton & Porter, 1831.

———. *Works.* 2nd ed., 12 vols.; London: John Mason, 1834.

Wesley, Charles. *Journal.* London: R. Culley, 1910.

———. *Sermons.* London: Baldwin, Cradock, & Joy, 1816.

Wesley, Samuel. *The History of the Holy Bible.* 3rd ed., in verse, 3 vols.; London: R. B. for Thomas Ward, 1717.

———. *An Hymn on Peace to the Prince of Peace.* London: F. Leake, 1713.

———. *A Letter from a Country Divine to his Friend in London Concerning the Education of the Dissenters.* London: Pecock, 1703.

———. *The Life of Christ, a Poem.* 2 vols.; London: A. Paris, 1809.

———. *Maggots: or Poems on Several Subjects, Never Before Handled by a Scholar.* London: printed for John Dunton, 1685.

———. *Neck or Nothing: A Consolatory Letter from Mr. D-nt-n to Mr. C--ill upon his being Tos'd in a Blanket, etc.* London: Charles King, 1716.

———. *The Pious Communicant Rightly Prepar'd; or a Discourse Concerning the Blessed Sacrament, to Which Is Added, A Short Discourse of Baptism.* London: Flower-de-luce, 1700.

White, Francis. *The Orthodox Faith and Way to the Church Explained and Justified: in Answer to a Papish Treatise, entitled "White Died Blacke"; wherein T. W. P. in his triple accusation of D. White for imposters, untruths, and absurd illations, is proved a trifler: and the present Controversies betweene us and the Romanists are more fully delivered and claimed.* London: printed by Richard Field for William Barret, 1617.

————. *A Replie to Jesuit Fisher's Answer to Certain Questions propounded by his most gratious Majestie King James*. London: printed by Adam Islip, 1624.

————. *A Treatise of the Sabbath Day, Containing a Defence of the Orthodoxal Doctrine of the Church of England Against Sabbatarian Novelty*. London: printed by Richard Badger, 1635.

WHITEFIELD, GEORGE. *Works*. 6 vols.; London: printed for Edward and Charles Dilly, 1771.

WHITEHEAD, JOHN. *The Life of the Reverend John Wesley, M.A., with the Life of the Reverend Charles Wesley, M.A.* 2 vols.; London: Stephen Conchman, 1793.

WILLEY, BASIL. *The Eighteenth Century Background*. London: Chatto & Windus, 1940.

————. *The Seventeenth Century Background*. London: Chatto & Windus, 1934.

WISEMAN, F. LUKE. *Charles Wesley*. New York: The Abingdon Press, 1932.

WOOLASTON, WILLIAM. *The Religion of Nature Deliniated*. London: Samuel Palmer, 1726.

WOOLSTON, THOMAS. *Works*. 5 vols.; London: printed for J. Roberts, 1733.

INDEX

INDEX

Calvin, John, 31, 35, 81, 88-92, 94, 100, 103, 117, 143, 193, 195, 199, 200, 208-10, 224-26

Calvinism, 31-33, 35, 45, 81, 89, 92-94, 97, 101, 102, 105, 116, 143-45, 149, 175, 210, 247

Calvinism *vs.* Wesleyanism, 35, 81, 90-100, 102, 105, 117, 143-45, 195, 199, 210, 225-26, 247

Calvinistic Puritanism, 33

Cambridge Platonists, 16

Canterbury, See of, 34

Castaniza, Juan, 250

Catholics, 188; *see also* Roman Catholic Church

Cato the Elder, 186

Cell, G. C., 61, 105, 116

Chalcedon, 205-6

Character; *see* God, character; Man, character

Character of a Methodist, The, 119

Charity schools, 22

Charles I, 31

Chesterfield, Lord, 23

Children of God; *see* Sons of God

Chinese, 187-88

Choctaws, 72

Christ; *see* Jesus Christ

Christian, 56-57, 59, 65, 70-71, 73, 97, 123, 138, 139, 217, 221, 224-25, 227-28, 230-31, 233, 236-38, 241, 244, 246

Christian apologetics, 154

Christian development, 223-24, 227

Christian ethics; *see* Wesleyan system of ethics

Christian life, 42, 47, 58-59, 75, 97, 120, 122, 134, 143, 147, 159, 222, 224, 228, 237, 240, 244

Christian Pattern, The, 56, 57

Christian Perfection, 57, 59

Christian perfection; *see* Perfection

Christian social order, 235-37

Christianity, 15, 18-21, 24, 34, 52-53, 59, 105-6, 154-55, 227

Christians, 20, 37, 48, 135, 158, 173, 188, 224-25, 237, 240

Church, 236-37

Church of England, 30-34, 42-44, 46, 48, 51, 70, 85-88, 125, 127-29, 215
  Catechism, 125
  Theology, 30-31, 36, 39-40, 85; *see*

Church of England—*continued*
  also Homilies; Thirty-nine Articles

Church of Rome, 31-34, 100, 135, 200, 245, 250

Circulation of the blood, 183-85

Circumcision, 122

Clarke, Adam, 46, 49, 51

Clarke, Samuel, 19-20, 178

Clergy, 20, 24, 95

Comets, 176, 180

Communion, 52, 57, 61, 71, 147; *see also* Sacraments

Condemnation; *see* Damnation

Conditional redemption; *see* Jesus Christ, redemption

Confession of Augsburg, 41, 88

Confidence, 221

Conscience, 101, 108, 114-15, 135, 140, 142-43, 153, 159, 218

Conversion, 38, 67-68, 114, 120-21, 126, 130, 134, 138-39, 222, 237, 248-52

Conviction of sin, 96, 109, 113

Co-operation, 36, 114-16, 248

Copernicus, 176

Corruption; *see* Evil, Sin

Council of Nicaea, 205

Council of Trent, 88, 200, 251

Cranmer, Thomas, 31

Creation, 162, 171-72, 176, 178, 180-81, 185, 194-97, 202, 205, 206, 212-13, 249

Creator, 30, 156, 162-64, 168-69, 171, 179, 180, 182, 192-94, 197, 199, 202, 205, 232

Crime, 22-23

Criminals, 22-23

Curnock, Nehemiah, 60, 62

Custom, 191

Cyprian, St., 181

Damnation, 46, 74, 86, 90-92, 94, 99, 100, 130, 142, 208, 247

Dartmouth, Lord, 23

David, Christian, 75

David, King, 137, 142

Death, 55, 70, 83, 119, 196-98, 202

Deism, 15-21, 38, 52-53, 86, 97, 153, 155, 157, 160, 204, 210

Deists; *see* Deism

Deliverance from sin; *see* Atonement

Depravity, 199, 202, 204

276

INDEX

277

INDEX

Gentiles, 98, 137, 186
Georgia, 60, 62, 69-74, 187
Gilbert, William, 176
Gloucester, Lord Bishop of, 86
God, 17-18, 21, 25-26, 29, 34-40, 42-46,
    49, 52, 55-56, 58-61, 63-69, 73, 76,
    78, 80, 82-84, 89-98, 101-7, 109-10,
    112-15, 117-25, 127, 130-40, 144-
    49, 153-64, 166-75, 177, 180, 185-
    89, 192-209, 211-22, 224-26, 228-
    36, 238-39, 242, 244, 246, 254
care; see God, providence
character, 153-54, 156, 162, 171, 174,
    175, 182, 203, 209, 249
existence, 17, 21, 38, 81, 112, 153-55,
    161, 169, 210
foreknowledge; see God, prescience
forgiveness, 34, 46-47, 49, 59, 76, 83,
    123-24, 144
goodness, 17, 45, 161-62, 165-68, 199
holiness, 175, 195, 201, 203, 221, 226
immanence, 214, 220, 232
judgment, 25, 37-38, 83, 90-93, 99,
    117, 142, 200
justice, 38-39, 45-46, 99-100, 102,
    162, 199-202, 208-9, 211
knowledge; see God, omniscience
love, 38, 74, 84, 93, 98, 100, 110, 118,
    124, 133, 138, 162, 173, 179,
    182, 202, 204
mercy, 83, 90-93, 98, 104, 112, 116,
    122, 133, 144, 149, 162, 186,
    200-201, 208-9, 230-31, 244,
    246-47
metaphysical attributes; see God, ex-
    istence, omnipresence, omniscience,
    prescience, unity, wisdom
moral nature; see God, nature
nature, 37, 153-54, 156, 160-74
omnipotence, 92, 116, 146, 161, 168-
    69, 171-72, 203, 206, 214-15
omnipresence, 55, 103, 169, 214, 240
omniscience, 83, 162, 169
perfection, 18, 165, 253
power; see God, omnipotence
prescience, 45-46, 163, 169, 173, 199,
    203
providence, 57, 153, 161-79, 229, 234
reconciliation, 26, 46, 76, 80, 83, 88,
    117, 217, 224
relation to man, 14, 20, 42, 46, 108,
    110, 124-25, 128, 144, 146, 160,

278

God—*continued*
    165, 169, 173, 179, 182-83, 197,
    207, 213
sovereignty, 92-94, 161, 163, 169-73,
    195, 209
truth, 20, 77, 83, 156
unchangeableness, 174
unity, 169
will, 20, 30, 39, 46, 50, 61, 66, 84,
    93-95, 104, 140, 159, 162, 163,
    168, 170, 175, 183, 193, 199,
    207, 222
wisdom, 83, 92, 102, 106, 159, 162,
    166, 168-69, 171, 175, 183, 204,
    206
wrath, 92, 109, 121, 209
Golden Rule, 178, 236
Good works, 30, 35, 42, 45, 57, 61-63,
    65, 69, 73, 75, 77, 80, 84, 89-90,
    96, 146-50, 239, 247
Goodness, 63, 146, 149, 175, 191, 247,
    251
Grace, 26, 29, 32, 34-37, 42-43, 57, 65,
    68-69, 76-77, 79-82, 86, 89-93, 100-
    108, 113-16, 118, 123-24, 134, 137,
    139, 141, 144, 149-50, 159, 200,
    216, 224, 241, 243, 245-49
Grammar schools, 22
Gratitude, 141, 253
Greek Church, 188
Greek Orthodox Church, 135
Green, J. B., 23, 24, 31
Grotian theory, 209
Guilt, 37, 39, 76, 140-41, 195, 231

Hagen, F. F., 75
Hali, 187
Hall, Joseph, 42
Halley, Edmund, 15
Hammond, Henry, 40
Hampson, John, 13
Happiness, 18, 39, 48, 195
Harmens, James; see Arminius, Jacobus
Harmon, Nolan B., 127
Harmony, 29, 164, 178
Harrison, A. W., 13, 32, 36
Heart, 183, 184
Heathen, 38, 72, 78, 92, 154, 170, 173,
    186, 188
Heaven; see Eternal life
Hebrews, 186
Hell; see Damnation

INDEX

Helplessness, 110, 141
Herbert of Cherbury, 16, 17
Hernhuth, 75-76, 88
Hervey, James, 210
Hilary of Poitiers, 205
Hill (the Calvinist), 94
Holiness; *see* God, holiness; Man, holiness
Holy Ghost; *see* Holy Spirit
Holy Living and Holy Dying, 54-55
Holy Spirit, 24, 26, 36, 74, 92, 120, 121, 124-28, 130, 132, 138-39, 155, 161, 201, 206, 213-19, 222, 229, 246, 250
Homilies, 85, 87-88
Hooker, Richard, 31, 34-35, 42, 243
Horne, 86
Hottentots, 159, 163, 188
"Hound of Heaven," 118
House of Israel, 98, 142, 186
Human body, 183, 202
Human depravity, 199, 202, 204
Human freedom; *see* Man, free will
Human initiative, 38, 43, 116
Humanistic center of faith, 60
Humility, 141, 160
Hunt, John, 31

Imagination, 184
Immorality, 22-23
Immortality; *see* Eternal life
Imitation of Christ, 56-57
Impatience, 229
Incarnation; *see under* Jesus Christ
Indians, 62, 71-73, 187
Infant baptism, 127-29
Infinite duration, 59, 162, 174, 181-82
Inspiration of Scripture; *see* Bible
Intellect; *see* Mind
Inward sin; *see* Sin
Irenaeus, 207
Islam, 187
Israel, 98, 142, 186

Jacob, 98, 118
James, St., 41, 137
James, William, 66
Jenyns, Soame, 165-66
Jesuits, 188
Jesus Christ, 34, 39-43, 46, 56, 68-69, 72, 74-76, 78-80, 82, 84, 89, 94, 98-99, 108-10, 115, 120-21, 124-25,

Jesus Christ—*continued*
130-31, 134-36, 138, 143-49, 159, 160, 161, 173, 204, 206, 208-9, 214, 218-19, 223-28, 230, 238, 241, 245
death, 40-41, 46-47, 64, 74-76, 79, 85, 98, 110, 117, 132, 146, 204, 206-10, 213, 229, 236
divinity, 34, 41, 56, 101, 117, 205-6, 213
human form; *see* Jesus Christ, incarnation
incarnation, 34, 40, 78-79, 206-8, 211
love, 40, 75, 99, 217
person, 56, 80, 83, 91, 161, 201, 204-7, 211
place in history, 204
redemption, 14, 18, 26, 30, 32, 38-42, 46-50, 52, 64, 66, 69, 71, 73-74, 76-79, 82-83, 90-91, 94, 98, 101-2, 113-15, 117, 121, 148, 200-201, 203-8, 210-14, 216, 223, 246, 250
resurrection, 79, 82, 207
righteousness, 34-35, 56, 66, 82, 131, 146, 205-8, 213, 224, 241
work; *see* Jesus Christ, redemption
Jews, 98-99, 122, 159
Johnson, Samuel, 14
Judgment; *see under* God
Justification, 26, 30, 32-33, 39-40, 48-50, 62-63, 69, 71, 74-76, 80-92, 102-4, 111, 119-24, 138, 142, 149, 153, 176, 213, 216, 222, 240, 242-46, 248-49, 251, 254
concomitants, 120-21
conditions, 39, 41-42, 73, 84, 87-88, 104, 108, 110-11, 114, 147
definitions, 34, 75, 82-83, 88-89, 110, 150, 201, 248
effect, 120, 125, 142, 145, 215, 222
God's own act, 35, 38, 43, 46, 103, 116, 239, 247, 250, 252
legalistic conception, 36-38, 121
man's part, 35, 38, 41, 43, 64, 104-6, 114-17, 145; *see also* Man, free will
scope, 14, 83-85, 91, 245
significance, 38
theological term, 43
Justification by faith, 33, 41, 47-48, 68, 77, 80-82, 86, 88, 102-20, 146, 226, 247, 250

INDEX

Justification by grace, 68, 80, 89, 110, 247

Justification by works, 34, 41-42, 47-48, 80-81, 85-86, 89, 110, 247

Justification through the Church, 33

Justifying faith, 114-15

Justifying grace, 115-16, 118, 144, 248

Kepler, Johannes, 176

Kingdom of God, 109-10, 119, 121, 130, 143, 226, 228, 250

Kirk, John, 44

Knowledge, 156-57

Koran, 187

Lapland, 187

Laud, William, 31-33, 35-36, 38, 42, 47

Law, William, 57-59, 63, 67, 240

Law of God, 37, 56, 59, 63, 83, 113, 137-38, 142, 147-48, 245

Law of Moses, 37, 39

Lecky, W. E. H., 22

Lee, Umphrey, 108, 215, 242

Leger, Augustin, 67

Levity, 229

Leyden University, 101

Liberty, 105-6, 171, 173, 194

Limited grace; see Predestination

Lincoln College, 57

"Linnaeus of his age," 167

Literalism, 153

Locke, John, 17, 19, 158

Lord's Supper, 42-47

Lot, 186

Louis XIV, 15

Love, 140, 150, 230-31, 241; see also under God, Man

Luke, St., 92

Luther, Martin, 31, 68, 76, 88, 103, 147-48, 193, 200, 223, 225, 250

Luther-Calvin thesis, 105, 117

McConnell, F. J., 13

McGiffert, A. C., 16, 21

Maltby, W. R., 200

Man, 37-38, 42, 47-48, 57, 80, 82, 95, 101, 106, 115, 117-18, 123, 127, 132, 134-35, 139, 142, 145, 180, 184-85, 189, 194-95

character, 25, 72-73, 77, 83, 100, 133, 140

Man—*continued*

co-operation, 36, 107-8, 114, 116, 249, 251, 253

evidence of fitness for salvation, 39, 46, 252

free will, 35, 38, 40-41, 43, 45-46, 54, 64, 105, 107-8, 114-16, 138-39, 173, 185, 194-95, 200, 203-4, 212-13, 243, 246, 248-50, 253

good works; see Good works

holiness, 24, 61, 83, 87, 95, 119-25, 129, 132, 149, 159, 194, 207-8, 214-15, 223, 225, 234, 237, 239-40, 245-46, 250-51, 253

impotence, 34, 39, 102, 111-13, 144

love of fellow men, 133, 140, 150

love of God, 35, 66, 84, 133, 140, 150

part in salvation; see Man, free will

place in nature, 163, 165, 167, 171, 173, 176, 178-79, 182, 197-98

rational being; see Reason

relationship to God, 14, 20, 26, 35, 38, 46, 48, 55, 76, 77, 83, 88, 91, 104, 113, 137, 139, 144, 173, 179, 226

religious life, 14, 37, 47, 57-59, 74, 77

"Marks of the New Birth, The," 127

Marlborough, Duke of, 14

Mary, Virgin, 206

Masses, 77

Materialism, 16

Matthew's Gospel, 227

Meakness, 229

Memory, 184

Mercy; see under God

Methodism, 22, 49, 77, 149, 156

Methodist conference, 108

Methodist Connection, 148

Methodist discipline, 148

Methodist Revival, 77

Methodist societies, 66

Methodists, 243, 251

Methuselah, 180-81

Mind, 15-16, 35, 44, 171-72, 196

Misery, 189

Montesquieu, Baron de, 23

Moral achievement, 81

Moral development, 240

Moral order, 129

Moral restoration, 14

Morality, 24, 37

280

INDEX

281

INDEX

M